Fighting the
Good Fight

Fighting the Good Fight

The Story of the Dexter Avenue
King Memorial Baptist Church
1865–1977

HOUSTON BRYAN ROBERSON

Routledge
Taylor & Francis Group

NEW YORK AND LONDON

Published in 2005 by
Routledge
Taylor & Francis Group
270 Madison Avenue
New York, NY 10016

Published in Great Britain by
Routledge
Taylor & Francis Group
2 Park Square
Milton Park, Abingdon
Oxon OX14 4RN

© 2005 by Taylor & Francis Group, LLC
Routledge is an imprint of Taylor & Francis Group

Printed in the United States of America on acid-free paper
10 9 8 7 6 5 4 3 2 1

International Standard Book Number-10: 0-415-94920-3 (Hardcover) 0-415-94921-1 (Softcover)
International Standard Book Number-13: 978-0-415-94920-0 (Hardcover) 978-0-415-94921-7 (Softcover)

Library of Congress Cataloging-in-Publication Data

Roberson, Houston Bryan
  Fighting the good fight : the story of the Dexter Avenue King Memorial Baptist Church, 1865–1977 / by Houston Bryan Roberson. — 1st ed.
      p. cm.
  Includes bibliographical references and index.
  ISBN 0-415-94920-3 (hardback : alk. paper) — ISBN 0-415-94921-1 (pbk. : alk. paper)
  1. Dexter Avenue King Memorial Baptist Church (Montgomery, Ala.)—History. 2. Montgomery (Ala.)—Church history. 3. African Americans—Religion. 4. Race relations—Religiousaspects—Christianity. 5. Reconciliation—Religious aspects—Baptists. 6. United States—Racerelations. I. Title.

BX6480.M6R63 2005
286.1'76147—dc22   2004026365

Taylor & Francis Group
is the Academic Division of T&F Informa plc.

Visit the Taylor & Francis Web site at
http://www.taylorandfrancis.com

and the Routledge Web site at
http://www.routledge-ny.com

For their unfailing love and support,
this book is dedicated to my parents,
Ralph and Madelene Ziegler Roberson

CONTENTS

ACKNOWLEDGMENTS

My debts are many. First, numerous libraries and archives have made my research possible, including the Alabama State Historical Archives and Montgomery Public Library, Montgomery, Alabama; the Selma University Library, Selma, Alabama; the Samford University Archives, Birmingham, Alabama; the Howard University Archives and the Library of Congress, Washington, DC; and the American Baptist–Samuel Colgate Library, Rochester, New York. Librarians and archivists at these institutions cheerfully responded to numerous research requests and gave of their time generously to help me locate many valuable sources.

I received several grants in support of this work. A Mowry Grant and a Kaiser Fellowship from the University of North Carolina helped me jump-start this project. I thank Dr. Anne Mitchell, Dr. Joseph Mitchell, and Dr. Norma Taylor Mitchell for providing shelter for several months during the initial research for the dissertation that served as the basis for this book; they were gracious hosts and delightful emotional support during the early phase of this project. I was given a generous research fellowship from the Southern Poverty Law Center that allowed me to complete most of my Alabama research. A University of California Regents Grant gave me six months of unfettered time to complete an initial draft of this manuscript. Crucial to my productivity were the staff members at the University of California–Santa Barbara's Center for Black Studies: Marnean Adams, Ina Huggins, and Dr. Charles Long. The George Lurcy Deep South Regional Humanities Fellowship enabled me to finalize my research for this project.

ix

Several members of Dexter Avenue King Memorial Baptist Church and the Montgomery community were fonts of information, including Edna Doak King, who at the time of our interview was 104; she spent many hours sharing her lucid memories of Dexter Avenue and Montgomery at the turn of the twentieth century. Her rich descriptions of the Judkins pastorate and turn-of-the-century Montgomery were invaluable. As well, I am grateful to Dr. Ralph Bryson, Dr. Zelia S. Evans, Robert Nesbitt Sr., and Thelma Austin Rice, who were willing to talk to me for many hours about the church and their lives growing up in the Montgomery community. Their insights imparted much needed perspective on the relationship between Dexter Avenue and other churches in Montgomery. A chance meeting with Janice Denton—who was visiting from Amherst, Massachusetts, but had grown up in the church during the 1940s and 1950s—proved very helpful in telling the story of this church. Always gracious and pleasant, Addre Bryant met me each morning for several weeks to escort me to the trailer that housed most of the church records and minutes, and words seem inadequate to acknowledge my debt to the Reverend Richard Wills Sr., who helped me to convince skeptical Dexter Avenue members of the importance of a critical history of the church; despite his busy schedule and many family responsibilities, for more than three months Reverend Wills sat patiently with me as I surveyed church minutes and records. Johnnie Carr and Virginia Durr told me many helpful stories about Montgomery, Dexter Avenue Baptist Church, and the civil rights movement.

Several persons read and offered valuable critiques of this text at various points in its development: Will Alexander, Martin Ferrell, Keith Kocher, Marla Miller, Laura Jane Moore, and Everette L. Webb. Sarah Gardner not only read parts of the manuscript but has been a wonderful conference panel critic and companion. Several other persons have offered informal advice and warm encouragement over the years: Ralph Luker, Charles Marsh, Barbara Savage, Pat Sullivan, and Ula Taylor.

There have been many extraordinary teachers in my life: Jon Crawford, Laura Flippin, Kay Gregory, Lucille Hicks, Betty Hughes, Phyllis Lemke, Jim Lenberg, Mary Lee Mitchell, Claudette Thompson, Mary Ihrig Whithers, and Evelyn Underwood. While a graduate student at the University of North Carolina–Chapel Hill, I was fortunate to have talented faculty and dissertation committee members who offered guidance, encouragement, and collegiality. Raymond Gavins provided effective and sustained critique of the text, and has been a quiet and constant presence. Peter Filene's writing seminar helped to create among Americanists entering the department in the fall of 1990 a spirit of cooperation and mutual support. Don Mathews, whose wonderful book on Southern religion and whose class further piqued my interest in the study of religion, was always ready with another hard question or unusual perspective to consider. My numerous conversations with him helped to sharpen the analysis in this project. My director, Genna Rae McNeil, was tireless in her support of me and of this project. Patiently, expectantly, and enthusiastically she guided me through the first draft of this manuscript.

I am grateful to the University of the South for faculty development grants to support my research, and a sabbatical leave to complete this project. My colleagues in the history department have all been encouraging, but special thanks are due Julie Berebitsky, Charles Perry, Woody Register, Sue Ridyard, and John Willis.

I am blessed with an extended family of remarkable individuals who were constant sources of support and, at times, much-needed diversions: Cynthia Baker, Al Baldwin, Jonathan and Elizabeth Clark, Gary Frost, Phyllis and Steve Gordon, Judy Haig, Michael Hickman, Melva Hicks, David and Shelby Ingram, Peggy Price, Sonya Ramsey, Sheria Reid, Beverly Tatum, Robert Tinkler, Jonathan Young, and numerous others have encouraged and supported me over the years in more ways than I can recount. The greatest gift and blessing of my life has been my loving and supportive family of six wonderful brothers and sisters: Elaine, Larry, Mitchell, Olivia, Sheila, and Teresa; each in her or his unique way has enriched my life and challenged me to seek my dreams.

Finally, I would like to thank the Routledge and Taylor & Francis staff members, past and present, for all their help and support, and especially Joanne Blake, Bill Germano, Kimberly Guinta, Brendan O'Malley, Daniel Webb, and Karen Wolny.

INTRODUCTION

Black churches, as they developed in the United States, emerged from a general matrix of varied religious experiences—indigenous African, Judeo-Christian, and Islamic.[1] From their creation as an "invisible institution" during black enslavement to their profoundly visible and dynamic existence during the era of black emancipation to their crucial presence in the struggle to procure full citizenship rights for African Americans, black churches have been a vital force in African American life and community.[2]

Much of the historical work on black churches has acknowledged a primary place for them in the history of African Americans since the eighteenth century. In 1926, Carter G. Woodson, in his path-breaking work *The History of the Negro Church*, initiated the historical debate on the role of the independent black church in American life (see note 1). Using the biographies of numerous ministers and discussing the formation of the state and national conventions of several black denominations, Woodson argued that the Negro church was an affirming space in an otherwise oppressive society and as such was a liberating and identity-giving institution. Almost ten years later, in their sociological study of the black church, Benjamin Mays and Joseph Nicholson reinforced Woodson's conclusions, asserting that black churches offered African Americans "the opportunity to be recognized ... to be somebody."[3] They noted as well that despite the growth of black membership in non-Christian religious organizations after World War I, black membership in Christian churches continued to increase, especially in Baptist churches in urban areas of the South.

During the 1940s, E. Franklin Frazier completed a scholarly study in which he posited that the black church was a "nation within a nation." Frazier contended that in the absence of a strong historical tradition, languages, or sentiments comparable to various European nationalities, the black church filled a void in the black community. He argued that black churches were the means through which previously enslaved African Americans were being assimilated into the mainstream of American society. In 1974, C. Eric Lincoln, building upon the work of Frazier, insisted that after World War II many mainstream churches abandoned their conciliatory or accommodationist approach in opposing racism. Rather, they took on the bold, daring, and confrontational demand that the nation recognize African Americans' full citizenship rights (see note 2). Works in the 1990s like *The Black Church in the African American Experience* have sought to update much of the sociological analysis of black churches. Studies like Donna Irvin's *The Unsung Heart of Black America* and Samuel Freedman's *Upon This Rock: The Miracles of a Black Church* emphasize the importance of local churches in African American community life. The picture that emerges from these and the other voluminous studies on the black church is one that compellingly demonstrates the preeminence of black churches in the lives of African Americans. *Fighting the Good Fight: The Story of the Dexter Avenue King Memorial Baptist Church, 1865–1977* chronicles six generations in the life of a historically significant African American Baptist church: the generation of postbellum emancipation, the erosion of many of the gains of the emancipation era, the accommodating activist response to the turn-of-the-twentieth-century nadir, the growth of an activist consciousness among African Americans who came of age after World War II, the confrontational activist demand for full citizenship rights during the apex of the twentieth-century civil rights movement, and, finally, the aftermath of that struggle during the mid-1970s.[4]

Dexter Avenue Baptist Church, in Montgomery, Alabama, became a place where members would embrace but exceed the traditional functions associated with religious institutions. The members accommodated, but more often contested, the white racism that circumscribed their community. One enduring characteristic has been the church's struggle with the symbiotic callings of providing expressly religious ministry—Christian salvation and regeneration—versus encouraging social activism. Over the years, the church aided in the push for radical change by consistently providing a sanctuary and a space for those who directly confronted the political and social status quo, but only a few of its congregants were ever in the vanguard of social change. In

Dexter Avenue's story we see both the promise and the foibles of the emancipationist strategies of racial uplift, an enduring faith in the American ideal of progress, and the accommodating activism of a black middle class committed to transmitting "proper" values and conduct to persons labeled by the larger society as "damaged." The church, in its labors to promote uplift and direct African Americans toward contemporary notions of improvement, sometimes shunned certain black expressive cultural forms. The sanctified church or holiness movement's approaches to worship, including shouting and preacher–congregation call and response, garnered little enthusiasm at Dexter Avenue. Most members also eschewed black musical expressions like blues, jazz, and, to some extent, gospel. It becomes clear why, years later, Dexter Avenue traditions and protest strategies offered much to the Martin Luther King Jr.–dominated component of the civil rights struggle, but proffered a tepid response to challenges by radical preachers like Vernon Johns. Still, we should not ignore, underestimate, or fail to appreciate the degree to which Dexter Avenue's presence in Montgomery immediately broadened black freedoms, kept hope alive, and provided a corpus of leadership and protest traditions that enhanced the daily lives of African Americans in Montgomery.

Dexter Avenue Baptist Church emerged from a biracial church—First Baptist, Montgomery, Alabama—that had formed in 1829. In 1842, whites at the church rewrote its constitution and rules of decorum to formally segregate African American members of the congregation. Under the watchful eye of white church members, the black congregation was permitted to have a separate service with its own deacons and pastor. Almost immediately after the Civil War, African Americans in the congregation left First Baptist to form the first independent African American Baptist congregation in Alabama, Columbus Street Baptist Church. Dexter Avenue was born of a second exodus ten years later. [5]

Two features characterized independent African American churches as they developed in the postbellum United States: a strong ethos of equality, an atavism from African American religious gathering during slavery, and a charge to meet both the spiritual and secular needs of the community. James M. Washington has explained that resistance to inequality was embraced by black Baptist ministers during slavery but was more symbolic than actual. During the period of emancipation, claims Washington, black ministers preached that God's righteousness required protest against a caste society based on racial distinctions. [6] Other independent black denominations also stressed the importance of equality. Reginald Hildebrand, in *The Times Were Strange and Stirring: Methodist Ministers and the Crisis of Emancipation*, explains that ministers in the African Methodist Episocopal and African Methodist Episcopal Zion Churches created a theological imperative for equality by preaching a gospel of freedom.[7]

These instructive studies focus largely on the activities of denominational conventions and do not portray fully the role of individual congregations in accomplishing the goals of the black church. The story of Dexter Avenue illuminates the ways in which institutional religion provided both moral training and service to the community in a local setting over time. We shall see as well how certain values emerge, are sustained, or fade over time. Early in its history Dexter Avenue became a place where an oppressed people reinforced their shared history and culture and discussed and realized community goals. In fact, the tradition of service to the community began almost as soon as the congregation opened its doors. During the 1870s in Marion, Alabama, the state legislature built the first State Normal College for Negroes (later renamed Alabama State University), but racists set it aflame. The state legislature ordered the school moved to Montgomery, but its presence was not warmly received, and legislators could find no available place to reopen the school. Church members at Dexter Avenue offered use of their facility for the first registration for classes, and ASU continued to use Dexter Avenue's facility for more than two years. We clearly see that this church consciously went beyond meeting spiritual imperatives to address the secular hopes and dreams—individual and collective—of the community it served. Black churches like Dexter Avenue, then, come to belong to congregants in very intimate ways.

Dexter Avenue's history not only reveals the powerful bond between members and church, it also illustrates the ways in which values were established and maintained through generations. For example, Dexter Avenue members are proud that their church began both as a Sunday school and a regular school, Langridge Academy. Over the years, the congregation continued the tradition of privileging education. In my interviews with them, members were quick to point out that all of the men who pastored the church were well educated and that members had always stressed the importance of being good church members and responsible citizens. In fact, we shall see many examples of members' faith in the morality of American institutions and their belief that hard work inevitably leads to progress and improvement. The ministry of R. C. Judkins, which created a cadre of Christian workers to prove African Americans worthy of first-class citizenship status, exemplified the development of and perpetuation of the values of education and patriotism.[8]

Related to Dexter Avenue's emphasis on the importance of education, we shall also observe the emergence of black middle-class life in the Deep South, as best pointed out in the music program and worship format at the church, as well as in the ladies' missionary society, which fostered particular attitudes and decorum. While whites saw African Americans as an undifferentiated mass of inferiors, blacks in Montgomery were aware of differentiated class status within the community and that some measure of stratification had been present even during slavery. We shall see this reality in the early struggle at Columbus Street Baptist (later First Baptist Montgomery, Colored), and we see it in Dexter Avenue's reticence to embrace the singing of spirituals or even offer the preacher a responsive "Amen" during Sunday sermons. In many black churches, especially those in urban areas, congregants worked to create an elite, what W. E. B. Du Bois has called the "talented tenth." Many believed that if blacks attained the typical middle-class values of hard work and self-restraint and the attributes of polite society they would earn respect for the community and, in turn, equal rights would be acknowledged. Although Dexter Avenue members provided a ministry to all members of Montgomery's black community, it would never shake the reputation of being the church of the town's "big shots."[9]

The church's story highlights sociological issues related to the development of black protestant churches in the United States at the turn of the twentieth century—namely, self-help programs for racial uplift. To be sure, some whites, most working for the American Missionary Association, invested a portion of their life's work to improving the political, economic, and social circumstances that newly emancipated African Americans faced. Yet, just as protection provided blacks by the presence of federal soldiers disappeared in 1877, by the early twentieth century, most white missionary efforts on blacks' behalf diminished. It became clear that efforts to improve African Americans' condition rested with black institutions. From J. W. Beverly's Sunday school classes, to the missionary society's health fair and midwives' clinic, to Ralph Riley's interracial day programs, racial uplift was an integral part of the church's ministry.

Helping in the work of racial uplift at Dexter Avenue were numerous noteworthy figures who spoke on race relations and a few other topics. Among them were leading intellectuals such as Sutton E. Griggs, educators like Nannie Helen Burroughs, and political personalities like Ella Baker, William Pickens, and America's most powerful spokesman in race relations during the early twentieth century, Booker T. Washington. Later, this list would include Daisey Bates, Miriam Wright Edelman, Clarence Jordan, and Kaka Kalelkar, former assistant to Mahatma Gandhi. The self-help, racial uplift program became a mainstay in the struggle for equality and freedom.

The pages that follow provide some analysis of the important role and function of black ministers. Over the years, numerous stellar figures graced the Dexter Avenue pulpit; the church earned a reputation, and rightly so, of driving out ministers and vesting greater power in the official board—dubbed by some the "Dexter barons"—than most Baptist churches. The power of the "Dexter baron" was most conspicuous in the painstaking searches for new pastors and in dismissing those men judged, for whatever reason, to be unsuitable. Still, it was always the minister who developed the programs for the church. There are, of course, numerous biographies of black ministers that provide us with excellent analyses of how ministers developed leadership styles and strategies as a result of their pastorate of various churches, but our consideration draws attention to how different ministers functioned in the similar setting of one religious congregation. Discussion of various ministers who pastored the church provides some new information on pastoral leadership in the black church and creates an opportunity for an exacting inquiry into the relationship between black churches and black pastors.

In some cases we rescue from historical invisibility remarkable persons like G. Murray Branch and R. C. Judkins, while at other times we get new insight into the biography and contributions of ministers of reputation. In fact, various pastors at Dexter Avenue epitomized certain leadership styles: R. C. Judkins combined intellectual and religious training with political action; Frank Jacobs highlighted the importance of personal holiness and professionalized the record keeping (it is no mere coincidence that extant church records date back to 1926 when Jacobs became pastor). Charles Arbouin was a remarkable preacher and, by all accounts, possessed the intellect and stellar credentials that always impressed Dexter Avenue members, but his life was so troubled that eventually he was taken to court to be removed from the pastorate. Vernon Johns, too, was profoundly intelligent and a gifted orator, but also brash and acerbic. Johns's impatience with what he judged the banal pretenses of black middle-class life pushed him to intentionally offend members' sensibilities.

Martin Luther King Jr. and G. Murray Branch had strikingly different experiences with Dexter Avenue members than their immediate predecessors. While Johns was a prophet, King was the long-awaited Moses who had both the vision and administrative acumen to lead the challenge against Pharaoh. King and Dexter Avenue had a powerful mutual relationship: for members, King at once restored calm and reinvigorated a level of activism among its members that had not been experienced in more than a generation; for King, Dexter Avenue, because of its similarities to Ebenezer, was a comfortable milieu that allowed the kinds of opportunities Ebenezer would have afforded him, but out from under the controlling thumb of his father, "Daddy King."

Finally, G. Murray Branch's prophetic but measured voice reminded members that even after passage of the 1964 Civil Rights Bill and 1965 Voting Rights Act the harvest was still plentiful. Branch pushed members to balance the symbiotic relationship that existed between the spiritual and secular imperatives of the church. In particular, he reminded members that they must weigh efforts memorializing the accomplishments of King's tenure with endeavors to live according to biblical principles and to apply those ethics to contemporary challenges in the continued struggle for freedom, equality, and spiritual growth. Branch regularly reminded members that they must read the Bible daily, vote, and—most important—commit to vigilantly fight against anything that threatened "to block or hinder the Godward reach of the human spirit."

As we move through six generations of congregational life at Dexter Avenue, we see that there was neither consistent congregational growth and spiritual emphases nor steady progress in race relations from the emancipation era to the direct demand for African Americans' basic civil rights. On the contrary, there was a regular waxing and waning of congregational growth. Unlike many black Baptist churches in Alabama just after the Civil War, it took almost ten years for Dexter Avenue to acquire a stable and sizable congregation. The early part of the twentieth century was then marked by a virtual explosion of congregational growth, with the church gaining as many as six hundred members one year. Between 1920 and 1948, for many reasons, the congregation decreased. These fluctuations in size obviously affected the amount of money the church had for basic operations. There was also a process of gain and loss of a racially tolerant climate—a rhythm of black gains and white backlash. While Dexter Avenue had been active in the fight for civil rights since the emancipation era, between 1920 and the late 1940s external forces in American society like the Great Depression and internal problems with finances and pastoral leadership led to the church's diminished, though not abandoned, efforts in the civil rights struggle. Dexter Avenue members, on the whole, remained within their segregated world and were relatively undisturbed by whites. Even the slightest transgression of racial etiquette, however, could provoke an overwhelmingly harsh response from the white world.

Dexter Avenue's story helps us understand religion, race, and culture during the civil rights movement, providing us with an "in-house" perspective. Aldon Morris, in *The Origins of the Civil Rights Movement: Black Communities Organizing for Change*, contends that black churches functioned as institutional centers for the movement, providing it with an organized mass base, leaders whose livelihoods were not dependent upon the larger white society, and a meeting place in which to strategize and raise money.[10] Some scholars assert that most analyses of black churches during the civil rights movement have presented a monolithic, oversimplified portrait suggesting that most black churches were eager to become involved in the movement. There are complaints that discussions of black churches' roles in the civil rights struggle ignore King's frustration with the "quiescent nature" of many churches.[11] Dexter Avenue during the 1950s and 1960s provides at least one scenario of a church transformed from accommodation to activism. A youthful twenty-five-year-old King arrived at the church in 1954 just as it had dismissed its pastor because he was too outspoken about how church members should respond to racial segregation. King had plans to make extensive changes in the church's program, but he was as surprised as most members when agitations against racial discrimination led to a bus boycott and ultimately a nationwide movement. We see in this story a plethora of responses to racism over time, and even though the urgent nature of the movement in the 1950s caught members and pastor alike by surprise, like the *Brown v. Board of Education* decision itself, the civil rights movement had been a long time in coming. This church's story provides an intimate examination of how pastor and church came together to become symbols of protest for justice.

Still, *Fighting the Good Fight* is not a biography of Vernon Johns or Martin Luther King Jr., and it is not a history of the civil rights movement in America. It is the story of a journey of believers who set out, more than 125 years ago, on their own distinctive journey of Christian faith and American citizenship—a sojourn intimately connected with important historical persons and events. This church's greatest significance is not found in the dramatic turning points in its life, but in the tedium of board meetings, missionary society activities, and pastoral searches. It was the day-to-day regular activities that anchored and stabilized life for church members as they experienced and endured the oppression of racism and segregation. The church was for them a world; a sanctuary; a place to seek power, become leaders, and affirm themselves and others as worthwhile, capable beings.

Dexter Avenue's story enables us to see liberation theology at work. In fact, we see the importance of liberation theology not just during the 1950s and 1960s, but as a force giving life to the black church when African American members left the white First Baptist Montgomery in 1867. The second-class membership status did not comport with their own notions of what emancipation demanded.[12] Over the years of Dexter Avenue's history, we shall see many instances where pastors and members' faith become the basis for action.

Past studies of African American churches active during the civil rights movement have not provided much prospective discussion, but we shall canvas more than ten years of the church's post-movement story. Once the spotlight moved away from the church, Dexter Avenue was left with important issues related to its identity and questions it is still struggling to resolve. On the one hand, there was the enormous celebrity of this church and the temptation to take on a museumlike character, memorializing its contribution in the struggle for the nation to acknowledge the basic rights of all persons; yet such a move would destroy the broader—and, most would argue, more germane—mission as a religious institution: providing Christian salvation.

As we examine the latter years of the church's history we also see its struggle to remain a relevant force in its community. Liberation theology posits that an African American church cannot effectively minister to its congregants without addressing issues of racism. Yet like any other church, its identity cannot preeminently become a vehicle through which to fight racism. It must develop specific understandings of salvation, righteousness, freedom, justice, ministry, and mission that reflect members' belief in and discipleship to Jesus Christ, as well as its commitment to Baptist doctrine and approaches to worship. Members must create a religious institution that reflects their notion of the church as God's instrument in society. In so doing, they must provide an environment that is meaningful to a generation that has little memory of the 1960s. The aging congregation and paucity of youthful presence in the church suggests that these issues are far from resolved. As we explore in the final chapter and conclusion the struggle between the memory of a celebrated past and the effort to remain a living church, we bring full circle the discussion of questions and issues related to religion and race in Montgomery, Alabama.

The complex circumstances that created Dexter Avenue King Memorial Baptist Church left no doubt that it would be a powerful force in American society. Its story is inextricably tied to the post-bellum struggles of African Americans and the history of the United States.

1

CALLED TO FREEDOM, 1865–1905

So then … we are not children of the bondwoman, but of the free.

Stand fast therefore in the liberty wherewith Christ hath made us free, and be not entangled again with the yoke of bondage.

… ye have been called unto liberty; only use not liberty for an occasion to the flesh, but by love serve one another.

—Galatians 4:31; 5:1, 13 AV

On August 20, 1865, an "old Negro woman" entered one of Montgomery's "principal" churches, walked down the aisle, found a seat, and sat down. Perhaps she believed this was a new day, a time to be particularly thankful. Three months earlier in Citronelle, Alabama, General E. R. S. Canby had accepted the surrender of the last Confederate forces east of the Mississippi River—the war was over. Two years earlier, Abraham Lincoln had issued the Emancipation Proclamation—the enslaved hoped that freedom had come. Whatever her meditation, whatever her thought, the calm of the moment was suddenly interrupted when this "old Negro woman" was "politely told that the church had prepared another place for her to sit." She would celebrate this new day in an old place, a familiar place: the gallery formerly designated for enslaved and free African Americans.

Two days later this event was noted in the *Montgomery Daily Advertiser.* The columnist seemed stunned that this African American woman "having found a seat exactly suited to her mind, proposed to herself to take possession," and relieved that "she moved off quickly and took her place in the gallery." The reporter continued, "The old woman was hardly to blame. She knew no better and probably had been told that she was as good as the whites and entitled to as many privileges." This willful African American act and indignant white response dramatized the sharp contrast between what emancipation meant to most African Americans and its limitations to the majority of whites. Coupled with a persistent determination on the part of African Americans to establish their autonomy, such incongruous perceptions of African American freedom gave rise to the establishment of religious institutions chartered and sustained by African American vision, initiative, and hard work. These irreconcilable interpretations of emancipation meant that blacks and whites would be separate, even in their prayers to God. The woman's sense of entitlement and her decision to sit among white worshipers can be interpreted as an act of resistance and protest, as well as an act of self-expression and self-determination.[1] Her action embodied many of the core principles upon which independent black churches were formed during Reconstruction: a prophetic appropriation of Christianity that shunned racism, advocated equality, and insisted upon the kinship of all people.

Moreover, the editorialist's language renders visible many historical complexities of the day. The phrase "proposed to herself to take a seat exactly suited to her mind" suggests the writer's belief that this woman willfully transgressed cultural conventions forbidding promiscuous seating in public facilities, including churches. Ultimately the writer concluded, however, that the woman "knew no better." The idea that this woman's actions were described as simultaneously intentional and innocent signifies that whites understood that blacks felt a new sense of entitlement. Yet while there was no intention of recognizing black equality, white paternalism was far from dead; that the woman "probably had been told that she was as good as the whites and entitled to as many privileges" indicates the writer's belief that the woman was not acting of her own volition, and "that she moved off quickly" insinuates that, like an innocent child when corrected, she acceded to the instruction of the wiser adult presence.

The formation of Dexter Avenue Baptist Church bears out many of these same realities: blacks' resolve to assert self-will and to determine the contours of emancipation's meanings amid an atmosphere of white assistance and desire to define the parameters of black freedom. It follows, then, that any expectations African Americans may have had that Christian fellowship might allow for the creation of a sacred space in which blacks and whites might worship as equals were quickly dashed. Blacks embarked upon a process of creating community spaces in which they could worship without being relegated to basements and former slave galleries.[2]

Officially established in 1877, the Second Colored Baptist Church (now Dexter Avenue King Memorial Baptist Church[3]) was born in the post-war era when African Americans throughout the South were establishing black religious institutions largely independent of white control. This independent church movement became an important step in answering the call to freedom, to "fight the good fight." C. O. Boothe, Dexter Avenue's first pastor, captured the essence of what African Americans believed emancipation demanded when he wrote, "We had to look to our own heads for light, to our own hearts for courage, and to our own consciences for moral dictation."[4] The formation of Dexter Avenue Baptist Church in many ways was a distillation of the black hopes and self-determination as well as the white angst and paternalism that characterized Reconstruction-era Montgomery, Alabama.[5] The pages that follow chronicle the story of an African American congregation whose past was yoked to a biracial church—First Baptist, Montgomery—where, by 1840, blacks lost democratic voice and standing as it was defined in the Baptist tradition. In 1867, blacks left First Baptist to form Alabama's first independent African American congregation, Columbus Street Baptist Church. Less than ten years later, for reasons more rumored than factual, a few in this same group broke away from Columbus Street and set out on a distinctive journey of Christian faith. In this chapter we shall see how competing notions of the meanings of black emancipation, white paternalistic largesse, and black efforts at self-determination and self-definition come together to create this important religious institution.

At the close of the Civil War, most white churches in Alabama, as in other parts of the South, expected business as usual despite the confederacy's defeat and the abolition of slavery. White Southern Baptists often looked to their pastors for guidance concerning relationships with African American members of their churches. In Montgomery, the Kentucky-born and -raised Isaac Taylor Tichenor, pastor of the First Baptist church, advised, "The changed political status of our late slaves does not necessitate any change in their relation to our churches

… their highest good will be served by their maintaining their present relation to those who knew them, who love them and who will labor for the promotion of their welfare."[6] Tichenor asserted that "former masters of slaves were their proper instructors and that Baptists above all others should exert themselves in the matter." Despite the genuine, albeit paternalistic, commitment Tichenor and other whites at First Baptist had toward African American members, historical race relations at the church explain why, by 1867, African Americans sought a separation from their white sisters and brothers.

First Baptist Church (originally Montgomery Baptist Church) emerged from the early-nineteenth-century frontier world of Montgomery, Alabama, and associations between blacks and whites—while largely segregated—were fluid; church relations mirrored the same reality. African Americans, free and enslaved, were part of First Baptist, Montgomery, since its earliest institutional beginnings. In the late 1820s church members first held services in a tavern, then shared the local courthouse with a thespian group, and next shared a common building with Methodists and Presbyterians. In the fall of 1832, a small, unpretentious frame building became their first official house of worship. In the first church constitution, no distinction was made between the rights and privileges of members based upon race.[7] Even in the mid-1830s, when black congregants came to outnumber whites, black votes counted equally in church conferences in which new church members were received and business decisions were made. Such parity was especially surprising, since the Baptist tradition vests local congregations with final authority on all issues, and decisions result from a simple majority vote. Sunday mornings at First Baptist found a biracial congregation worshiping at the same time and in the same building, with whites seated in the front and blacks accommodated in the back, as was common in the North. At least on some occasions, communion and baptisms were shared.[8]

By the 1840s, Montgomery was growing rapidly and sloughing off its status as a primitive outpost. State legislators voted to move the state capitol from Tuscaloosa to Montgomery. Concurrently, First Baptist had come to occupy a prominent place in the city and now counted several city leaders among its members. The same years saw white leadership take measures to bring about a more rigid racial segregation at the church. The actual precipitating cause for the changes is not recorded, but in February of 1840 a committee reported on charges that had been leveled against some African American members for drinking and working on the Sabbath. Two black members were excommunicated, and a committee was created to revise the First

Baptist Church Constitution and Rules of Decorum.[9] In April, one of First Baptist's founders and a prominent deacon, A. B. McWorther, made a motion to excommunicate a black member accused of running a "house of ill fame," lying, and working on the Sabbath. Church members voted: seven whites and one black for excommunication and five whites and five blacks against the motion. The motion failed. Later that month, new articles were added to the Church Constitution and Rules of Decorum: African Americans were barred from regular church conference meetings, but were to congregate at a different time; six white church members, the pastor, and one deacon were to oversee the separate black meetings; in all church matters, a majority of white members would decide all questions and "colored" members would be allowed to vote only on matters affecting other blacks; black members could give evidence in the trials of other black members only; and, except in extraordinary cases, new black church members would be received at the separate black church conference meeting.[10]

This pivotal change in race relations at the church betrayed the precarious state of black equality, which rested on the pleasure of whites and made it clear that whites would not long tolerate the possibility of being outvoted by African Americans. After the fateful dispute, black congregants became a church within a church and met separately for worship service. Throughout the 1850s, church minutes of the black conference meetings record the separate congregation accepting new members through letters and baptism, disciplining members for "disorderly walking," and ordaining leaders to the deaconate. They called their own minister—first an enslaved man named Caesar; then A. Ellis; and, finally, Nathan Ashby, who became pastor to the congregation when it broke off from First Baptist. Ashby had been brought from Virginia as a slave in 1810, but managed through his carpentry work to purchase his freedom for nine hundred dollars. Though Ashby was in the position of pastor to the black flock, he was not ordained by a presbytery until 1865. Blacks also selected (and Tichenor ordained) Fayette Vanderville, Jerry Fry, and Peter Miles to the deaconate. Even before 1865, African Americans at First Baptist were used to making their own decisions. This arrangement gave African Americans some autonomy, but only within a circumscribed sphere, since decisions made at the all-black conference meetings had to be presented to and ratified by the separate white conference, which sometimes reversed black decisions.[11]

It is not difficult, then, to understand how blacks and whites at First Baptist may have had different notions of what emancipation meant for the society at large and for church life in particular. We do not know if First Baptist was the church the writer referred to in the August

1865 editorial, but we do know that it was one of Montgomery's "principal" churches, so a similar sentiment prevailed there. Such a feeling was discordant with African American notions of what emancipation meant. Most blacks believed that emancipation required conscious and intentional acts of self-determination and meant sloughing off the remnants of slavery, which included relegation to the galleries and basements of white churches. As late as 1870, Alabama's governor, Robert Lindsay, complained that African Americans "were disposed to ... rush into a church ... where white people were sitting; not that they had no place to sit but simply to show their equality."[12] The actions that white Alabamians construed as audacious effronteries to contemporary racial etiquette African Americans saw as rightful and necessary expressions of their new status as freed persons.

The intensifying post-bellum black expectations and white anxieties were among the many dramatic political changes that characterized the times. In fact, Reconstruction-era Alabama society was characterized by black protest and resistance to white efforts to retain all political, economic, and social power. With assistance from federal authorities, blacks were successful in gaining some measure of political power. On June 1, 1865, when Louis E. Parsons was appointed provisional governor of Alabama, he called for the election of a convention to ratify measures that would permit Alabama to be readmitted to the Union. The presence of Union soldiers reminded elected governor Robert M. Patton that neither Northern sentiment nor the government in Washington, D.C. would long tolerate his efforts to fight passage of the Thirteenth and the Fourteenth Amendments to the U.S. Constitution.[13] Patton's distressed compliance with the all-white convention's actions to ratify the Reconstruction Act signaled that the state "accepted the war's political verdict" but not its "social judgment."[14]

The accommodation of radical political changes alongside the rigid opposition to even modest change in social relationships between blacks and whites bracketed the early years of Reconstruction in Alabama. Throughout the state, African Americans made the most of this brief period of political opportunity. Meeting in an all-black convention in 1865 and again in 1867, delegates called for the creation of a public school system as well as relief for poor and aged former slaves. The convention further held that it was blacks' "undeniable right to hold offices, sit on juries, ride on all public conveyances, and to sit at public tables in places of amusement." In Montgomery, demographic realities sharpened whites' fears of African Americans acquiring equality. By 1860, 41 percent of Montgomery's population was African American. Five years later, as African American freed persons began to settle throughout the city, a few black majority voting districts were created. Indeed, changing demographics led to rather profound alterations in the political makeup of the city and the state. Between 1865 and 1877, African Americans in Montgomery were always represented in the state legislature, and at least two of the twelve city councilmen were black. In August 1868 the city council of Montgomery appointed, for the first time, African American police officers. In fact, the force consisted of twelve white and twelve black men. Through these offices and positions, blacks were able to wield some power to secure opportunity for members of their community.[15]

Sufficiently removed from the direct arm of federal influence and authority, social relations developed differently from the brief respite of these temporary political gains. More important, rather than these gains leading to movement toward social integration (equal access to public facilities), the rigidity of social separation created a milieu that eventually reversed most such gains.[16] Even with federal support and the sincere goodwill of some white Alabama politicians, it was still a struggle for African Americans to sustain political offices, and there were from time to time attacks by white democrats abjuring the notion that African Americans could be effective officials. Furthermore, all steps toward granting African Americans some say in political affairs were taken in the shadow of a set of laws bent on circumscribing black freedoms—namely, the Black Codes.[17] As African Americans migrated from rural areas to the cities, they had to contend with strict vagrancy laws. Under these edicts people could be arrested, jailed, or fined for a panoply of offenses: not showing up for work, quitting a job, breaking the town curfew, and so on. Often these laws were not race-specific on the books but only in their enforcement. African Americans were prohibited from purchasing or renting certain properties and from serving on juries. Though black politicians tried to thwart these measures, they rarely won more than a reprieve, and by 1877, when the last federal troops were removed from the South, these codes became the corpus of a structure of rigid segregation and discrimination that white politicians imposed on African Americans as a means of "redeeming the South," or restoring the old order to power.

While African Americans envisioned a new role for themselves in society and the federal government successfully forced some black voices into the political arena, many whites believed that control would be maintained only through a rigid segregation in all aspects of social life, to be enforced by law and sometimes by terror. It quickly became apparent that "former slave holders never intended to accept the 'freedom' of Negroes without the reservation that (Negroes) continue to be wards ...

of the class which had owned them." By the late 1860s, given the nature of race relations at First Baptist, Montgomery, and the troubled political and social state of affairs, blacks' decision to separate from their white-dominated congregation, and whites' acceptance of that decision, reflected the adjustment processes taking place in the larger society.[18]

On July 27, 1867, African American congregants, at their regular Saturday evening meeting, agreed to withdraw from First Baptist, "passing a resolution, couched in the kindliest of terms suggesting the wisdom of the separation." The next day, after the Sunday morning church services, church clerk John Stratford presented a resolution "in compliance with a request made by colored members of the church at their regular meeting." Stratford stated, "Whereas our colored brethren are erecting a house of worship and contemplate establishing an independent church ... and whereas the colored members shall make applications ... letters of dissmission [sic] are herby granted to Rev. A. Ellis, Pastor; Holland Thompson, Richard Williams, Abram Blackshear, Joseph Jackson and Jesse Figh, and Ned Tillman, deacons and to all the colored members hitherto holding connection with the First Baptist Church, for the purpose of organizing a separate and inde-pendent church." African American members took with them the seats and pulpit from their former worship space in the basement and more than twenty years experience as a de facto separate religious body. More than six hundred African Americans—two-thirds of the congregation, led by Tichenor, Ellis, and Ashby—moved from First Baptist Church on Court Street to Columbus Street Baptist Church, a wooden, Gothic-revival structure with large windows, a high ceiling, and a tall steeple.

Separation allowed for a large measure of autonomy for African Americans. It took a few years, however, before members of the church would develop the financial means to sustain themselves. Until 1868, when Tichenor resigned his Montgomery pastorate, he remained closely involved in Columbus Street affairs. Other whites at First Bap-tist volunteered to help as well, especially with teaching Sunday school. Here whites' involvement in securing separate religious facilities for blacks at once appealed to their paternalism and helped eliminate the possibility that African American majorities in white congregations might agitate for parity. African Americans had taken a giant step toward shoring up the possibility of defining emancipation in broad terms. We also see that exercising political and social independence became tied to controlling institutional expressions of spirituality.[19]

The early years of church life at Columbus Street Baptist were characterized by the excitement and newness of the venture but also by fragility and challenge. Ashby was reputed to have been an able administrator, pastor, and preacher who urged the congregation to consider that Christianity was more than emotion and Sunday morning church attendance but also "faith in the gospel and right-doing." Church membership grew rapidly, and within a year the congregation joined with twenty-seven other new independent African American Baptist churches to form the Colored Missionary Baptist Convention of Alabama. Ashby was elected as the convention's first president. Columbus Street also took the lead in securing the help of the predominately white American Baptist Home Missionary Society to augment efforts of the Freedman's Bureau to help African Americans establish new lives.

The initial excitement that Ashby and members experienced soon gave way to tensions and even tragedy. Ministering to the large diverse congregation created by the steady influx of thousands of blacks into the city was difficult. The same stratifications that had existed among African Americans during the slavery era persisted. The congregation included formerly enslaved persons and those who had been free long before 1865. Among the formerly enslaved members were those who had worked in the fields and others who had been house servants as well as those who had held positions of authority within the slave system. Pastor and members struggled over how best to fashion a congregational life to accommodate this diverse membership, address pressing social and political needs and comport with traditional spiritual functions of a church, like instructing and supporting members in their Christian walk. Intensifying the fragility of church life, Ashby suffered a paralyzing stroke, and while he continued to be involved in Columbus Street affairs until his death a few years later, James Foster became the new pastor.

Columbus Street Baptist Church weathered the struggles and uncertainty of the early years and eventually flourished. Still, internal pressures and the assorted needs of the membership led to differences of opinion among congregants, and factions developed. For numerous reasons, then, groups broke away to form separate congregations.[20] This difficulty was not unique to Columbus Street or to Montgomery. New black Baptist churches were forming so quickly throughout Alabama that the state Colored Missionary Baptist Convention created a committee to stem the proliferation of new congregations. Committee members visited new congregations to evaluate their resources. If a congregation was judged to possess insufficient assets to sustain a healthy independent church, it was encouraged to disband and join in with a nearby already-established church. On the other hand, if the congregation showed potential, it was encouraged to send delegates to the state convention. Dexter Avenue Baptist Church was born in this flurry of Reconstruction-era church growth.[21]

In the early 1870s, the departure of a group of disgruntled Columbus Street Baptist Church members—namely, H. A. Loveless, John Phillips, Samuel Phillips, Charles Sterrs, Alfred Thomas, Alfred Thompson, Holland Thompson, and William Thompson—set a series of events into motion that culminated in the establishment of the Second Colored Baptist Church (later renamed Dexter Avenue Missionary Baptist Church). Beyond the stresses that challenged most black churches during Reconstruction, the precise reasons for the second exodus are not known. Rumors persist that among this group were the more privileged members of the Columbus Street congregation and those who disapproved of the church's emotional worship format. There was even a suggestion that those forming Dexter Avenue left Columbus Street because it was located in an area that flooded after heavy rains, thus forcing persons entering the building to muddy their shoes. Church historian Zelia Evans explained that those who left wanted a more dignified access to the building. At first the group met informally in Samuel Phillips's home on 630 High Street for regular prayer meetings. By 1875, they sent a delegate to the Colored Missionary Baptist Convention of Alabama, where they were formally recognized as a fledgling but promising independent congregation.[22] Two years would pass before an official dedication ceremony was held in Montgomery. In the interim, Holland Thompson, at the request of the white Southern Baptist Convention, established a separate Sunday school, which opened February 25, 1877, in a former slaver trader's pen on Dexter Avenue.

Like many other independent African American churches Dexter Avenue Baptist Church was indebted to the presence of missionaries. Joining Thompson on the Sunday school staff were white Northern missionaries, two sisters and a brother: Ann, Clarinda, and John Wilkins. They came south from Patties Run, Ohio, just after the war to establish a school for African American girls. During the week, the family taught the rudiments of education in an apartment rented from Mr. and Mrs. Henry Campbell on Bell Street. The Campbells' three daughters Annie, Gertrude, and Louise all attended the regular school and the Sunday school. A short time after the Wilkinses began their work in Montgomery, they were joined by other white missionaries Kate Nutting and John Langridge, who frequently came to the school and gave instruction to the students. Langridge helped the Wilkins raise money to move the school into a building on Dexter Avenue. Soon, the school was renamed Langridge Academy.[23]

It remains a mystery exactly how the disparate elements all came together to form a single congregation, but Phillips and the others who left from Columbus Street Baptist Church combined their prayer meetings in his home with the Thompson Sunday School to officially organize the second African American Baptist congregation in Montgomery. In January 1878, surrounded by the remains and ashes of an old slave trader's pen, the Second Colored Baptist Church rose as a phoenix of freedom. For the community in general and members in particular, the new church was a second citadel from which to push for a broad interpretation of emancipation's meaning. At the ceremony officially recognizing and dedicating Dexter Avenue, the African American community was represented by James Foster, pastor of Columbus Street Baptist Church, while J. B. Hawthorne (Tishenor's successor at First Baptist) and several of his deacons offered the good wishes of Montgomery's white Baptist community. On January 30, 1879, Dexter Avenue trustees Eli Langston, H. A. Loveless, and Samuel Phillips purchased, for $270.00, a small piece of land on South Decatur Street (which intersects Dexter Avenue), and it officially became the home of the church.[24]

We know little of the day-to-day life of the congregation before 1905, but available sources on Reconstruction-era Alabama, the black clergy, black education, and information on some members provide a window into the church's character formation during its early years. Four factors worked together to create the distinctive personality of Dexter Avenue Baptist Church: the worship format, the relationship between deacons and pastors, the comparatively elite status of many of its founders and members, and the presence of two colleges nearby, which provided sources of employment and education.

One principal source of conflict rumored to have existed among the diverse congregation at Columbus Street Baptist Church was the question of what constituted appropriate worship in this new day. How should new, independent congregations distinguish themselves from so-called slave-religion or biracial churches where blacks were assigned to the galleries? Positions ran along a fault line demarcating "conservatives" who embraced an emotional worship approach with shouting and preacher–congregation call-and-response versus "progressives" who advocated a formal worship format that privileged hymn singing over spirituals or Gospel music (which was in its infancy at this time). As "progressives," Dexter Avenue members wanted ministers to give them "thoughts rather than feelings" and argued that churches were called to overt social and political activism. The congregation believed that education was essential to a mature Christian faith, "as there can be little revelation of God where there is arrested mental development."

Perhaps as a result of its commitment to progressive Baptist doctrine, or simply to distinguish itself from most other black churches, Dexter Avenue consciously instituted a staid and formal worship format. Disapproving glances discouraged emotional displays during worship. Sunday services were punctilious and opened with a proper introit followed by the singing of traditional Baptist hymns. Some members claimed that emotional displays during worship, such as shouting and the singing of spirituals, were too reminiscent of slavery. The more formal worship format, they contended, appropriately marked a new day in African Americans' practice of Christianity. This worship format was appealing to some members of Montgomery's African American community, but others judged it as a thinly veiled rejection of black cultural survival practices forged in the crucible of slavery and a pretentious insignia of a middle-class sensibility and—perhaps most important—as an impediment to the church's claim to affirm all people. The approach likely contributed to Dexter Avenue's slow initial growth. While Columbus Street continued to deal with rapid growth during the 1870s, Dexter Avenue's membership did not stabilize until the late 1880s.[25]

Another distinguishing characteristic of Dexter Avenue was the power relationship that developed between deacons and ministers. Dexter Avenue's first pastor was called by its deacons. This founding group of deacons set a precedent of exercising great influence over the minister. The late nineteenth and early twentieth centuries were arguably an apex of the African American minister's authority and popularity. African Americans had just "broken forth from slavery…. There was no one to baptize their children, to perform marriage, or bury the dead. A ministry had to be created at once—created out of the material at hand."[26] The black minister, argued W. E. B. Du Bois, is "the most unique personality developed by the Negro on American soil. A leader, a politician, an orator, a 'boss,' an intriguer, an idealist…. The combination of a certain adroitness with deep-seated earnestness … gave him his pre-eminence and helps him to maintain it."[27] The power relationship between the deacons and the pastor at Dexter Avenue, when compared to contemporary post-bellum African American Baptist Churches, represented an unusual division of sovereignty and resulted in an unusually high number of pastoral resignations.

During Reconstruction, African American ministers were intimately involved in the lives of church members. They helped the Freedmen's Bureau teach newly freed men and women to read and write, find housing and jobs, and even choose new family names. Often they were the best-educated members (though not always formally, especially among Baptists[28]) of their congregation. Most African American preachers balanced seeking power and opportunity for their congregation with allaying whites' fears of blacks mobilizing their resources. Black preachers and exhorters were in the best positions, as respected members of the community, to advocate a liberal interpretation of emancipation; but because they were so influential, their very presence threatened white supremacy. African American clergy knew that in negotiating with whites in power, being too outspoken could cost them their lives; yet, too much capitulation to white authority eclipsed their congregations' freedom.[29]

Some black ministers were traditionalists; while they abhorred slavery and were dedicated to defining black emancipation broadly, many were comfortable with Southern values, customs, and religious beliefs. Most had grown up in the South and thus developed particular strategies for coping with racism. They established autonomous churches while maintaining a level of congeniality with their white sisters and brothers. Black ministers' efforts to placate whites did not hinder their preaching a "Gospel of Freedom." For example, Daniel Alexander Payne, bishop of the African Methodist Episcopal Church, maintained that any black person who would accept seating in "Negro pews" repudiated his own manhood. Payne and many other black ministers preached that African Americans should strive to "free themselves from the control of whites and become equal, independent, fully franchised citizens." Black ministers believed that emancipation had brought about the destruction of the old society. They preached that all things were new, and they committed themselves to help "regenerate" formerly enslaved African Americans from the intellectual and moral degradation of slavery. The "Gospel of Freedom" combined American middle-class notions of moral reform and self-help with racial pride. These ideas, as we shall see in subsequent chapters, were permanently imprinted onto the character of Dexter Avenue in its formative years.[30] We shall also see that, with few exceptions, the locus of power at the church rested with the deacons.

Dexter Avenue was also greatly influenced by the presence of a sizable number of achieving elites in its congregation and by the proximity of two colleges. In post-bellum Montgomery, a degree of social stratification developed among the city's black residents. African Americans attained status within the community by getting a formal education, securing a professional position in education, answering the call to ministry, or accumulating wealth. Several of the church's founding members were among the community's elite. Dexter Avenue owed its large percentage of relatively privileged members to the presence of two schools, Alabama State University (originally Lincoln Normal School) and the Tuskegee Institute. The stories of the founding of these schools provide insight into the struggles of establishing African American's educational institutions and the ways in which close relationships formed between black schools and black churches.[31]

It was the dream of Scotsman William Burns Paterson, born in 1849, to serve as a missionary in Africa, but in 1867, when insufficient funds prevented such a venture, he came to America.[32] Eventually he found his way to Alabama and started a school, Tullibody Academy, to teach freed blacks "to read and write and do figures."[33] In 1878, he accepted a position from the American Missionary Association to head Lincoln School at Marion, Alabama, which the state legislature had made the first State Normal College for African Americans. In the winter of 1887, white segregationists, bent on frustrating African Americans' educational opportunities, set the school aflame. The state legislature moved the school to Montgomery, and held its first registration for classes at Dexter Avenue Baptist Church.[34] In fact, for the first couple of years, classes met in various black churches, including Dexter Avenue, and in private homes throughout the city. In 1888, the Alabama State Supreme Court declared the funding arrangement for the university unconstitutional because the legislature had sought to pay for the college component of the school from common school funds (designated to be used for grade school education only). In 1889, the legislature abolished the university department of the school and renamed it the State Normal School for Colored Students.[35] Largely due to the commitment and persistence of William Paterson, the school grew and soon regained its college division.[36] Several Dexter Avenue members were on faculty at Alabama State, including Dora Beverly, J. W. Beverly, Annie Doak, J. L. Kirkpatrick, and Gertrude Watkins.

A Virginia-born and -educated former slave, Booker T. Washington, left his teaching position in the night school at Hampton Institute in Hampton, Virginia, to start an industrial training school for African Americans just fifty miles from Montgomery.[37] In 1881, with a two-thousand-dollar grant from the Alabama General Assembly, Washington founded the Tuskegee Normal School (later the Tuskegee Institute).[38] Upon arriving in Tuskegee, he had hoped to find buildings and teaching materials in place to begin his administration, but no preparations had been made for such. He was delighted to find, however, "that which no costly building and apparatus can supply —hundreds of hungry, earnest souls who wanted to secure knowledge."

Along with establishing a school, Washington also became a major proponent of a certain philosophy concerning race relations known as accommodationism. This conciliatory approach to the struggle for black progress counseled blacks to secure industrial skills and make themselves an essential component of the manual labor force in the United States. It discouraged African Americans from demanding social equality and cautioned them to delay their press for political rights. This philosophy formed an important part of the basis of Dexter Avenue's approach to race relations and social activism in the twentieth century. Along with Alabama State University, the Tuskegee Institute provided many African Americans living in Montgomery with opportunities for employment and to get a formal education. Over the years, several Dexter Avenue members were employed by Tuskegee. Along with Alabama State, Tuskegee helped create a population of blacks in Montgomery who were slightly privileged, and many of this group attended Dexter Avenue. Two church pioneers, Henry A. Loveless and William Watkins, were members of Alabama State's first board of trustees.[39]

Some Dexter Avenue pioneers attained economic status by owning businesses. William Watkins was a noted contractor in the city whose company built the present edifice at Dexter Avenue;[40] Charles Sterrs owned a successful upholstery business; and then there was H. A. Loveless. Born enslaved in Union Springs, Alabama, on November 24, 1854, Loveless remained with his former master's family for five years after the Civil War ended, but soon became convinced that he would be better off on his own. Leaving Union Springs in secret, he came to Montgomery, where he married Lucy Arrington in 1875. Working odd jobs, he saved his money and established a butcher's business, which he soon expanded to include a coal yard, an undertaker's shop, and a horse-and-carriage taxi. By the turn of the twentieth century he was estimated to have employed about twenty-five people and possess a net worth of over $25,000.[41]

Another of the Dexter Avenue founders, Holland Thompson, was a lawmaker. He served three terms in the state legislature and several terms on Montgomery's city council.[42] Born in 1840, for over twenty-five years Thompson was enslaved to a wealthy Montgomery planter, William Taylor, who taught him to read and write. After the Civil War, Thompson opened a grocery store located in the majority-black fifth district of Montgomery.[43] An early advocate of the self-help strategy of racial uplift, he spoke at the first black independence day celebration on January 1, 1866 (later called Emancipation Day). Speaking before a racially mixed audience, he warned African Americans, "The colored race ... must not stand waiting for others to push them [sic] along ... [but must] work industriously, educate our children, avoid whiskey and cease bickering."[44] This speech made Thompson popular among whites as well as African Americans, and it helped get him elected to the city council.[45]

As a politician, Thompson chose his battles carefully. He did not fight the white power structure on the issue of segregating much of public life in the city. He did not oppose plans to create a segregated public school system, city hospital, city graveyard, and municipal railway transit complex. He saw to it, however, that the Freedman's Bureau set aside funds to establish a black-owned bank in Montgomery. As a city councilman he insisted that black city workers (namely street hands) received equal pay for their work, and he oversaw the establishment of a public defender for the city as well as a soup kitchen to feed poor residents (often people who had recently arrived in the city from the countryside). He tried but failed to prevent the state legislature from passing acts that limited black voting, and he tried to thwart a state law that barred interracial marriages. Additionally, he challenged Northern missionaries who would not hire black teachers at local African American schools.[46] In many ways Thompson epitomized the status, ambition, and accomplishment of the kinds of people who helped to establish Dexter Avenue.

Features of Reconstruction were also part of Dexter Avenue's early history. The church's first pastor, C. O. Boothe, was a teacher for the Freedmen's Bureau.[47] He was born enslaved and in his early years was raised by his grandmother, but later he was taken to be a servant in the home of his master's son, Nathan Howard Jr. Teachers who boarded at the Howard home taught Boothe to read and write, and, at age fourteen, he worked in the law office of brothers James and S. H. Terrel. While in this position, he read numerous books from their library. His only formal training was in the medical department at Meharry College in Nashville, Tennessee.

Boothe's years at Dexter Avenue were difficult ones. It is probable that financial difficulties and his inability to reconcile disagreements among members of the congregation resulted in his leaving after a short time.[48] For all of his shortcomings as the pastor of Dexter Avenue, however, Boothe excelled as an educator and editor. He served as assistant editor of the *Baptist Leader* (the official newspaper of the Colored Missionary Baptist Convention of Alabama), wrote three theological pamphlets, and served as both a faculty member and president of the college that Baptists established in Selma, Alabama, for African Americans.[49]

To create favorable sentiment regarding Baptist activities and to garner support for Baptist ventures, Boothe wrote a historical and biographical work, *The Cyclopedia of the Colored Baptists of Alabama.* Typifying racial uplift efforts of the day, Boothe explained, "Appeals to Pharaoh and Caesar are not so wise as appeals to facts which prove the Negro to be man just as other races are men."[50] The book was illustrative as well of African Americans' embrace of the American progress narrative; Boothe hoped to exhibit the textures and maturity of "Negro Christianity" during and after slavery and to "chronicle Negro progress from 1865–1895 for black people, white people—friends and foes." He maintained ties with Dexter Avenue long after his tenure as its pastor, chiefly through his intense participation in white and African American Baptist conventions.

From the late 1870s to 1883, during the pastorates of J. W. Stevens, F. McDonald, J. C. Curry, Albert Franklin Owens, and Dr. John Langridge (white), Dexter Avenue became more involved in the Colored Missionary Baptist Convention of Alabama. Three issues concerned the convention in its first years: Baptist congregations in the state, establishing a home mission association to help with relief efforts in the African American community, and launching a training school. Founding a home mission board was not a source of controversy. With the financial support of the white American Baptist Home Missionary Society, a home mission organization was instituted to serve Alabama's African American community.[51]

Building a theological school to educate young African American men for the Baptist ministry, however, was contentious.[52] Establishing preaching credentials through formal education had never garnered the same support among Baptists that it had with Presbyterians and Episcopalians. Baptists believed that a person was "called" to preach, that divine inspiration provided exhorters and pastors with their messages and their training.[53] In November 1873, at the sixth session of the Colored Missionary Baptist Convention of Alabama, Boothe noted that the question of "whether God needed help in preparing his ministry" (which white Baptists had argued over many years earlier) was now "stirring the souls of black men."[54] White Baptists meeting in the same city at the same time advised against building a school. They argued it was too soon after slavery for African Americans to take on so large a project. Baptist minister and leader W. B. McAlpine and a few others forged ahead, ignoring the naysayers. The following year the Colored Missionary Baptist Convention reluctantly passed a resolution to build a school. It took yet another year before Boothe and McAlpine were given the charge to find a site for the theological school.

In 1878, in its tenth session, the convention purchased land in Selma. According to Boothe, the organization and influence of the Women's Baptist Convention of Alabama provided the drive, energy, and money necessary to build the school. He maintained that the Baptists "occupy advanced ground with regard to the questions which involve the powers and rights of women."[55] Mary V. Cook agreed that there was an important role for women to play in the effort to educate Baptist ministers, explaining that women must be allowed to "do the heart and hard work.... Give women the scope the Bible gives them and let them throw the influence of their spiritual power into churches. ... Let them feel that they have a higher calling than the love of fashion and worldly pleasure, that God has called them to minister unto him."[56] Dexter Avenue's Sallie H. Wright spoke passionately and persuasively on the value of an educated clergy, noting that "knowing the terrors of ignorance and superstition and seeing demonstrated around them each day the power of education and enlightenment, they [women] in their poverty and weakness have undertaken to make our school what it should be." S. A. Stone, another Dexter Avenue member and first president of the Woman's Baptist Convention of Alabama, was responsible for raising a substantial amount of money for this effort. In 1878, the Alabama Baptist Normal and Theological School (later renamed Selma University) opened its doors to students.

While members of the Colored Missionary Baptist Convention strongly disagreed over some issues, such as an educated clergy, their struggle to get white Baptists to recognize them as equals was a uniting force.[57] For example, African American ministers wanted those capable among them to be allowed to write Sunday school literature for dissemination. White ministers and conventions contended that Alabama's African American ministers had inadequate understanding of Christian theology to write Sunday school lessons for publication. African American preachers, claimed their white counterparts, placed too much significance on the biblical figure of Moses, had an inadequate understanding of the importance of Jesus Christ, were too emotional and superstitious, and had an insufficient understanding of the concept of Christian atonement. Boothe countered this attack, arguing that "black Baptists recognize and establish religion around the belief that Negroes are human, sinful, accountable, in need and capable of redemption through Christ." Boothe held that African American Baptist preachers worked to achieve in their followers "individual human essence leavened by divine essence." One of Dexter Avenue's ministers, Jacob Tileston Brown, was among the first African American ministers to write Sunday school literature. He wrote the first Sunday school lessons for the newly established National Baptist Publishing Board, an independent organization founded in 1895 to provide Sunday school literature for African American Baptist churches.[58]

The convention movement, as it developed from a local association to a state and finally a national organization, took on great significance among African American Baptists. The formation of the National Baptist Convention, U.S.A. in 1895 was the culmination of more than thirty years of organizational work. This convention allowed for the creation of national racial self-help programs. Just as the independent African American church carved out a sphere in which members could participate in all aspects of church life on a local level, national conventions provided the same opportunity nationally.[59] In these conventions, African Americans could exercise their right to choose their leaders. Those with leadership ability could run for offices. The convention allowed African Americans to pool their resources to build and support educational institutions. Most significantly, perhaps, efforts to bring together such a large body of African Americans led to the development and proliferation of a race consciousness of affirmation and self-respect.[60]

As the 1880s found the attention of Dexter Avenue's members focused on expanding the influence of African American sacred space by supporting state and national conventions, these same members had somewhat neglected activities at home. When A. N. McEwen accepted the call to the pastorate in 1883, however, he was able to breathe new life into the floundering congregation. He put the church's finances in order and brought a measure of reconciliation and cooperation to a congregation whose members "were entertaining such feelings toward each other that the work seemed to be at a stand still."[61] Upon his arrival, members were still using, for their religious and educational needs, a small frame building purchased and repaired by the trustees in 1880.[62] In 1883, pastor and congregants began to solidify Dexter Avenue's place in the neighborhood, and once again we see how black self-determination, measured white assistance, and a degree of white objection coalesced to influence black religious life during Reconstruction. We see, as well, black activism and black accommodation.

Using dray wagons, members of the congregation collected bricks discarded by city workers paving the street and in two years had enough bricks to build a one-story structure. In December 1884 members asked Pastor McEwen and Deacon H. A. Loveless to head a campaign to raise money. Noting that the "membership and congregation are made up of the best colored persons of our city and hope to be encouraged by our people," McEwen and Loveless placed an article in the *Montgomery Daily Advertiser and Mail* explaining that congregants intended "to commence building on their brick church on the corner of Dexter Avenue and Decatur Streets ... and are asking aid of the public."

The solicitation brought attention, support, and opposition. Some members at First Baptist, Montgomery contributed and encouraged other whites to give. When it became apparent, however, that this African American congregation would build a permanent worship facility one block from the state capitol, an editorial betraying many whites' belief that citizenship was a white possession appeared in the *Daily Advertiser*. Referring to himself as simply a "citizen," one person wrote, "This street will in the near future be one of the best improved streets in the city of Montgomery ... and nothing should be allowed that would deter citizens from building on Dexter Avenue." The white editorialist continued, "The Negro is demonstrative in his nature and noisy in his religious exercises ... they [*sic*] will hold their night meetings at a late hour when the whites as a general rule are asleep...." This was an ironic objection for a church whose reputation, at least in the African American community, was to frown upon even the slightest displays of emotionalism. The writer claimed "no race prejudice that would cause him to do any injustice to 'our brother in black'," but admonished white citizens to "refuse to contribute a nickel until [they find] out where the church is to be located." Harking back to almost twenty years earlier, when the African American woman took a seat exactly suited to her mind in one of Montgomery's prominent white churches, the editorialist explained, "In the years I have contributed to build churches and educational institutions for them. But Mr. Editor, I recognize ... a propriety and fitness in all things proper to be done ... it is not right for them to build nor for us to assist them to build every place." He concluded, "Fair minded and thinking ones among the colored people can see the justice of the foregoing remarks and the propriety of choosing some other place for a house of worship." Rumors persisted, as late as 1972, that state government officials and other prominent Montgomery citizens were plotting to force the congregation to sell this property, but members refused to be deterred.[63]

Still, there were efforts to demonstrate to the white community that black people were worthy and capable of negotiating shared public space. The persistent refusal to back down from members' plans permanently to locate their religious facility across from the capital building was a real and symbolic action that contested whites' determination to define public space as an exclusively white domain. Over the years, the church's being located in so conspicuous a place induced a routine ebb and flow of threats to force relocation. As we shall see in later chapters, church members' success in maintaining Dexter Avenue's location becomes even more significant when one considers that this building would become an important meeting space in 1919 when Montgomery's branch of the National Association for the Advancement of Colored People met to demand that the state take some action against lynching and improve the condition of African American schools. The church was an integral site as well for planning the 1955 Montgomery bus boycott and for refreshing and supporting the 1965 Selma marchers at the end of their tumultuous journey.[64]

The first worship service was held in the basement of the new church in July 1885. A white architect, Pelham J. Anderson, designed a red brick Gothic revival structure with white Victorian bracketing.[65] William Watkins, a deacon at Dexter Avenue and the contractor in charge of the project, was able to have the upstairs sanctuary ready for Thanksgiving services in 1889.[66] Typical of many buildings constructed in Alabama cities in the late nineteenth century, Dexter Avenue was a product of eclectic European styles of architecture (classic, Gothic, and Renaissance). The outline of the church building forms a simple rectangle with geometrically symmetrical openings—doors and windows, bell tower, and massive steps—indicative of the late English Renaissance. The building has a low gable roof with a decorative triangular pediment that hangs from the front edge of the roofline and extends across the front face of the building to its extremities, and keystones adorn the top of each window; these features reflect a classic design. The large, narrow window openings, pointed arches and inlaid glass are typical of Gothic architecture.[67] For the members of Dexter Avenue, their new facility was an object of pride. Many in the Montgomery community agreed. The *Montgomery Daily Advertiser* noted "the Colored Baptists" have erected "a handsome brick church."[68]

Seven years into his pastorate, McEwen left Dexter Avenue to accept a call to a large church in Mobile. A number of successful and able pastors followed him at Dexter Avenue: Jacob Brown, W. B. McAlpine, W. W. Colley and Thomas Pollard. Pollard was a strong advocate of foreign missions. He preached a sermon, "Baptist and Colportage," in which he told the Dexter Avenue congregation, "God has never presented to his children the dark side of providence but that he afterward presented the bright side." He went on to explain that taking this message to the world was an important component of Baptist responsibility and Baptist tradition. Baptist efforts to "spread the word" date back to 1840, when the Baptist Publication Society was created to send traveling agents into all parts of the world. The demands for work in foreign fields, Pollard preached to the congregation, were "frequent and urgent."[69]

In addition to his work in foreign missions, Pollard was also an editor of the *Baptist Leader* and later a president of Selma University. During his pastorate at Dexter Avenue, J. L. Kirkpatrick established a chapter of the Baptist Young People's Union (BYPU), and Henry Loveless's daughters Bertha and Henrietta were among its charter members. This organization's charge was to prepare the next generation to be spiritual leaders. Through it, Dexter Avenue youth learned about Baptist doctrine and church life. In its earliest configuration, this auxiliary held Sunday afternoon training sessions to augment young people's general education as well as their religious instruction. The BYPU symbolized that Dexter Avenue was here to stay, that the institution had successfully navigated the first difficult and uncertain years of its life.

Dexter Avenue was now a smoothly functioning, independent, African American Baptist church. Members of its congregation covenanted to "walk together in Christian love; to strive for the advancement of this church ... give it a place in our affections, prayers and service ... to sustain its worship, ordinances, discipline and doctrines ... to contribute ... for support of a faithful and evangelical ministry among us, the relief of the poor and the spread of the Gospel...." To carry out these functions the church was structured to have—in addition to a pastor—a board of deacons to work closely with the pastor, a board of trustees to be responsible for the physical structure of the church, a clerk to keep a record of church activities and meetings, a finance committee and treasurer to oversee the financial life of the church, a superintendent of Sunday schools to facilitate religious education training, a BYPU to insure the posterity of the church, a small choir, and a missionary society to evangelize locally while providing relief for the poor in Montgomery.[70] Firmly entrenched in the Montgomery religious community and actively associated with local, state, and national Baptist conventions, the church was now stable.

By the dawn of the twentieth century, Dexter Avenue Baptist Church was poised to launch a rigorous fight to define black emancipation more broadly. Members were earnestly prepared, some might say naively, to do the work of racial uplift, to promote education, and to advocate a faith in the morality and basic decency of democratic values and American institutions. This racially separate religious organization was a safe place for Montgomery's African Americans, a place where community leaders were trained and congregants were affirmed as worthwhile, capable individuals.[71] Dexter Avenue's founding, then, was a dramatic act of self-determination amid both white assistance and white objection.[72] Opening its doors on a structure formerly used as a slave trader's pen transformed a profane facility of enslavement and bondage into a hallowed shrine from which to exercise self-expression and to fight for African American freedom.[73] On the very space where blacks had once been held awaiting a life of slavery and illiteracy, the founders of Dexter Avenue established a religious institution that promoted education as indispensable to good Christian character, good citizenship, and personal liberation.

The early twentieth century also brought an end to stories of outraged white Alabamians decrying African Americans' "running into white churches" and taking seats "exactly suited to their minds" aggressively to demonstrate their equality. Jim Crow racial segregation was firmly and doggedly entrenched in the city and the nation. During Reconstruction, African Americans had set out to interpret their emancipation in a manner that gave them the greatest possible latitude. During this same period, however, whites in Alabama—as in other parts of the nation—insisted upon a circumscription of African American freedom that maintained a trenchant and inimical white supremacy in all aspects of society. African Americans' determination to "stand firm and not submit again to a yoke of slavery" in tandem with conflicting interpretations of African American emancipation compelled them to "fight the good fight" to answer the call to freedom by creating a separate space where African Americans could be affirmed and could work for their own improvement. This separate, supportive space operated within the boundaries of legalized and government-supported white supremacy, even as it sought to challenge it.[74]

2

WORKERS THAT NEEDETH NOT BE ASHAMED, 1905–1916

Study to shew thyself approved unto God, a workman that needeth not be ashamed....

—2 Timothy 2:15 AV

At the turn of the twentieth century in a widely circulated black newspaper, a Spanish-American War veteran, prominent Alabama physician and druggist Lincoln Laconia Burwell, issued a clarion call to African Americans throughout the state, declaring that "we as a race must make our own history ... so act that no excuse can be rendered why we may not enjoy the rights and privileges of Americans." Similarly, in a 1912 editorial announcing the upcoming observance of the fiftieth anniversary of emancipation, Dexter Avenue Baptist Church pastor R. C. Judkins, also the activist editor of Montgomery's black newspaper, the *Colored Alabamian*, reminded his church and community that "the eyes of the world will be turned upon the race with a deep and anxious inquiry; has the Negro manifested in this period sufficient evidence of his capability to be a full-fledged citizen of America?"[1]

Heeding these words, African Americans at Dexter Avenue Baptist Church in Montgomery, Alabama, as in other parts of the South, became more convinced than ever that their freedom depended upon the efficacy of the institutions, primarily religious and educational, that they controlled. At the turn of the twenty-first century such statements are open to criticism, riddled as they are with the insignias of traditional accommodationism—the racially conciliatory practice of postponing the demand for immediate recognition of African Americans' political rights and social equality. Booker T. Washington captured the essence of this approach to race relations in his "Atlanta Exposition Speech" when he stated, "The wisest among my race understand that the agitation of questions of social equality is the extremist folly, and that progress in the enjoyment of all privileges that will come to us must be the result of severe and constant struggle rather than artificial forcing."[2]

The kind of accommodation practiced by churches like Dexter Avenue Baptist was complex and fraught with problems, but it was also, in many ways, effective. Against the backdrop of persistent racial hostility and oppression, this strategy recognized and tried to allay white fears of African American efforts to become equal citizens, all the while resisting, contesting, and challenging the circumscribed niche into which white society placed African Americans. Through accommodating activism African Americans sought power and opportunity, organized and galvanized resources, and steadily pushed to enlarge black freedom with the ultimate goal of achieving an optimum measure of self-expression and empowerment. In this chapter we shall see that between 1905 and 1916, members and Pastor Judkins created important traditions of protest and activism—namely, petition, education, and cooperation with willing whites—that, despite seemingly insurmountable obstacles, nurtured a fragile but steadily emerging sense of self-empowerment. Accommodating activism helped lay the groundwork for the more direct, confrontational activism that characterized civil rights protest in the mid-twentieth century. In their early-twentieth-century effort to make Dexter Avenue Baptist Church an effective spiritual and intellectual beacon in the fight to secure basic rights and freedoms, pastor and congregation studied to show themselves approved—workers that needeth not be ashamed.[3]

In the wake of almost thirty-five years of hard-earned but seemingly steady movement toward institution building and the improvement of life within the African American community, the turn of the twentieth century ushered in a period of fomented political enervation, economic deprivation and social segregation for African Americans in Alabama—a nadir of post-bellum race relations. By 1900, though they were far from adequate in number, Montgomery had several African American educational institutions in the area, a health infirmary, and a host of African American churches. Nevertheless, political disfranchisement and the subsequent social segregation of this era heaped upon African Americans a harness of racial inequity. The trenchant nature of these political and social proscriptions and the use of violence in the form of lynching to enforce them created a hostile environment in which the physical oppression of slavery met its twentieth-century incarnation—the psychological and emotional oppression of second-class citizenship.[4]

Ratifying a new state constitution in 1901, Alabama Democrats, who had wrested control of state politics from the hands of Republicans, managed to overthrow state constitutional protections that had been granted African Americans in the years just after the Civil War. Ostensibly meeting to draft regulations to respond more effectively to economic problems in the state, Alabama state legislators in coalition with Democratic and some Republican leaders called for a constitutional convention. Delegates moved quickly to frame provisions that effectively excluded African American men from the state's electorate. As one delegate observed, "we have disfranchised the African in the past by doubtful methods; but in the future we will disfranchise by law."

The Committee on Suffrage and Elections dominated the proceedings. Former governor William C. Oates was the top contender for president of the convention, but he had opposed, on record, what he termed the "absurd grandfather clause" and subsequently had stated that the "disfranchisement of the whole Negro race would be unwise and unjust ... among them are many honest, industrious, and good citizens, capable of fairly understanding the issues of a campaign." Instead of Oates, the convention elected as its president Henry Knowles, who eagerly embraced African American disfranchisement.[5]

On June 30, failing to agree completely, the convention entered both a majority and a minority report, the former of which became the new state constitution of 1901. Delegates bent on disfranchising black men issued the following constitutional provision: until January 1, 1903, any veteran who met age, residence, and poll tax requirements could register to vote for life. Any man who had not served in the armed forces could also register provided an ancestor had fought in any military conflict from the American Revolution to the Spanish-American War. All other would-be voters were to pay a poll tax of $1.50, retroactive to

1901 or to the year at which the voting age was reached. Additionally, the voter or his wife had to own three hundred dollars of property or forty acres of land on which there were no outstanding taxes. Finally, voters had to be able to read and write any article of the constitution to the satisfaction of the registrars. These new measures rendered the overwhelming majority of African American men and more than 100,000 white men ineligible to vote.[6]

Four men—Stanley Dent, George Harrison, William Oates, and Frank S. White (later a U.S. senator)—boldly opposed the new constitution. Oates presented the dissenters' objections in the minority report; except for the new ordinances regulating voting, he pointed out, the new constitution brought no changes. It remained silent on all of the problem areas that purportedly had prompted the call for the convention. Oates noted that the dissenters did not necessarily oppose making it difficult for African Americans to vote, but they believed the plan, as presented in the majority report, was unethical. Oates candidly stated the crux of their opposition: "The ballot can be secured to the honest and dependable without resorting to this subterfuge."[7]

Not one African American was elected as a delegate to the convention, but many crowded into the gallery to hear the debate over their suffrage. Even the polite objections and measured pleas of prominent voices—like those of former Dexter Avenue pastor A. F. Owens and Booker T. Washington, who begged for "some humble share in choosing who would rule over them"—fell on deaf ears. Passage of the new state constitution successfully nullified any remnants of federal protection of black freedoms in the state, and it laid the foundation for "decades of reaction, injustice, recurring violence and sectional stagnation" for all Alabamians. Black disfranchisement was characteristic of much white Southern sentiment. Addressing a session of the American Bankers' Association in Atlantic City, New Jersey, in 1907, Virginia governor Claude Augustus Swanson declared that the "disfranchisement of the Negro and his consequent elimination from politics ... had been one of the greatest factors in the advancement of the South ... with God's help and our own good right arm, we will hold him where he is for his own good and our own salvation." Dexter Avenue Baptist Church entered its second generation of life amid these political and social realities.[8]

By 1900, Dexter Avenue members had erected a physical structure; established a stable congregation; selected several pastors; created a Sunday school and deacon and trustee boards, as well as a youth fellowship; and participated in domestic and foreign missions ventures.

The early years of the twentieth century were remarkably productive ones for the church, bringing improvements in various aspects of its life, from installing electric lights and a new Moller pipe organ, to establishing a seasonal revival and a spring lecture series, to more effective community outreach.

Leading the work of the church during these years was a passionate and dynamic young pastor and Alabama native, Robert Chapman Judkins. Born in 1868 on the Carter plantation in Waugh, Alabama, R. C. Judkins was the oldest child of Julius and Isabelle Judkins. The young Judkins found church work and school very compelling. He held positions as president of the Baptist Young People's Union and superintendent of Sunday school, and he was reputed to have been a gifted student. His junior high school studies were interrupted when his father died in the early 1880s, and thereafter as the eldest child Judkins helped raise his three siblings. In 1890 he resumed his studies, first at Mt. Meigs, a school patterned after the Tuskegee Institute, and then at Talladega College, which had both a classical and an industrial curriculum. Talladega officials boasted of training its future ministers in "how to build as well as establish" churches. Having both an industrial and classical education influenced Judkins and the ministry he established at Dexter Avenue.[9] Rather than privileging one over the other as the best route for the many challenges blacks faced, Judkins was pragmatic and would expose the Dexter Avenue congregation to competing ideas and diverse speakers and preachers.

Judkins's ministry was most profoundly influenced, however, by the intellectual and religious world he experienced at the Theological College of the Virginia Union University in Richmond. The amalgam of three former independent schools—and rated in W. E. B. Du Bois's famous study of African American education, *The College Bred Negro*, as a "First Grade" university—Virginia Union was founded and supported by the American Baptist Home Mission Society. In keeping with the emerging social gospel movement of the day, the school emphasized the "divinity of the gospel, its power in solving the problems of the world and the importance of living in such a way as to bring the world up to the gospel standard." The theological school's curriculum sought to create a "trained and consecrated" ministry, and saw this charge as the "most serious problem before the race." Black clergy, college administrators contended, should hold progressive attitudes toward life and racial uplift and must develop the talents and abilities to transmit those aspirations to their congregations. In turn, black congregations would serve and lead in religious life and devise social reforms to redeem the race. And so, officials concluded, "As teachers of the word, and as leaders of their people into larger faith and truth and righteousness of life, ministers of intellectual breadth and spiritual vision are needed." The students were, college officials touted, an "immense army of young men and women being trained in the very best manner ... to go forth to grapple with the great problems before them" and "rise to the full measure of just expectation and prove worthy of all the care bestowed" upon them. Students were told further that "the eyes of the world were looking at the race enquiringly [sic]; the eyes of the North expectantly; the eyes of God lovingly."[10]

Judkins thrived in this college milieu. He was active in Virginia Union's literary society, and as president of the Corey Lyceum he brought in speakers on a variety of topics, from religion and politics to ornithology and war. The lyceum also sponsored discussions on important social issues. Here we see the moral, intellectual, and cultural world that nurtured Judkins. As would be exemplified by the kind of ministry he'd later establish at Dexter Avenue, Judkins relished the idea of creating workers within the black community to prove African American worthiness. In his senior year, Judkins was selected to speak at the commencement services in May 1904. The day arrived amid clouds "dark and lowering" and eventually profuse rainfall. By the time he presented his speech, "Church Union and the Baptists," to the commencement audience, however, "the evening stars were seen twinkling in a clear sky and the assembly room of Coburn Hall was well filled." The weather trajectory of the day from ominous morning to peaceful evening seemed an almost metaphorical end to Judkins's rather long, hard struggle to obtain a formal education and then to begin a bright, promising and challenging career of service and leadership.[11]

In June 1905 Judkins married school teacher Virginia Harper, moved to Montgomery, and assumed the pastorate at Dexter Avenue. Enthusiastic about this new venture, he returned to his home state full of ideas and with a vision for every part of church life, from improving the physical structure to creating a series of religious and intellectual programs to broaden the ministry and mission of the church. He enlisted the aid of a relatively privileged African American congregation to help him establish his ministry of social justice and racial uplift. His earnest belief that churches must not only provide salvation for the soul but also serve as God's vehicle for political and social justice guided and directed him in cultivating church members' emerging sense of self-empowerment.[12]

During his years in the Montgomery community Judkins structured a ministry, sought out leadership and workers, and established community programs in the hope of achieving what he believed to be the earthly mission of a church. To these ends, he founded and published out of his home at 105 Tatum Street a weekly newspaper, the *Colored Alabamian*, that served the African American community in Montgomery and beyond. This newspaper aided Judkins both in his efforts to give vitality to the church's growing sense of self-determination and his undertaking to promote justice through his personal, as well as Dexter Avenue's collective, endeavors. Judkins and the congregation at Dexter Avenue regarded the newspaper as "in a sense an organ of the church." The newspaper's motto, "Equal justice for all, special privileges to none," clearly signified Judkins's determination to inform and try to marshal the community in a fight for fairness and for African Americans to determine their own destinies.[13]

In an editorial written shortly after establishing the paper, Judkins expressed his visceral motivation and belief concerning the relationship between justice and the work of the church. He began his editorial with a quotation from Matthew 7:12, which reads, "In all things whatsoever ye would that men should do to you do ye even so to them...."[14] He called this statement the "Christ rock that constitutes the foundation stone of the temple of justice." Therefore, he concluded, the "inculcation of this principle [justice] is the one concern of the earthward mission of religion...." Judkins used the pulpit, his newspaper, and trained Christian workers to accomplish his mission of religious and racial redemption, deliverance, and justice.[15]

In his ministry, Judkins sometimes presented his ideas about redemption and deliverance in the form of a jeremiad. One of his Sunday morning sermons was taken from Jeremiah 26:13: "Therefore now amend your ways and your doings ... and the Lord will repent of the evil that he hath pronounced against you." The week prior, Judkins instructed the congregation to read the entire twenty-sixth chapter of Jeremiah, where Jeremiah warned Jehoiakim, the King of Judah, to appeal to the people to repent of their ways or incur the wrath of God. Judkins, in a message that at once called congregants to work to prove their worthiness and called them to spiritual obedience to Christian principles, told members they could seek God's favor in the world.[16]

Judkins's belief in deliverance was made evident in a sermon he preached using a text from Isaiah 26:2, "Open ye the gates, that the righteous nation which keepeth the truth may enter in." From this text it is possible to discern more clearly how the three components of Judkins's ministry—redemption, deliverance, and justice—worked together. Particularly as demonstrated in the *Colored Alabamian*, Judkins intoned a cry for justice for his race. In a series of jeremiads, he preached to his congregation of the work it must do to redeem the race. Finally, he told his parishioners, if they could rightly divine the word of truth, they would be delivered to enter the gates as a righteous nation, to achieve salvation. Justice, redemption, and deliverance, the objectives of Judkins's ministry, were similar to the objectives of other African American churches at this time. As they guided and directed the activities and actions of church life at Dexter Avenue, their literal and figurative meanings for the congregation became apparent.[17]

The reality of oppression in conjunction with Judkins's commitments convinced him that he must design a particular kind of ministry at Dexter Avenue. He was persuaded that Christian duty required not only obedience to Christ for personal spiritual growth, but also a commitment to strive for social justice, redemption, and deliverance. More important, Judkins structured a ministry at Dexter Avenue that nurtured members' sense of self-worth and empowerment. He created a cadre of faithful Christian leaders and workers, in all areas of church life, who combined intellectual ability and professional success with a strong sense of morality, spirituality, and commitment to racial uplift.[18]

We see these efforts illustrated especially in the focus on education and programming for church youth. From its earliest days forward, Dexter Avenue's Sunday school had provided not only Bible study but also general instruction in reading and writing in order to supplement that of the inadequate public schools. Judkins appointed J. W. Beverly as superintendent of Sunday school programming. A Montgomery native, Beverly attended Lincoln Normal School in Greensboro, Alabama (the school later moved to Montgomery and eventually became Alabama State University) and had been an active member of Dexter Avenue before Judkins arrived. He taught math and philosophy at Alabama State, and later enrolled at Brown University; upon graduating in 1894, Beverly returned to Montgomery to become assistant principal of the laboratory school at Alabama State. He was particularly interested in training young children, and published two pamphlets, "Practical Ethics for Children" and "A Guide to English Oration," that he provided for the youth at Dexter Avenue and distributed to community children who for various reasons could not attend public school. In 1915, Beverly became the first African American president of Alabama State, replacing the school's first president, a white man named William Paterson. Beverly was just the kind of man Judkins was looking for, both capable and willing to help lead in the "spiritual and intellectual uplift of the race." Judkins ordained Beverly to the deaconate. Other deacons included John Calston, John Doak, King Kelly, J. R. Lawrence,

H. A. Loveless, Prince Ross, Robert Ross, Major Saxton, C. F. Sterrs, William Swanson, Frank Todd, William Watkins, and P. W. White.[19]

As a further means of vesting adults in the responsibility of helping train church youth, Judkins created what he called the Youth Musical and Literary Program, which was led by churchwomen Elizabeth Brown De Ramus and Agnes Jenkins. The two women developed a Youth Day program that once yearly placed church youth in charge of the regular Sunday service. The Youth Musical and Literary Program allowed church youth the opportunity to recite short poems and excerpts from pieces of literature as a prelude to the seasonal revivals and lecture series Judkins inaugurated. On some occasions BYPU members recited works by Lord Byron, John Keats, William Shakespeare, and Percy Bysshe Shelley; at other times they memorized works by African American authors like Charles Chestnutt, Paul Laurance Dunbar, and Sutton Griggs. Recitations provided young people with chances to perfect their memorization and elocution skills; but more important, in a society offering fewer and fewer prospects for African Americans to exercise leadership, church work like that created by the Judkins ministry afforded opportunities to lead and affirmed African Americans' sense of themselves as capable and thus contributed to their sense of self-empowerment.[20]

Along with helping to create Christian leaders at Dexter Avenue, Judkins also wanted to further develop some of the existing ministries and programs at the church. As a student in the theological division of Virginia Union, he had taken the required four semesters of vocal music. Students there were taught that music could enhance or detract from the worship experience; music was supposed to ready congregants for the sermon, focusing their attention away from the world outside. Musical training that members received at Virginia Union, Alabama State and other institutions, such as the Boston Conservatory, tended to reinforce the church's already established practice of limiting Sunday morning music to hymns and classical pieces.[21]

Dexter Avenue's music program had been started formally in the 1890s with the formation of an adult choir. Agnes Jenkins Lewis had acted as instrumentalist, playing the piano and a hand-pumped organ, and R. T. Grant directed both the congregation and the choir in hymn singing. Affectionately called Father Grant, he served as chorister at Dexter Avenue for more than twenty-five years.[22]

True to his training, Judkins devised a comprehensive music program. He created a regular season of special church musicals and performances in order to achieve a pleasing worship milieu. In 1905, he directed Elizabeth Brown De Ramus, a graduate of the Boston

Conservatory, to reorganize the adult choir. He also led the church in its effort to purchase a new Moller pipe organ and arranged for Edna Doak (King), then a teenager, to take music lessons from the organist at the local white First Baptist Church. By 1908 De Ramus had reorganized a formal adult choir, and by 1913 she added a junior choir. The music ministry grew to include three annual programs: Christmas, Easter, and summer cantatas. During the next few years, a small orchestra was assembled to accompany the choir and congregation on special occasions. Music became an important part of church life, and all special programs had some musical component. Choir members like Annie Jones Williams, who usually accompanied guest performers at the church and taught piano, worked to strengthen the relationship between the church choir and the university. Many of the choir members were on the faculty of Alabama State.[23]

Edna Doak King became an important and active force in this church for many years. King's background and life lend insight into the generation of African Americans who made up a large portion of the congregation during the Judkins years. Born in Shelby County, Alabama on June 12, 1889, Edna Doak's family moved to Montgomery and became members of Dexter Avenue several years before Judkins arrived. Her father was a contractor in town. One brother studied mechanical drawing at Tuskegee and in partnership with their father, designed and constructed some of the buildings in downtown Montgomery.[24]

King attended Alabama State between 1906 and 1910, the latter years of the school's Paterson presidency (1878–1915). In order to obscure class distinctions and create a sense of solidarity, Paterson had required that all students wear uniforms, which they did not like, according to King, and she recalled as well a strict code of discipline. Emphasis, she said, was placed on learning what was appropriate: "Everything had its place ... we had to watch every aspect of our behavior and attitude, including where we went and with whom we associated. We had to watch how loudly we walked or talked." King claimed that under the tutelage of their very dignified New England teachers, students "had to tip-toe ... we just didn't have that old kind of Negro talk; no kind of smoking and drinking, and no kind of loudness. You had to watch your diction. You had to watch your every movement. If you broke the rules, you would get demerits and were sent home after you accumulated too many points." In 1910, Edna King graduated from Alabama State and went on to teach in Alabama's public schools for many years, but also continued to study piano and organ.[25]

Remembering her years of organ study with her white teacher, Dr. Thomas C. Calloway (organist at the white First Baptist Church),

King explained that the social mores of the day demanded that Calloway "sneak into the church to give me lessons, and I had to sneak in as well. I hated that." She also recalled, however, the pride and elation of the entire community at the dedication of the Moller organ to Dexter Avenue: "When we first got the organ, there was not another Negro church in town that had one. At the first recital, the church was filled ... all the aisles and the balcony, with white and colored alike," King remembered. "The white people all sat together in the front, but they were there." Intermittently, she served as church organist from the early part of the century until 1954, when she resigned to look after her invalid mother.[26]

Recitals became another component of the music ministry Judkins helped to create. H. A. Loveless's daughters, Henrietta and Bertha, were often featured in voice recitals. Musical training at the church started early with the children's performances being a regular part of the music season. In additional to encouraging congregants' talents, Judkins brought in musicians with national reputation. Madame Marguerite Egbert, a Detroit opera singer described as "one of the race's greatest and sweetest sopranos with a wide and enviable reputation," gave several performances at the church during these years. She performed at the organ dedication in 1910, and was also featured in an Easter recital in 1911, and another recital in 1915. Another famous singer, Madame Martha Broadcus from Chicago, gave a recital that filled the Dexter Avenue auditorium.[27]

The congregation that had called Judkins to serve as pastor was reputed to attract the best-educated and most economically prosperous members of the Montgomery community. Several people were involved in commercial pursuits. In some instances, Judkins used the resources of these businesses to help support his ministry. For example, E. M. and Jonas Lewis, William Watkins, and T. H. Williams had construction businesses and each did repair work for the church at a discount. H. C. Ball, who owned and operated a grocery store, often donated food for the Christmas and Thanksgiving dinners the church hosted for the poor. Local druggist A. L. Hinson, surgeon James A. De Ramus, and dentist W. F. Watkins conducted health fairs at the church. L. Beverly, a teller at the black-owned Alabama Penny Savings Bank, arranged for Judkins to set up an account in order to purchase items for needy children at John Adams's store.[28]

Still, it was difficult to minister to the diverse African American community in Montgomery. In south Montgomery, a small but growing African American middle class of educators, a few physicians, and several local businessmen emerged around Alabama State.

The majority of African Americans—the working class and the poor—lived in west Montgomery. This demographic pattern becomes significant during the 1940s and 1950s, when African Americans begin to form competing political and civic organizations. Dexter Avenue was the church of the majority of the black elite. To be sure, it reached out to the poor, but would always have the reputation of being the church of the city's "big shots," and thus was often deemed as unwelcoming to the poor.

Against the reality of poverty and the lack of educational opportunities, many African Americans likely felt uncomfortable, perhaps even intimidated, by the Dexter Avenue milieu and leadership. The church's membership created an atmosphere that "placed great stress on ... the attributes of polite society, as personified by the Northern missionaries" who were often their college teachers and mentors. Poor congregants who struggled to sustain the basic necessities of life—such as food and shelter—likely had little time and energy to appreciate the accouterments of polite society. It was always a struggle for the church to provide the same level of spiritual, intellectual, and moral affirmation for poorer members of Montgomery's African American community that it did for those who were well educated and economically comfortable. And yet, Judkins's pastorate saw more than six hundred members added to the church roster.

Judkins worked hard to raise church members' consciousness of their need for spiritual development. In addition to Sunday services and various other weekly activities, he implemented a ritual of four revivals, held in the spring, summer, fall and winter. In preparation for an upcoming revival, a prayer and consultation service was held each afternoon at four during the week preceding the services. These one- and two-week-long revivals exposed the congregation to many of the great preachers of their day, such as William Gilbert, president of Selma University; Charles Henry Phillips, a medical doctor and a pastor in the Colored Methodist Episcopal Church; and members of the Baptist hierarchy, such as E. D. W. Edward and evangelist S. M. Dawson, who was blind. Above all, these occasions were reminders of members' Christian and community commitments.[29]

Judkins's efforts often extended beyond the pulpit to contest community concerns. He used the *Colored Alabamian* to express his outrage over disfranchisement, editorializing, "Ten million Negroes of the United States live in a land that knew them in times past as slaves, now scornfully proclaim them to be of ... unacceptable blood ... denied representation in law making.... This decision," he continued, "is not a crime against man but a sin against man's maker…." He explained that "Negro religious organizations have thus felt it their responsibility to point out the golden rule to the politicians of society." Later he stated that "deprived of the protection of the very law we are called upon to obey and respect … Negroes in this community have … borne it all with patience." He appealed to state lawmakers, noting that "every spirit of justice and fair play demands that the law be upheld…."[30]

Often pictured in his newspaper in a stiff-bosom, high collared shirt with a bow tie, dark vest, and jacket, Judkins appeared the epitome of erudition, the embodiment of the Victorian values of restraint and propriety that characterized his proper education at the hands of Northern missionaries. Yet his fervent indignation at the injustices experienced by African Americans sometimes drove him to exchange his usually proper and measured demeanor for sarcasm. In yet another editorial decrying the injustice of social segregation he queried, "When President [Theodore] Roosevelt and his fellow Negro hunters were away in the swamp hunting bears, what became of the colored brethren when they stopped for lunch … how far apart did they have to sit before it was settled that there was no social equality?" Judkins reveals here that in the same way Roosevelt worked alongside African Americans in his hunting ventures, white and black Montgomerians encountered and worked with one another in their daily lives in ways that probably transgressed the rigid boundaries of racial etiquette observed in public. Conscious that racial segregation was more concerned with conferring a badge of inferiority on African Americans than it was with literally keeping black and white people separate in all avenues of life, here Judkins contests social segregation by highlighting its illogicality and impracticality.[31]

In 1908, Judkins joined the voice of his church with the voices of other community leaders when he aired the concerns of a group of local African American ministers responding to a series of attacks on local African Americans. Along with Judkins, W. A. Blackwell, J. B. Branam, W. C. Branton, N. N. Nealy, and E. E. Scott wrote a letter of protest to the city council. The ministers laid out several complaints. First, they condemned the assault on an honored and highly respected black woman by a strong white man because she boarded the street car ahead of him. The man received a minor fine and the woman apparently was charged with breaking segregation laws. Second, they denounced an incident in which a white man who killed a black man, for no stated reason, was released without a trial. Third, they condemned the killing of a black man by a white policeman because the man failed to drive as far to one side of the road as the officer felt he should. Finally, they protested the brutal treatment suffered by African Americans while in the custody of the police.

The group "viewed with grave concern the widespread spirit of lawlessness and violence which has manifested itself … within the past few weeks." Accommodating white fears, the ministers "vow[ed] to do all in their power to suppress evil and lawbreaking committed by Negroes." For this accommodation, however, they demand that "Negroes charged with misdemeanors or minor crimes have a fair and impartial trial." "Fair treatment," they pointed out, "was essential" to insure that African Americans would not soon believe "that laws are not made for their protection but their punishment."[32] Clearly, these ministers' trenchant and provocative actions were confrontational beyond our traditional notions of accommodation. They were insisting that the community recognize and honor the equal protection clause of the Fourteenth Amendment.

Judkins used the *Colored Alabamian* to highlight another injustice he perceived. In 1913, white businessmen in Montgomery launched a program to bring white foreigners—mostly from Austria and Hungary—to Montgomery to purchase and farm some of the land. Judkins exclaimed, "we regret the spirit and attitude of our white neighbors … [who] have at their very doors hundreds and thousands of the best peaceable farmers anywhere in the round world." He was particularly indignant at white Montgomerians' readiness to "break up sizeable plantations" to make them affordable for whites in other countries. The message to the world, Judkins protested, was that "whites in Alabama view the Negro as thriftless, ignorant and undependable."

Judkins not only refuted what he perceived as an unfair characterization of hardworking African Americans; he also took the opportunity to condemn the inadequate education system, writing, "Montgomery County's total expenditure for Negro school buildings will not equal what it has expended to build one jail to incarcerate Negro men." Any lack of preparation on the part of blacks to be good farmers or competent in other areas, Judkins posited, was due to the fact that "in the noon day sun of the twentieth century, the city of Montgomery owns only one black brick school building." Still, he insisted, "There are thousands of thrifty Negro farmers who can not afford a whole plantation, but could purchase smaller pieces of land." "Why," pondered a baffled Judkins, "are white businessmen helping people they do not know but ignoring the Negro whom they do know?" This editorial highlighted several critiques Judkins had concerning the mistreatment of African Americans and the tools he employed to try to improve local conditions. There was an obvious reference to 1 John 4:20 in which

Judkins wrote, "For whosoever hates his brother whom he has seen cannot love God whom he has not seen," and also allusions to a citizen's civic duty to another resident. As always, there was the fervent cry for racial justice. It would be easy to conclude that, since this editorial only appeared in the *Colored Alabamian*, Judkins was simply "preaching to the choir." To do so, however, would underestimate the article's power to promote a race consciousness of affirmation and inform African Americans about important happenings in the community. Here we see, then, an example of Judkins's concern with religion, race, education, and community.[33]

We must keep in mind that the accommodation and the activism that we see here are products of a particular historical moment. Jim Crow laws and the racial etiquette that they demanded were only then in the process of being firmly solidified. Many African Americans, though it might seem naive from a present-day vantage point, still believed that their ability to embrace and espouse Victorian bourgeois values were outward signs of their inner worthiness to the white community and evidence of their potential to be useful and productive citizens. Modeling such behavior, blacks hoped, would gnaw away white prejudice and crumble the walls of segregation. But, as Glenda Gilmore points out, "white men reordered southern society through segregation and disfranchisement in the 1890s because they realized that African American success not only meant competition in the market place and the sharing of political influence but also entailed a challenge to fundamental social hierarchies...." Many black activists did not believe that the system of racial oppression would become even more entrenched in the years after World War I.[34]

Judkins sometimes featured, in his newspaper, editorials on social concerns too sensitive for the pulpit. Walter S. Buchanan, a black Harvard University graduate and later a president of Alabama A and M University, often wrote passionately of injustices perpetrated against the African American community. In 1910, Judkins printed the text of a Buchanan address given in Birmingham to commemorate the forty-seventh anniversary of emancipation and attacking miscegenation perpetuated by white men. In addition to having lost the ballot, Buchanan pointed out that black men in Alabama also lost the power to protect themselves and black women from victimization, exclaiming, "we are powerless to protect our women and so avoid being the dumping ground for this superior garbage which is forever mudding our streams of virtue, poisoning the fountains of our race and dignity." He noted that "so long as a lofty public sentiment does not operate to keep white men from Negro women, every black child born with a white face should be christened by the government and supported at public expense." Buchanan explained that his indignation was not "directed at innocent children" but at white society's refusal to acknowledge and protect black women from sexual exploitation by white men. He pleaded for "the protection of Negro women and a recognition of the sanctity of the Negro home." Buchanan's speech is audacious and confrontational, and clearly calls for the state to live up to its obligation to protect its residents equally.

Even in a forward-thinking and provocative speech like Walter Buchanan's, however, we find a continued faith in the decency of democratic institutions to prevail over racial oppression. Buchanan explained that post-bellum America was characterized by "a period of readjustment in relations between the races in the South" and that while both blacks and whites had made mistakes, "in the main the period has been one of steady progress in the right direction." More important, he explained, "signs are encouraging for a fair and complete readjustment during the next half century." We see exemplified, once more, a faith in progress that characterized Dexter Avenue during its founding years. Still, Buchanan's adamancy that, "[a] fair chance and civil justice are all the Negro wants" insinuates that along with faith in democratic institutions and progress was an unrelenting expectation that African Americans were entitled to equal privileges.[35]

Judkins's ministry included a tenacious effort to expose his congregation to contemporary ideas about political equality and social justice for African Americans. As part of his commitment to education and racial uplift, he inaugurated a seasonal lecture series at the church, using this opportunity to bring in some of the most famous and influential African Americans in the country to speak on race relations. United in their belief that race relations were in crisis, these lecturers represented a variety of professions, including the ministry, and exemplified the rich and varied points of view on this complex issue. Sutton Elbert Griggs, a novelist and the pastor of First Baptist Church of East Nashville, Tennessee, presented one of the first lectures. When he addressed the audience at Dexter Avenue on November 18, 1907, Griggs had written five novels, the most famous of which was *Imperium in Imperio*, a fictional tale about a group of African Americans who created a secret, separate country within the United States whose purpose was to protect African Americans from injustice when the federal government refused to do so.[36]

Griggs spoke at Dexter Avenue on November 18 to "a large assemblage of Montgomery's cultured, educated and progressive Negroes." After church youth performed a musical and literary program, Griggs presented his speech, "The Race Problem." In many ways, his talk embodied accommodating activism: it contested African American disfranchisement even as it tried to accommodate white fears. Griggs began by stating that, "the problem of the races will be solved when the Negro is granted every right guaranteed him by state and federal constitutions." He called for intensified self-help, beginning with as many Negroes as possible qualifying themselves to vote. Yet he cautioned that those who vote must always vote "in the interest of their community"; this was his way of responding to whites' justification for denying African Americans franchise by claiming that blacks always vote Republican.[37]

As well, parts of Griggs's speech attempted to reason away virulent white racism. He told the crowd that "the Southern white man has a heart and Negroes must strive to find it…. If a white man mistreats you, in a straight-forward, non abusive way, tell him of it—chances are he will hear you." Even so, Griggs's concluding comments—which began with a litany of black achievements in scholarship, the arts, the military, science, and sports—asserted a faith in African American potential and equality. "The Negro," he contended, "has demonstrated by every test that prejudice and incredulity has [sic] set up that he is a man in the fullest, broadest application of the term." Judkins observed in his newspaper that Griggs's well-received speech was neither bitter nor abusive but impassioned, and went far in trying to "mould correct and just public sentiment to lift up the race."[38]

Over the course of the next few years, speakers included minister and humorist Reverend D. Webster Davis, who gave the lecture "Jim Crow's Search for the Promised Land"; celebrated intellectual and dean of Howard University Kelly Miller; and John Milton Waldron, a Baptist minister who was a member of the 1912 Woodrow Wilson Presidential Inauguration Committee. Waldron, who had attended the 1909 Niagara Conference, was a charter member of the National Association for the Advancement of Colored People (NAACP), and he opposed Booker T. Washington's ideas about gradualism improving race relations. Each of these speakers expounded upon the importance of African Americans getting their due political rights and complained of how social segregation placed a badge of inferiority on African Americans. Each also strongly advocated the immediate recognition of African American equality and of the important contributions African Americans had made to the health of the nation.[39]

On February 22, 1913, Booker T. Washington, president of the Tuskegee Institute, spoke at Dexter Avenue's lecture series on what African Americans and whites could do to help one another. Not only did Washington address an interracial audience, but he was introduced by Alabama governor Emmet O'Neal, who claimed that "an officer of the state should be willing ... to work harder for Negroes than for members of his own race" and promised that the state would do more to support black education.

Washington began, "I am anxious that here in Alabama each white man do all he can to contribute to the happiness and usefulness of the colored race, and that each colored man do all he can to make himself of value to the white race so that ... both are helping each other forward toward a happier life." He spoke of the enormous contributions African Americans made to the state of Alabama though their productivity in the industrial arts. The many prizes African Americans won at state fairs, Washington suggested, brought pride to the state and were evidence of their thrift and ability to contribute to the community. Continuing to work even harder in these areas was, claimed Washington, what black Montgomerians could do to help their city. Whites, he noted, could help by providing more schools and funds in order to lengthen the school terms in black schools so that they might equal the length of white school terms. And finally, there was a need for better training of teachers in African American schools and for increasing their pay.

Washington stated, "There is exceptional opportunity in a city like Montgomery to show the world how two races different in color and separate in their social affairs, still can live side by side in peace and harmony, and each race in its own separate way contribute toward the prosperity of the city." His speech was true to his notions of traditional accommodationism. Unlike any of the other lecture series speakers, Washington openly embraced the practice of social segregation, and he made no mention of political rights for African Americans.

Nevertheless, Judkins, though a strong advocate of immediate recognition of African Americans' political rights (typical of accommodating activists), greatly admired Washington. In particular, he respected Washington's encouraging African Americans to be productive and independent by doing such things as growing their own gardens. In editorializing Washington's lecture, Judkins reported that the main auditorium of Dexter Avenue was filled to overflowing with the "best blood of both races. Hopes were high that the meeting would give impulse to a new understanding." In inviting Washington to address the Dexter Avenue congregation, we see Judkins's pragmatic strain. As pastor, newspaper editor, and avid gardener himself, Judkins modeled Washington's notion of the black productive citizen.[40]

The only woman to speak at the lecture series was Nannie Helen Burroughs, then president of the National Training School for Women and Girls. Burroughs was born in Virginia, moved to Washington, D.C., and attended high school there. Upon graduation, she became a bookkeeper and an editorial secretary for the Foreign Mission Board of the National Baptist Convention. At the age of thirty she realized her dream of opening a school for young women in Washington, D.C.—the National Training School for Women and Girls. At the time of her lecture at Dexter Avenue, she was traveling on the lecture circuit in Europe and the United States. While she was in Montgomery, she gave a special address to the women of the community on the issue of suffrage. She also spoke on race. Her speech acknowledged the power of institutional racism but asserted that an individual's determination and will were more powerful and more important to that individual's success. Burroughs "paid high tribute to the progress already made" by African Americans and encouraged her audience to keep faith that progress would continue.[41]

These educational programs, in conjunction with editorials in the *Colored Alabamian* and Sunday sermons, were part of Judkins's activist ministry. Such presentations and writings always focused on the issue of race—sometimes to lament and bitterly complain of injustices, and other times to create a milieu in which to encourage black agency and optimism. It seemed important to Judkins to expose the congregation to various opinions within the black community concerning the best way to cope with and address the problem of race in America. The people who spoke at the seasonal lecture series provided a rhythmic succession of spiritual and intellectual affirmation for the congregation and the community, encouraging them to contest the current state of affairs. As well, these speakers' stories were success stories that helped to counter extant perceptions of African Americans as incompetent and unworthy of sharing the rights and privileges of American citizenship. Each speaker, in many ways, embodied the hopes and dreams of the congregation; each found a way to remind the audience of the work that was yet to be done. And each offered a solution in which church membership was essential.

Judkins and the congregation were willing, it is important to note, to work with cooperative whites. On at least two occasions, white lecturers addressed Dexter Avenue audiences. On October 21, 1911, Reverend Dr. Samuel Riley spoke on the state of race relations. "No matter what our prejudices … be, it [race relations] is purely a question of humanity," Riley began. Shoring up his comments on a notion of religious equality, he noted that the ten million blacks then residing in

America were "ten million humans for whom Christ died ... [whose] souls are of equal worth to God as ours [whites]." Riley used this opportunity to point out three debts that whites owed to African Americans, the first of which was "gratitude for ... laboring for white people [and allowing whites to] enrich and educate seven generations while they [African Americans] remained in bonds and ignorance." The two other debts, Riley continued, were "justice by every consideration human and divine ... and the chance of a man in the race of life."[42]

Another white voice to address the congregation and community at Dexter Avenue was that of J. C. Manning, an Alabama native who had been active in an attempt during the 1890s to fuse the Populist and Republican Parties in the state. Manning was described as a "man whose views differ from many whites in Montgomery but most of these same people esteem him personally." Speaking in 1914, he directly addressed the issue of voting, telling the audience that he "had studied voting patterns among Negroes in the North where they have the ballot and found that Negro votes were diverse...." Manning went on to say that white fears that the Negro vote would always be Republican were not necessarily true, and that even if blacks tend to vote in a block, "Negroes in Alabama have acquired land and education in sufficient number that they should receive the vote." Arguing that it was only through the state's allowing of blacks to get involved in government that they would have the opportunity to experience the responsibilities and obligations of political power, Manning concluded with the warning that "the move to repress Negroes was wrong and will hurt the South in the long run."[43] Judkins praised Riley's and Manning's well-received messages and assured the Dexter Avenue congregation that some of its white peers could be relied upon for assistance in the work to uplift the race. But more important, Judkins was exposing his congregation to whites who believed in black equality and who understood that efforts to suppress African Americans hurt all Southerners.

The *Colored Alabamian* was used to encourage African Americans to actively participate in Montgomery's civic life. The paper always listed the names of newly elected town officials and city council members. Establishing a tradition of petitioning city officials that would be carried into the 1950s by people like Jo Ann Robinson and Rufus Lewis, Judkins urged African Americans to "get to know these men," to write to them to enlist their "cooperation and assistance in the great work of racial uplift." He advised the black public to make a particular effort to get to know the sheriff and the police force. He wrote, "This department of our county government ... can become the iron gauntlet of oppression and injustice, or the velvet glove that guarantees peace and protection to all citizens." Here is another example of cooperation with willing whites, further instituting a tradition of interracialism. Also, encouraging church and community members' to be familiar with city leaders and to enlist their assistance and cooperation were ways in which Judkins aspired to empower African Americans.

Judkins's newspaper and ministry at once affirmed and informed African Americans in Montgomery and helped spur them into action. This is best illustrated by the quotidian activism of the women of Dexter Avenue. As with many other religious institutions during the early years of the twentieth century, women's presence and contributions were essential to the day-to-day functioning of the church in service to its membership. Moreover, as Evelyn Brooks Higginbotham argues in her analysis of black Baptist women's undertakings, women's work was critical to African American churches' effective service to the community at large. Much of the effort of the women at Dexter Avenue was expressed through the ladies' missionary society, established in the late nineteenth century. Like other church activities, women's missionary work also illustrates accommodating activism. Even though the members of the ladies' missionary society accepted that African Americans should have to prove their worthiness through adhering to certain Victorian bourgeois standards, they were even more determined to broaden black freedoms and opportunities and improve the quality of African American life through their daily activism.[44]

Early on, the ladies' missionary society concerned itself with fostering certain standards and attitudes among the women in the church that illustrated its embracing traditional ideas of accommodationism. One of their special meetings for women was called "What I Can Do to Make Myself More Attractive". At this meeting women discussed various beauty tips of the day as well as informed members about what was available in the area of hair care and cosmetics. At another such meeting a speech was given: "Has My Tongue Been a Blessing to the Community?" The speaker began by reading scripture taken from James 3:2–10, which warns that while no one can tame it, the tongue can be used as either a blessing or a curse. Following the talk, a discussion was held. Mrs. Edna King, who was 104 years old at the time of our 1993 interview, recalled that between the rules at Alabama State and the behavioral and attitudinal expectations promoted by the missionary society, her life was lived within the confines of very strict rules. As Higginbotham argues in her work on black Baptist women, standards for such discussions on attitudes, styles, and fashions—like most ethical and moral values—were examples not just of Christian but also of Victorian and accommodationist insignias on church life. Even though the ladies' missionary society advocated this kind of strict behavior, it still labored unrelentingly to improve the quality of life for African Americans at the church and in the Montgomery community.[45]

Missionary society work at Dexter Avenue dates back to the very beginnings of the church's history with its commitment to help newly emancipated slaves. The church's decision to officially incorporate as Dexter Avenue Missionary Baptist Church meant that it would participate in both domestic and foreign outreach programs. The missionary society was defined at Dexter Avenue as "a place for showing love through obedience ... with God's plan [to give] ... each disciple a part in saving the world."[46]

Missionary society activities during these years were varied. In the area of home missions, the society created programs to help the poor in the community. Each year, usually on December 27, the missionary society prepared and served a traditional Christmas dinner for the poor. The society would sponsor a service of prayer and song, Reverend Judkins would give a short sermon, and then all would sit down together for a meal in the basement of the church. Also part of the missionary society's holiday ministry was to prepare and serve a Christmas dinner at the county poor house, and to donate groceries to the Hale Infirmary so that workers there might prepare a holiday meal.[47]

Concerns with standards of beauty and preparing Thanksgiving and Christmas dinners for the poor fall within our notions of traditional accommodation, but two other instances of Dexter Avenue's women's missionary society work illustrate ways in which the organization sought to empower the African American community and contest white racist notions: cosponsoring the church's Health Week program and supporting universal suffrage.

The ladies' missionary society sought to educate community members on various issues that confronted it. During the early years of the twentieth century, disease and death disproportionately affected persons living in the Gulf Coast South. Among African Americans, the infant mortality rate was 27 percent, and the four leading causes of death were tuberculosis, pneumonia, heart disease, and Brights (or kidney) disease. In late March 1915, the ladies' missionary society cosponsored a health information week in which they invited health officials in the community, most of them members of the congregation, to speak at the church on various ways to improve health habits and sanitary practices: Dr. R. T. Adair spoke on "Dissipation as Cause of Disease"; Dr. James De Ramus explained the importance of proper home ventilation to good health; Dr. David Norcross spoke on the problems of infant mortality in the state; Dr. D. H. C. Scott discussed the importance of proper nourishment; and Dr. W. F. Watkins talked on the ways to maintain healthy oral hygiene. A question-and-answer session followed each presentation, giving the audience an opportunity to engage in a discussion of what the *Colored Alabamian* described as "vital questions" about health.

This program contrasted sharply with the stereotypes that abounded in academic and popular discourse about African Americans' physical and intellectual inferiority. From Edgar Rice Burroughs's creation of the idealized white male body in his *Tarzan* novels, to the ideas propagated in D. W. Griffith's film *The Birth of a Nation*, to the degradation of black bodies through lynching, African Americans in the early twentieth century faced an image of the black body as inferior and as the transmitter of disease, especially tuberculosis. In the Health Week program, then, we have another example of missionary society action that helped empower African Americans to contest extant notions that suggested they were inherently physically weaker.[48]

Activities sponsored by the ladies' missionary society sometimes provided an opportunity for more women's voices to be heard at the church. In 1914, the society brought in Cornelia Bowen, Judkins's former teacher at Mt. Meigs and then president of Alabama's State Federation of Colored Women's Clubs, to speak. Bowen had a close association with another member of the Dexter Avenue family; she had worked with Henrietta Gibbs to establish the State Boys Industrial Center Reform School at Mt. Meigs. Such ventures were common among African American women during the first quarter of the twentieth century. Most African American women believed that "to be fully participating members of American society" they needed to work to "establish long lasting educational and social service programs for poor and uneducated blacks." In a presentation titled "The True Test," Bowen reminded the packed audience at Dexter Avenue that the success of African Americans' integration into society was the "true test" of democracy. Bowen's visit to the church also included a special address to the church women on the issue of women's suffrage. Dexter Avenue women supported women's suffrage: they organized information sessions to raise awareness and support in the community and sponsored a community debate on women's suffrage as a way to raise money for the cause locally.[49]

The women at Dexter Avenue had their pastor's support. In fact, Judkins strongly supported the efforts of all advocates of women's suffrage with regular editorials in the *Colored Alabamian*. "[T]he universal suffrage movement like the movement against slavery, will not down until it has accomplished its full purpose," he wrote. "We [in the black community] are glad to see this movement take root and begin such a healthy growth right here in the South." He further contended that "white men of Alabama met ... and greatly restricted the electoral privileges...." Their actions, he explained, "placed many citizens in the position of bearing the burden of taxation without representation." Judkins complained that "when Negroes are taxed for everything white men are taxed for but deprived of public institutions that are kept up by taxes, it is robbery." And yet it was Judkins's hope and belief that "this narrow, ignorant and short-sighted statesmanship on the part of Alabama will be overcome and finally overruled by the spirit of universal suffrage." As has been suggested by Rosalyn Terborg-Penn, African American women were indeed anxious to get the ballot. Missionary society member Henrietta Gibbs was the first African American Alabama woman to cast a vote in the 1920 election.[50]

We can see that even though the ladies' missionary society accommodated some white racist notions, it more often challenged them. For the most part the society seemed to accommodate some white beauty standards and embrace the strict Victorian moral code of whites, but we must not lose sight of how the society aspired to enlarge the autonomy of African American ministers by agitating for universal suffrage. Of equal import, missionary society members rejected the idea that African Americans were weaker or more susceptible to disease.

In 1916, perhaps feeling that his work in Montgomery was done or maybe believing that another place needed him more, R. C. Judkins tendered his resignation to accept a call from Salem Baptist Church in Jersey City, New Jersey. Judkins and the congregation at Dexter Avenue had had a remarkably productive working relationship in the eleven years of his pastorate. Judkins had seen to it that noteworthy ministers, intellectuals, literary figures, politicians, and performers regularly graced the Dexter Avenue pulpit as speakers at the seasonal revivals and lectures series. He carefully and consistently—through his newspaper and church ministry—encouraged members' sense of themselves as competent, worthwhile people entitled to the same rights and privileges enjoyed by white Americans.[51]

Church members and Judkins had a mutual affection and were proud of all they had accomplished together. H. A. Loveless noted that Judkins was a "faithful, honest and upright Christian minister and citizen ... that he had preached against the sins of the people ... which made him unpopular at times, but that he was a sincere man ... that in the ... years of his leadership, the church had been able to pay all of its operating expenses...." Likewise, Judkins told congregants that "on the whole you have been a people of industry and honest report ... [whose] spiritual deepening is serving to elevate the entire race."[52]

The Judkins ministry to fight for political and social justice was at once religious and political. As Alexis de Tocqueville noted of religious expression in America, "every religion has some political opinion linked to it...." Nevertheless, it is important to understand that Judkins regarded his work as profoundly spiritual. When he spoke of equality and justice he did so out of what he believed was divine imperative. As he stated, he saw injustices directed toward African Americans as "not a crime against man but a sin against man's maker." It must also be considered, however, that in the *Colored Alabamian*, which Judkins considered an extension of his ministry, he stated that the newspaper was a "race journal and race defender with the object ... to strenuously contend for the Negro's political and civil rights."[53]

The newspaper's advocacy of black civil rights was something Judkins considered an essential part of his divine calling. When some members of the congregation, perhaps believing that their adherence to middle-class sensibilities or their status in the community at large was somehow compromised by having their names on the roll as paid subscribers to the *Colored Alabamian*, Judkins protested, editorializing, "Negroes who feel it a disgrace to have their names on subscription rolls of Negro newspapers should ask white editors to publish their social news...." Some church members' reticence to openly support the newspaper, brought on by their belief that the white community somehow felt threatened by its existence, attests to the power of this publication and the courage of its editor to confront and denounce the racism of the day. Judkins's newspaper and his work at Dexter Avenue were typical of what John Brown Childs has identified as "two major tendencies characteristic of the turn-of-the-century black church: an outward secular involvement in community activism and universalistic principles, and an inward spiritualistic and localized withdrawal from the wider society." As Carter G. Woodson has noted, "Negro churches gradually realized the necessity for connecting the church more closely with the things of the world to make it [the world] a decent place to live in." Woodson was quick to add, however, that these same churches did not go "as far as the white man in divesting Christian duty of spiritual ministration and reducing it to mere service for social uplift."[54]

When Judkins arrived in Montgomery in 1905, he found a church poised to serve its congregation and community. His extraordinary vision and skillful leadership equipped congregants with the moral, spiritual, and intellectual agency to become effective disciples in the fight for spiritual equality and racial self-help. Important traditions were established during these years. We have seen a continual emphasis placed on education, exemplified in the appointment of J. W. Beverly as superintendent of the Sunday school and the comprehensive program of religious and secular education he developed, and the ladies' missionary society's health fair. As well, the tradition of cooperating with willing whites, bringing them in as part of the lecture series anticipated other progressive whites like Koinonia Farm's Clarence Jordan and Robert Gratetz of Trinity Lutheran Church, Montgomery, who would speak at Dexter Avenue in the 1950s; it marked the beginning of a new kind of interracial cooperation at the church. It is true that whites were a part of this church's history from its earliest beginnings, but the whites that Judkins invited believed in a kind of social and political equality earlier whites involved in the church could not have imagined.

Judkins's encouragement and the church members' willingness to work hard to prove that African Americans were worthy of first-class citizenship attest to their continued faith in the effectiveness of racial uplift and inevitability of progress. Yet the realities of life for African Americans in Montgomery when Judkins left the pastorate suggests the limits of these strategies in bringing about change within the time frame anticipated by Judkins and the congregation. It would be almost thirty years before blacks in Montgomery had a publicly supported high school or a real hospital, and more than fifty years before the right to vote was secured for all. It is also true that, in their activism, Judkins and Dexter Avenue's members sometimes accommodated white fears of black equality, but this accommodation was accompanied by an activism that helped enlarged black opportunities within the Montgomery community.

Moreover, Judkins left the congregation with an emerging sense of self-determination and empowerment. Nowhere was this more evident than in church members' participation in initiatives just after Judkins's pastorate to help found the state's first NAACP chapter, to agitate for a compulsory education law, and to protest lynching in the state. Robert Chapman Judkins, indeed, had been the chief architect of a congregation of workers that needeth not be ashamed.

3

WAITING FOR A NEW DAY, 1916–1948

But they that wait upon the Lord shall renew their strength;
they shall mount up with wings as eagles; they shall run and not
be weary; and they shall walk, and not faint.

—Isaiah 40:31 AV

Between World War I and World War II, Alabama was the model of a
state marshaling all of the resources it could deploy to insure that
power would remain in the hands of reactionaries. The infamous state
constitution of 1901, rather than "a document of fundamental powers
and general processes," was a "constitution of minute specifications
designed to freeze change...." Emmet O'Neal's gubernatorial campaign
and his administration between 1911 and 1915 helped to solidify the
state's reactionary political and social disposition. In his campaign,
O'Neal lectured voters on "the virtues and glories of doing nothing and
the evils of doing anything." Alabamians were encouraged to "fear and
thus oppose the new and the alien and the different." In the economy,
"agriculture remained mired in—a world of sharecropping, one-mule
farms, slavish reliance on cotton and ruinous economic cycles."
Though industrialization and urbanization brought some changes to
the cities, most Alabamians lived in the countryside. Prohibition was a

political issue around which many—black or white—agreed. African American Baptists, at their 1888 state convention, had declared that "the church was the greatest agency by which intemperance" would be destroyed, and members covenanted to abandon their practice of using fermented wine for communion.[1] Racism flared, however, as many white Southerners insisted on segregated organizational meetings. Furthermore, white unification around prohibition hurt the African American struggle for freedom because it gave common cause to white evangelical Protestant groups and the Knights of the Ku Klux Klan, creating a coalition that intensified the effort to restrict black freedoms.[2]

Despite the gargantuan efforts among African Americans at Dexter Avenue and in the Montgomery community to prove blacks worthy of first-class citizenship status, outside the walls of the church, blacks continued to lose political, economic, and social power. By 1919, African Americans in Alabama knew their place, and there was relative peace as long as there were no challenges to racial etiquette. Along with problems created by racism, mainstream independent black churches—the powerful religious institutions that had dominated organizational life among African Americans after 1865—faced new challenges in the years after World War I. Randall Burkett notes that these churches were "being marginalized by external creative energies from below and also from above."[3] Many black Baptist and Methodist churches in the South began losing portions of their congregations to the Northern black migration.[4] Storefront churches attracted a following among the black lower classes in the urban North.[5] There was also a rise in de-Christianized groups, such as black Jews in New York's Harlem, the Moorish Science Temple, the Nation of Islam and deific figures like Daddy Grace.[6] Some middle- and upper-class blacks united with Congregational, Presbyterian, and Episcopal churches.[7] Moreover, a perception emerged that mainstream denominational black churches had "bought into a white Christian notion of a self-effacing white Christ."[8] Some African Americans believed that southern black churches became a foil of the white power structure, unwittingly enabling white oppression by encouraging only cautious challenges to segregation.[9]

While such themes validly characterize general trends among black churches in the early twentieth century, it is also true that these churches continued to grow—especially the Baptist churches in urban areas of the South.[10] And though these trends were indicative of serious problems and shortcomings on the part of black churches, these churches remained institutionally vital to African American life. For Dexter Avenue Baptist Church, the years between World Wars I and II were a time of mounting internal strife prompted by the Great

Depression, which hit the African American community and the South earlier and harder than it did other groups. A controversial pastorate also colored these times. In this chapter, we get our first in-depth picture of the day-to-day workings at Dexter Avenue, and we see some of the church power dynamics in the struggle between the deacons and pastors. We see the affirmation of African Americans as individuals in the rise of men's, women's, and youth-day celebrations. Outreach challenging the racism of the day diminished appreciably but was sustained in smaller, less dramatic ways. In this period of instability leadership passed from the generations who remembered the founding years and ideals to new leaders who were more reluctant to challenge the current racial mores than their forebears, who, at least in memory, had reigned over a "glorious" past. This chapter encourages us to consider how the tedium of church life—through board meetings, pastoral search committees, missionary societies, and other organizations—helped stabilize communities and make life more routine during tumultuous times. In the midst of these struggles, African Americans at Dexter Avenue fought not to lose hope but to wait for a new day and a better time.

Dexter Avenue had been accustomed to ministers coming and going. The frequent turnover of pastors was not uncommon among African American congregations at this time. R. C. Judkins's eleven-year tenure as pastor was an important distinguishing characteristic of his ministry. It had brought stability and heightened the expectations of what could be accomplished. It would be difficult to sustain Judkins's remarkable legacy, so members sought a candidate with experience, reputation, and impressive credentials. They endured a year of guest preachers before finally, in 1917, extending a call to a mature, South Carolina native, Peter Andrew Callahan. Edna King noted that the fifty-five-year-old pastor, who forgot her name at her wedding, "was rather old to be beginning a ministry at a new church." Still, he had much to recommend him; a graduate of the Richmond Theological Seminary, his reputed eloquence and erudition earned him the nickname "the apostle of Dixie," and he had served as a pastor at large churches in Florida and South Carolina.[11]

When Callahan arrived at Dexter Avenue in the summer of 1917, he found an active, well-organized congregation. The church held a week of celebrations to install its new leader, and local ministers were invited to "deliver messages on the importance of the church and race." Once the new pastor was official, church members focused on internal improvements and purchasing a parsonage. At the church, a group of men, the Men's Church Aid Band, had organized a few years before

Callahan arrived. In October 1914, this organization repaired the ceiling and carpeted the floor of the sanctuary. A year later, the church purchased a parsonage, a one-story clapboard cottage with a truncated pyramid roof, on 309 South Jackson Street in the Centennial Hill neighborhood. Since the 1870s, many of the professors at Alabama State University, as well as professionals and local business owners, had purchased homes in this area. Grocery stores, dry good shops, and other black-owned businesses dotted this part of town, bordered on the north by the First Congregationalist Church and on the south by Alabama State. Here we see the church functioning smoothly and situating its pastor's residence, like those of most of its members, in the heart of Montgomery's black middle class. These years would be the last calm before a generation of storm and struggle.[12]

Like Judkins, Callahan was able to bring in notable preachers for the revival series at the church. In April 1918, Dr. J. W. Bailey of Marshall, Texas, an evangelist with the Home Board of the Southern Baptist Convention in Atlanta, led the revival. Following the earlier custom, there was a week of services culminating in an all-day service on Sunday. Special separate services were held for the men and women. Among the new converts added to the church in this revival was ten-year-old R. D. Nesbitt. Nesbitt—whose family members had been among those in the exodus from First Baptist Church that led to the establishment of Dexter Avenue—had wanted to join earlier, during the pastorate of the Reverend Judkins, but his parents believed he was too young to make such a commitment. Nesbitt admits that even later, when he joined Dexter Avenue, he did not understand the gravity of his decision and "went to the altar following some of the older boys in the church." His parents saw to it, however, that he and his brother would deeply understand exactly what joining the church involved. Recalling his early years, Nesbitt said of himself and his brother, "Every Sunday we walked from our home on 1015 Tuscaloosa Street up to Dexter Avenue Baptist Church for Sunday School and church in the morning. Then we walked over to the Episcopal Church on Jackson Street for a three-o'clock service and then came back to Dexter Avenue in the evenings for the BYPU [Baptist Young People's Union] meetings." And so began R. D. Nesbitt's involvement with and service to Dexter Avenue, which lasted until his death in April of 2002.[13]

In tandem with internal activities, church members kept up their community activism. Soon after Callahan's arrival, congregants became involved in efforts to support American soldiers fighting in World War I. Ironically, in this era of austere segregation and restrictions on the freedoms of African Americans, a new black newspaper, the

Emancipator,[14] urged church members to "show patriotism and escape the bondage of German chains by subscribing to American Liberty bonds." Black churches in Montgomery organized the Central Committee of Colored Montgomery Citizens to devise ways to "entertain the colored soldiers stationed in the area." Victor Hugo Tulane, a local businessman, chaired the Central Committee. Dexter Avenue members J. W. Phillips, H. C. Scott, and W. F. Watkins sat on this important committee. The Dexter Avenue choir, along with the choirs of other black churches, created a 250-voice chorus to entertain the troops. Dexter Avenue's superintendent of the Sunday school, J. W. Beverly, directed the food conservation program in Montgomery's African American community. In early November 1917, Dexter Avenue expanded its participation in the war effort to include national and state involvement. Kelly Miller, dean of Howard University, organized the Colored Comfort Committee to "aid the dependents of our soldiers and sailors" who were killed or disabled fighting for the nation. Victor Hugo Tulane was in charge of the Montgomery chapter, and Dexter Avenue held programs to raise money for this cause.[15]

In 1918, Dexter Avenue led Montgomery's Emancipation Day celebration. Meeting in the Dexter Avenue sanctuary, the Emancipation Association Committee planned what it hoped would be "the greatest celebration ever," which included a parade with floats to represent all phases of "Negro development and activity" since emancipation. Intensifying the festive mood of the 1918 celebration, the compulsory education law, the result of an exacting twenty-year struggle, went into effect on the first day of January. African American leaders hailed the regulation as "the greatest blessing to ever come to the commonwealth of Alabama." It should be noted, however, that the compulsory education bill that finally passed was weaker than the original bill, which had guaranteed free public education for all Alabama children. This final bill included some exceptions: no community could be compelled to build a public school; and people in rural areas with no school nearby, as well as families who demonstrated financial hardship and needed their children to work, were not forced to send their children to school. As well, the state provided public support for education only though the eighth grade. For a high school education, students had to pay tuition to private schools, like the lab school at Alabama State. Here we see again the promise and limits of uplift work and faith in the democratic process. Persistent efforts produced a compulsory education law, but a rather weak one.

Still, there were reasons to celebrate. Dexter Avenue members planned floats that marked progress in agricultural production, education, and health and medicine, including a float with doctors and nurses from Montgomery's only African American health facility, the Hale Infirmary. Local merchants and business owners marched in the parade as well. The parade began in downtown Montgomery, proceeded up Dexter Avenue toward the state capitol, turned right and headed down Decatur Street, and ended on the campus of Alabama State University, where several speakers addressed the audience. The meanings of such celebrations were complicated. On the one hand, they literally represented a presenting of black achievement and progress for white approval and proof of African Americans' worthiness of first-class citizenship. Still, barely more than fifty years from slavery and in light of so much loss of the political gains of Reconstruction, these celebrations were opportunities for African Americans to publicly commemorate their freedom and to remind the community of their presence.[16]

In these years, Dexter Avenue's activism was sometimes confrontational. On August 31, 1918, several Dexter Avenue members were part of a group of sixty people who met at the First Congregational Church to establish a local chapter of the National Association for the Advancement of Colored People (NAACP). Along with the Minister's Alliance and the Negro Betterment League, the NAACP convened a group of African American leaders from across the state. Meeting at Dexter Avenue, they petitioned the state legislature to enforce the compulsory education law and pay more than two dollars per year for the education of each black child. (The legislature paid five dollars per year for each white child.) The group requested that conditions be improved on Negro train cars and in waiting areas. Finally, this group expressed grave concern over the escalation of lynchings. Using NAACP statistics, they determined that 3,785 persons had been lynched in the United States between 1885 and 1918, and that 95 percent of the victims were African American. They suggested a number of actions to deter further lynchings: to immediately fire the sheriff of the county and his assistants, to pay ten thousand dollars to the lynched victim's family, and to provide sure and certain punishment for all perpetrators. This group also endorsed the prohibition amendment, and requested impartial enforcement of the constitutional provision for enfranchisement.

In June 1918, at another NAACP meeting held at Dexter Avenue, Pastor Peter Callahan and James Julian led the charge to get more African Americans registered to vote. They created a brief pamphlet clearly laying out the requirements for voting and distributed five thousand copies throughout the state. Callahan, whose son Andrew had lost his life in the war, said he wanted "to remind men, especially the returned soldier of his duty and his opportunity" to vote.[17] What's important here is that we see continued faith in the morality of democratic institutions and the power of the vote to improve conditions for African Americans.

The years between 1917 and 1926 were an important time of challenge and change in the history of Dexter Avenue Baptist Church. The church saw many internal improvements and purchased a parsonage. The missionary society, Sunday school, and most other organizations continued to grow, and the seasonal revivals continued. A few church traditions, however, including the lecture series, were discontinued.[18] More significant, the church suffered two losses that symbolized the close of an age. In August 1919, members learned that former pastor R. C. Judkins had died. Judkins and the congregation had maintained close relations. Members were saddened and felt a deep sense of loss.[19] In many ways his leadership had stabilized and given direction to the church. Most important, during the Judkins ministry, Dexter Avenue's founding ideals of racial uplift and hard work as avenues to progress and full participation in American democracy had flourished.[20]

Before church members recovered from losing Judkins, H. A. Loveless, one of the church's most active pioneers, died at his home on August 8, 1921. Loveless had attended the 1877 founding meeting of the church at Samuel Phillips's home. He was one of the church's first deacons and an original trustee, who had helped purchase the land for the original church building, and he led the fund-raising campaign for construction of the permanent church building. Loveless was among those helping to craft the character of the church. He was often a spokesman for the congregation and he had risen from slavery to become one of the most prosperous African Americans in the city;[21] he won appointments from the governor and served on the trustee boards of the Swayne School and Alabama State.[22] He was always willing to share the honor and prestige he received with the whole church body. To honor Loveless's memory, Elizabeth De Ramus organized the H. A. Loveless Working Club.[23] This auxiliary, opened only to women, raised money to foster programs and projects to develop better Christian fellowship;[24] Loveless's daughter Bertha served as president of the club until her death in 1937.

The death of these two prominent actors in the life of Dexter Avenue coincided with changes in the character of the church. By the end of the Callahan pastorate, in 1926, internal and external forces were beginning to diminish the church's stability and activism. For the next twenty years the church became far less involved in overt civil rights activities and racial uplift, but continued to be a vital force in the African

American community. The financial starkness of the Depression, which hit the African American community in Montgomery by the mid-1920s; the many challenges to the new generation of leaders; and the frequent changes in pastoral leadership combined to threaten the stability that had marked the early years of the twentieth century for Dexter Avenue.

In May 1926, Dexter Avenue called another Virginia Union graduate, Frank Walter Jacobs, to the pastorate. Jacobs, a native of North Carolina, was ordained to the ministry at an early age, and had served as a chaplain to troops stationed in Camp Lee, Virginia, during World War I. Similar to his immediate predecessor, Jacobs came to Dexter Avenue after having led large churches. As always, the installation of a new pastor at Dexter Avenue involved the whole community. Each night of the eight-day celebration featured a community group; public school teachers and fraternal lodges like the Eastern Star and the Black Elks were featured as guests to meet the new minister. Guest pastors from local churches gave the sermons. On June 6, 1926, former Dexter Avenue pastor Dr. Robert Thomas Pollard opened the installation services. A week later, on June 13, the day of installation, another former Dexter Avenue pastor, sixty-three-year-old A. F. Owens, gave the morning sermon, and that afternoon Dr. R. J. Langston formally installed Jacobs and closed the service. Church member and Alabama State University president H. Council Trenholm served as master of ceremony. On the evening of June 14 a reception for local pastors and their wives was held in the basement of the church. Such celebrations were a tradition at Dexter Avenue, but they were also markers and displays of the church's middle-class status. It also assured that the new pastor, as a community leader, would immediately become familiar with influential African Americans in Montgomery.[25]

The Jacobs pastorate infused a new excitement and energy into the church. Jacobs believed this to be a pivotal moment in the church's history and that the congregation was experiencing a malaise. He was passionate about two things: standardizing and professionalizing the church's finances, and ensuring that church members understood and adhered to Baptist doctrine. Within two weeks of Jacobs's arrival, at his first meeting with church officials, he drafted resolutions for the officers' "most careful consideration and adoption; believing them to be of great good for the church." Among these was the appointment of a missions and benevolence treasurer to "receive and bank all moneys taken up for such purposes." Jacobs advised that the church bond its treasurers, "not to be construed as prompted by any suspicion, but as a practical common sense business form." Further, he suggested members place offerings in envelopes and that all checks be drafted by the treasurer, who would report all financial activity to the board. Finally, Jacobs urged members to form an auditing committee to oversee all financial transactions.[26]

At the pastor's direction the board rented a safety deposit box from the First National Bank for the safekeeping of important church documents such as mortgages, warranty deeds, copies of the deeds for the church and the parsonage, and insurance policies currently in force. These recommendations were just the beginning of the financial reform implemented by Jacobs. In June 1926 Jacobs launched an every-member canvass and set the budget at $5,800.[27] Church officials presented members with a detailed explanation of how moneys would be spent.[28] Officers approached "every member under the most favorable circumstances ... [to] impress upon each member that giving is a necessary part of worship."[29] At the year's end, Jacobs noted that "Dexter Avenue Baptist Church owes no one anything but love." In reviewing the first year of their relationship as pastor and church, he wrote "let opposition spur us to larger and higher things. Let our past achievements serve as a guide, pointing us to larger tasks."[30]

During the Jacobs years members continued church and parsonage repairs and purchased insurance for the church automobile. Members also constructed a new restroom and new steps that were less steep, allowing easier access. Finally the church constructed a wall around the edifice to drain off the excess water that accumulated during the rainy season;[31] these repairs and many other endeavors were accomplished through special fund-raising campaigns.[32] Jacobs's campaigns to raise money were successful because he had inherited a well-organized congregation. Along with the regular church officers—clerk, treasurer, chorister, organist, board secretary, and board chairman—the deacon board, trustee board, and an advisory board worked closely with him. To better serve the community, the missionary society divided the town into units; members were assigned to acquaint themselves with all the people living in their town unit and personally invite them to church. Leaders were to report activities within their unit at the bimonthly meetings of the missionary society.[33] Jacobs refined the church's organizational structure to run even more smoothly. The church held quarterly conferences on each fourth Monday night; here officers were elected and auxiliaries submitted reports to the board that included membership, scheduled meetings and attendance, activities and participation, money collected and money spent, and projected expenditures for the next quarter.[34]

Jacobs's pastorate was also characterized by beginning new church traditions. Most notably, on October 10, 1926, the church held its first homecoming service, an all-day affair. Elderly church members and shut-ins were asked to make a special effort to be present because they would be recognized during the morning service. People who had been members of Dexter Avenue at some other time but were currently living out of town were invited to return home to attend this service. On this day of celebration, the choir prepared special music, and all major organizations of the church gave reports and made presentations. The highlight of the evening services, however, was the "roll call of the sainted dead," where the names of all of those who had died in that calendar year were read.[35] One of the early goals of the Jacobs ministry was to promote adherence to and understanding of the doctrines and disciplines of the Baptist faith. He made an especially vigorous effort to help acclimate new members, providing each with a copy of *Bailey's Manual of Instruction for Baptists*. This religious primer, published by the American Baptist Publishing Society in Kansas City, Missouri, provided a brief history of Baptists in America and laid out fundamental principles of the faith, like the importance of individual conscience and adult baptism, and the democratic decision-making process. Jacobs urged the board to adopt a uniform procedure for receiving persons from other denominations into membership—namely, that such persons be "immersed by a Baptist minister (which means that a candidate's body is fully immersed in water at baptism)."[36]

To better educate church members concerning the responsibilities of Christian living, Jacobs implemented changes in the Sunday school curriculum and the communion ritual. Initially Jacobs wanted to establish a leadership training school for members. This organization would provide instruction for participation in the church's auxiliary life, educating Sunday school teachers, deacons, trustees, and others about their particular responsibilities and commitments. While this plan did not come to fruition, Jacobs did arrange for Sunday school teachers to meet on the Tuesday before the Sunday they were to teach to go over the lesson in order to ensure uniformity in the interpretation of and approach to the lesson. Additionally, Jacobs revived the midweek prayer service as a time where members could come to church, sing a few hymns and read scripture, but most of the hour was spent in meditative (silent) prayer usually led by one of the lay members.[37]

Changes were also implemented in the service of communion. Traditionally, at Dexter Avenue, the deacons served communion and church members consumed the wine and bread individually as they were served. Jacobs wanted to make the service more sacred by creating a closer sense of togetherness. He requested that at communion "'all eat and drink together and remain until the Pastor reads Matthew 26:30: 'When they had sung a hymn, they went out.'" At a later board meeting, officers decided that they would wear white gloves when serving communion. Indeed, Jacobs inaugurated a ministry that emphasized accountability in all facets of the church life—financial, organizational, and spiritual. While he did not completely capture the dynamic vitality of the Judkins ministry, his efforts breathed much-needed energy into the church. What we see here is a shoring up of the infrastructure of church life to achieve a level of stability, not in anticipation of trouble to come, but in the hope of providing a sanctuary from the world's troubles for members and being of greater service to the community.[38]

In the midst of these reforms, the church tried to address the economic difficulties so many faced in the wake of the Depression. By the mid-1920s African Americans were feeling the ravages of hard times. Agriculture entered a depression in the early 1920s and would not recover for the next twenty years, and by 1926, industry had sunk into depression as well. During the early and mid-1920s, the church devised specific measures to relieve congregants and community members who had fallen on hard times. The board "adopted" a blind and indigent man who often attended services, providing him with a meal after church each Sunday. They paid a month's rent for a family in north Montgomery and sent ten dollars to a destitute woman in Lowndes County. The Dexter Avenue board also provided aid to financially troubled members of the church; it gave money directly to one member, and on another occasion paid for the repair of an elderly member's home; in yet another case the church even arranged to pay for the funeral expenses of one of its members.[39]

Contributing to the difficulties the church was experiencing, in July 1928, Dexter Avenue lost another of its pioneer members. R. T. Grant had been largely responsible for organizing the choir and developing the music program. Father Grant, as he was affectionately known, had been chorister for more than twenty-five years, and had assisted practically "every church in town in its music arrangements." In a fitting tribute to Grant, Bertha Loveless, whom he had helped train and encouraged to complete a music degree at Fisk University, sang at his funeral, and he was buried in Oakwood Cemetery in a special vault the church purchased for him. Grant's death was not only a personal loss for Dexter Avenue but one more indicator that another generation of church life was passing. Soon there would remain only a handful of charter members. In the years immediately following Grant's death, economic hardship forced church leadership to struggle to maintain a healthy infrastructural auxiliary life, to keep guiding ideals and principles before members; internal important founding ideals—like that of the church as a "free space" to foster spiritual affirmation and racial uplift as well as a place to develop workers—diminished in intensity but fortunately did not disappear in the years between the two world wars.[40]

Frank Jacobs's ministry reflected his belief that black churches occupied "a distinct place in the development and well being" of African Americans. He saw the church as the most important institution in African American life, believing that ministers at most churches were "prepared and consecrated to their life's work" and that black congregations were "for the most part earnest and zealous of good works and 100 per cent loyal to their respective church." Jacobs's ministry emphasized organization and accountability in all their activities involving church work and in some instances, in their private lives.

He stressed issues of personal holiness, encouraging members to avoid smoking, drinking, dancing, and playing cards. In Montgomery, as in other parts of the nation, jazz and juke-joints were common parts of the social lives of some African Americans. He requested that board members disallow dancing in their homes, but failed to persuade a majority to support his admonition. Board members, however, fully endorsed Jacobs's position favoring prohibition. Jacobs inspired a dynamic spirit among church members that encouraged them to examine their individual consciences and strengthen their commitment to Dexter Avenue. Meanwhile, evidence emerged that the church was experiencing dire financial strain.[41]

By 1930, the church's financial condition succumbed to the faltering national economy. Dexter Avenue experienced serious financial problems and struggled to meet its obligations. The board immediately streamlined the budget, abolishing—at least temporarily—some paid church positions, like those of treasurer and financial secretary. Overseeing the finances now fell to the regular church clerk, whose salary was reduced from eight dollars to five dollars per month. By January 1931, the church could pay the pastor only one-third of his $150 monthly salary. During the next year, the church's financial stability deteriorated further, and the church only paid its pastor half of the promised fifty dollars. Jacobs sympathized, but explained that he could not meet his personal financial obligations on what the church was paying him in 1931 and 1932.[42]

In February 1932, Reverend Jacobs resigned to become pastor of Messiah Baptist Church in Bridgeport, Connecticut. Deacons and church members voted unanimously to reject his resignation and offered him three hundred dollars of the back salary owed him. Jacobs had resolved to leave, and on April 20 again tendered his resignation, which the church now accepted. Church members noted that Jacobs's administration had been marked by "phenomenal and miraculous strides in all phases of our complex social, political, economic and religious life." They wanted "to make special mention of his honesty, uprightness, sincerity of purpose and the warm constructive interest which he has manifested in everybody—from the infant to the aged."[43]

Difficult and uncertain times marked the summer of 1932 for the nation and for Dexter Avenue. The church struggled to settle its financial obligations to Jacobs while seeking new pastoral leadership; it strained to raise money to keep its ministries functioning and to relieve mounting debt. The church still owed Jacobs a substantial amount of money and an astringent dispute ensued over the exact amount of indebtedness. It took one year to reach an acceptable settlement, and the church had to sell the car that it maintained for the pastor's use. To minimize cost for care of the parsonage in the absence of a pastor the board allowed a church member to move there and live rent free in exchange for maintenance and utility payments.[44]

These temporary solutions provided minimal relief, and problems escalated. Strong disagreements emerged among board members over how to restore congregants' confidence in their leadership. Some board members urged that all church leaders stand for reelection believing that such a move would result in increased giving. To be sure, board members understood that economic hardship was the primary culprit in diminished financial contributions, but they also believed that a crisis of confidence existed in the current board's leadership.[45]

Other members of the board believed that new elections would only add to the current confusion and instability and that the real problem was the absence of pastoral presence at the church. The deacon board brought in a temporary minister to help alleviate the confusion and discord, calling upon a local man, A. F. Fisher. Naively, Fisher enthusiastically offered his suggestions for ways the board could restore members' confidence and raise money. The clerk did not bother to include Fisher's suggestions in the minutes, instead only noting that the board had flatly rejected them and had restricted his role to Sunday morning preaching until a permanent pastor could be found. In October 1932, the pulpit committee found Reverend E. G. Thomas and brought him in to speak for two Sundays, but then lost him in salary negotiations. The board managed to keep the church doors open on Sundays, but it continued searching for a new pastor and struggling to pay church debts.[46]

The year 1932 had brought much frustration, but with assistance from the president of the Alabama Baptist State Convention fortunes changed. In December, the pulpit committee found Arnold E. Gregory, a professor of religious education at Talladega College. Gregory was an immigrant from Jamaica who had come to the United States in 1906 as an instructor at the Berea Training School in Kentucky. In 1911, he enrolled at Oberlin College, which he identified as the most important and formative experience of his life and Christian walk. After completing his bachelor's degree in divinity he wrote, "Oberlin has given me a deep conviction of the reality of the Christian faith and (Christian) purpose." Gregory had led churches in Montreal, Canada; Savannah, Georgia; and Philadelphia.

In negotiations with Gregory, the board emphasized that until economic times improved, the church could only offer him one hundred dollars per month, a parsonage, and coal for the winter. He assured pulpit committee members that he understood the difficulty of the times and "welcomed the opportunity to serve the church." At the close of Sunday services on December 18, 1932, the church committee members placed Gregory's name before the church body, which voted unanimously to issue him a call to the Dexter Avenue pastorate. For the first time in its history, Dexter Avenue called a minister who had not been raised in the Baptist faith, and one of the first orders of business was to baptize Gregory in a simple service at Dexter Avenue.[47] One sign of the austerity of the times was the simple, one-day service officially installing Gregory as pastor. Local ministers and civic groups were invited, but there were none of the elaborate displays that had characterized the Callahan and Jacobs weeklong installation services.

Gregory restored order and stability to the board and helped the various auxiliaries of the church meet their expenses, though financial problems continued to plague Dexter Avenue. The church paid Gregory a portion of his salary, and the pastor was not the only officer asked to make sacrifices; all church officers who received money for their services agreed to take reductions in salary.[48] Gregory assured the membership of his confidence in church leadership, and that he had not come to the church with a plan for changing traditions and practices but wanted to lead and enable the church to continue as it had for many years.

Despite the economic privation of the stark Depression days, Dexter Avenue maintained a flurry of activity to sustain its regular programs and provide some level of community service. Organizations such as the H. A. Loveless Working Club and the missionary society held various fundraisers. Community services, such as the Thanksgiving food drive and Christmas community dinner, remained regular parts of church life. Henrietta Gibbs, acting on behalf of the board of trustees, asked church members to bring baskets of food on the Sunday before Thanksgiving; the public was then invited to purchase the food at significantly reduced prices, and the funds raised were used for general expenditures. Church auxiliaries brought in doctors for yearly health clinics and lectures, and from June 25 to June 27, 1935, the church permitted the federal government to hold an institute for midwives in its basement. Two years later, Dexter Avenue allowed the Association of Domestic Employees to use church facilities for bimonthly meetings. The church also consented to a request from the state's Vocational Rehabilitation Department to use the Sunday school rooms to host a clinic for crippled children. One Sunday in November 1937, the church aided U.S. census workers by having church members who were either unemployed or partially employed fill out cards that were then turned over to government workers. In 1937, the missionary society sent Katie Reynolds as its representative to an interracial and interdenominational conference of Christian workers, meeting in Tuscaloosa, Alabama to talk about how churches could better meet the needs of the poor and how they could more effectively spread the Gospel in their various localities. The BYPU sponsored a program on important historical Negro women. The Sunday school began sponsoring an annual picnic for the church family at a local black park.[49]

Along with the H. A. Loveless Working Club and the missionary society, the board took several actions to raise enough money to meet the church's expenses. Each Sunday, before collecting the regular tithes, a benevolence offering was collected in order that the pastor might discreetly help community people or church members who had fallen on hard times. Allowing the pastor such discretion was a significant change for a board that traditionally required a strict accounting of all church funds. To further support its fragile treasury, the board decided that all church clubs should turn over their money to the general church fund to aid in paying for running expenses.[50]

To maintain financial solvency, Dexter Avenue adjusted some of its traditions. Rather than discontinue marking noteworthy occasions like church anniversaries, homecomings, and pastor anniversaries the church members voted to combine the celebration for the church's and pastor's anniversaries. Since the church could no longer afford week-long lecture series and revivals, it established some new traditions. In May 1938, the church celebrated its first Men's Day. R. D. Nesbitt, having been recently elected church clerk, was the master of ceremony for the historic event. The Dexter Avenue men began their program by reading from Romans 12:1–3, which says that they must present their lives as a living sacrifice to God. The theme was "Men maintain strength as trees do, by remaining sound at heart." The men presented three speakers who gave brief addresses. First, J. S. Burch of the Atlanta Mutual Life Insurance Company spoke on "Negro Business in Montgomery"; he was followed by Eugene Lyon; finally, T. S. Lambert, director of Negro education for the State Board of Education, spoke on the educational challenges that lay ahead for African Americans.[51]

A few weeks later, the women celebrated the first Women's Day at Dexter Avenue. Henrietta M. Gibbs served as mistress of ceremony. The women chose for their special scripture reading the Second Book of John which is a letter to Christian women living in Asia Minor during the first century, warning them against showing hospitality to false teachers. For their theme, the women chose, "Better to be great in little things than little in great things." The special guest speaker was a community activist, a Mrs. Greeson, who was a member of Montgomery's Recreational Council and spent most of her time volunteering to help poor families and juvenile delinquents living in Montgomery; she spoke about the challenge of serving others.[52] These Men's and Women's Days provided opportunities for the men and women at Dexter Avenue to raise money, but more important, they were also days of affirmation of African American womanhood and manhood.

During Gregory's pastorate general conditions improved even flourished at times, but the church still struggled to maintain a stable church life and congregation as faithful members of the first two generations continued to pass away. J. A. Lawrence, who was only the second superintendent of the Sunday school died on New Year's Day in 1937. Lawrence was an educator for many years, and was honored at his funeral service by the teachers of Booker T. Washington High School and by school superintendent C. M. Dannelly.[53] In December 1937, the church lost Bertha Loveless, who had headed the H. A. Loveless Working Club since its founding in 1921. Finally, long-time deacon and leader J. H. Phillips died in May 1938. The passing of Loveless and Phillips signaled the beginning of the dying out of the first generation of people who had been born and raised in the church. Both Loveless and Phillips were members of the original BYPU, which had formed in 1892.

Concurrently, however, new leaders emerged. Gregory had come to rely on W. W. Streety, head of the deacons, for leadership of the official board.[54] As well, R. D. Nesbitt assumed the first of several positions of leadership he would hold during his life at Dexter Avenue. Nesbitt, carrying on the tradition established by his father Joseph Nesbitt (who had served as secretary of the board), became clerk of the church.[55] He replaced J. T. Alexander, who relinquished his position as temporary clerk in order to focus his attention solely on the Dexter Avenue Sunday school.[56]

It appeared that the new leaders at Dexter Avenue were of two minds. The Dexter Avenue that these men and women remembered most clearly was a church plagued by uncertainty and defined by its financial struggle. Stability and faith in church leadership were the chief concerns of these leaders as they guided Dexter Avenue into its next decade of life as a religious institution. In large measure, they believed that stability depended on strong leaders who could maintain calm. The new leadership was also inspired by the stories told by the church's elders—particularly Henrietta Wade Austin, Henrietta Gibbs, King Kelly, and Edna King—about the "glory days" of the creative and innovative ministry of R. C. Judkins. New leaders' childhood memories of the Judkins years at the church, embellished by the nostalgic recollections of their elders, motivated them to work to challenge the status quo.[57]

These competing influences, focusing church leadership attention at once backward and forward, explain the choices and the complex nature of church politics that characterized life at Dexter Avenue from the 1930s through the 1950s. On the one hand, in looking for new pastors and electing new officers the church wanted to find persons who would not be controversial or particularly challenging to congregants. On the other hand, they wanted leaders to revive the dynamic spirit they believed had once existed. This combination helps explain why a conservative church like Dexter Avenue brought in controversial ministers.

While new leaders contemplated possible paths and directions for Dexter Avenue, unanticipated circumstances altered the course of events. In 1938, Gregory's wife became very ill, requiring hospitalization in New York City. Called away suddenly to attend to his wife, Gregory put W. W. Streety in charge of filling the pulpit and leading the official board in its meetings.[58] For almost a year, Gregory commuted between Montgomery and New York City. It came as no surprise when on June 2, 1939, Gregory read his letter of resignation to the church. Still, T. H. Randall asked Gregory to turn the letter over to the board for its consideration. Gregory explained that his mind was made up, and it was not a matter for the board but for the church to decide.

J. A. Gibbs then moved that the church body accept the resignation, and after the motion was seconded by Randall, the church, with some regret, passed the motion.[59]

On June 19, 1938, Streety called a special meeting of the official board to form a pulpit committee. Remembering the confusion that had ensued when Jacobs resigned, Streety asked for the "whole-hearted support of all members" in the absence of a pastor. T. H. Randall was asked to chair, and J. A. Gibbs and D. D. Williams were asked to sit on this committee. The board decided that until they found a permanent minister, the church would pay forty-five dollars to guest ministers invited to fill the pulpit. Frank Jacobs returned for a few Sundays to help out his former church, and also helped the church schedule other ministers. Jacobs's return suggested that a measure of reconciliation had been achieved between himself and the church regarding the dispute over the exact amount of back salary he had been owed when he left.[60]

Streety's leadership and his plea to the board to avoid confusion eased the pastoral search process. One problem remained, however: Dexter Avenue's enduring debts, despite its best efforts to recover. Board members harbored concern that the church would appear insolvent to any new pastor. Nevertheless, T. H. Randall and the pulpit committee requested permission from the board to visit two Georgia ministers they knew were in search of pastorates. The committee first met with Reverend Ralph Waldo Riley and were so impressed they believed that they needed to look no further. They invited Riley to speak on the fourth Sunday in October. Deacon Streety urged board members to make sure as many church members as possible would be present and that members make a special effort to give generously, emphasizing that "it takes money to bring a minister here."[61]

Despite Streety's and others' efforts to maintain calm and good feelings among church members, strong reactions to minor issues suggested that there was some dissatisfaction with church life. Weariness of the financial struggle and uncertainty of the past ten years had created a malaise. The first crisis surfaced, seemingly out of nowhere: for almost a year, the Dexter Avenue choir had been without a leader, and while there had been some confusion and division, the choir had managed to lead the congregation in music each Sunday, but tensions finally reached a breaking point a few Sundays before Riley was to preach. Choir members disagreed over the music to sing each Sunday and were angry that they had to sit in ragged chairs while perfectly good choir chairs were stored at the parsonage. One choir member,

Emery Liverette, approached the board to report that the choir was "in a state of unrest." Streety appointed a committee of three, Henrietta Gibbs, Reynolds Moore, and Randall Wood, to resolve the problem. Choir members wanted new leadership, and the board was able to persuade Professor J. T. Brooks, a Dexter Avenue member who taught music at Alabama State, to serve as chorister. Custodian William McGee also replaced choir chairs in need of repair with those at the parsonage. In the absence of pastoral leadership, many of the details of life at the church got lost.[62]

Board members were confident that the Dexter Avenue pastorate had much to recommend it. Despite financial problems, it remained a highly sought-after pulpit. J. A. Wilson, pastor of the First African Baptist Church of Savannah, Georgia, wrote to the deacons to offer himself for consideration. As well the presiding bishop of the Eighth Episcopal District of the Colored Methodist Episcopal Church wrote to Henrietta Gibbs requesting that the board consider Reverend Oscar Lee, a professor at Hampton Institute in Hampton, Virginia. Board members remained interested in Riley and turned their attention to arranging Riley's visit. Streety wanted Riley's election to the pastorate to be put before the church body the same Sunday he preached his trial sermon. Other board members, however insisted on a second visit from Riley.[63]

Streety persisted in efforts to move quickly in selecting a new pastor, perhaps believing that a prolonged consideration might result in disharmony. A majority of ten to three favored placing Riley's name before the church. T. H. Randall pleaded unanimity before approaching the church so that Riley could be the unanimous choice of the board because "we now have a man who fits our needs. He's our kind of man." Riley's profile was typical of most ministers Dexter Avenue had called. He was born on January 12, 1900, the youngest of the three children of Abe and Abie Riley of Valdosta, Georgia. After completing his secondary education at Florida Memorial College, he earned a bachelor of arts degree from Morehouse College, a master of arts in history from Atlanta University, and a divinity degree from the Gammon Methodist Theological Seminary. Riley had not only pastored large churches, but had also helped organize the campus Young Men's Christian Association (YMCA) at Bethune-Cookman College (later University). Later, as a college student in Atlanta, he convened an interracial conference of students at Atlanta's colleges and universities.[64]

On October 22, 1939, Streety asked the congregation to remain after the morning service. Church clerk R. D. Nesbitt presented Riley's name as the unanimous choice of the board for Dexter Avenue's next pastor. Essie Mosley Jette, head of the missionary society, proposed that the recommendation coming from the board be accepted unanimously by the membership. T. H. Randall wrote a letter inviting Riley to accept the pastorate of Dexter Avenue. Riley replied that he would "take this matter under prayerful consideration" and respond when he had made final his decision. A month later, on December 4, Riley accepted the offer and requested meeting with the officials to work out an acceptable agreement. The church now had a new pastor, but finances were still precarious. T. H. Randall suggested that the pastor be paid a flexible salary valued at about $125 per month. The amount of cash he received might vary each month, but the board agreed to pay Riley's bills if he needed assistance. On the one hand, this arrangement might allow the church great latitude in meeting its financial obligations to the pastor each month, but such an arrangement would place Riley at the mercy of a very powerful board.[65]

Dexter Avenue's official board, especially deacon T. H. Randall and trustee Henrietta Gibbs, was famous in Baptist circles for being difficult and controlling ministers. Riley, having no doubt learned of the board's reputation, came prepared for his first meeting with the board. He explained that he believed that a pastor must be a strong figure in a church and in "pastoring all departments and that all things must be under his charge." He hoped "that he had made it clear what kind of leader he was, and if they did not want a strong leader for the church, they should not have called him." Riley then asked the clerk for a full report pertaining to all of the indebtedness and financial condition of the church. He assured the board that if it cooperated with him, "things can boom again at Dexter." Next, the board presented its idea of the flexible salary to Riley, but he rejected it outright, insisting on a flat salary and that he would take care of his own expenses. When Riley asked what the church could pay, there was a long silence. He stated that "a church like Dexter should be able to pay $152.00 per month." Rather than responding directly to Riley's suggestion, Gibbs asked, "[W]hat methods might you suggest for raising money?" Riley noted that his policy was "to make certain that someone see each member of the church every week" to encourage him or her to be present and to pay tithes. He further stated that "each fifth Sunday be designated as a special drive day to raise extra money." Noting that the new pastor had some fine ideas, T. H. Randall suggested a compromise figure be considered for the pastor's salary with the understanding that it be increased as the church became more stable. J. T. Alexander proposed—and Riley accepted—that the church pay him $132 monthly until its financial situation improved.[66]

On the next Sunday, December 10, 1939, church members again were asked to remain after the morning service, where they were informed of the salary settlement the board had reached with Riley. The church body and the official board noted that the transition from Gregory to Riley, on the whole, went more smoothly than when Jacobs had left, due in large part to the atmosphere of cooperation that Streety and Randall had promoted. Riley's pastorate was a real victory for the new leaders.[67]

On December 19, Dexter Avenue held its last quarterly meeting of the year and the first church conference at which Riley acted as moderator. After he led the members in prayer and the singing of "Joy to the World," Riley explained that "he wanted all members to feel free to speak when they wished, and to call his attention immediately to any problem they might notice." With hope and enthusiasm members moved into a discussion of the activities for the coming year. Riley requested that all clubs and auxiliaries elect new officers, and then he shared his ideas of how to reach all members each Sunday to encourage them to come to services and to pay their tithes.[68]

The new pastor asked J. H. Gilchrist to select two people to help him divide the city into wards. Members were placed in a particular ward according to where they lived in the city. Each ward was assigned a team and a team leader who would see that each church member in the ward was visited every week to encourage regular attendance and giving. The church decided at this meeting to form a committee to write a constitution. Members voted to place a sign board in front of the church to advertise the church's Sunday services and special activities. Riley closed the meeting by requesting members' cooperation in making Dexter Avenue the best it had ever been. These changes represented Riley's attempt to lift the congregation out of its lament over its past "glory days" and troubled present to focus it toward a new day. Notably, the sign board was a new invitation to the community to join in the life of this institution. More important, changes such as the attempt to rewrite the church constitution suggested that perhaps the new generation of congregational leaders at Dexter Avenue now hoped to redefine life at the church.[69]

The ward system improved the financial condition of the church and brought both welcomed and unanticipated changes. Board members reported increased contributions, and ward leaders collected some money from inactive church members by threatening that unless financial hardship prevented attendance or giving, their names would be dropped from the church roll after a period of more than three months without some interest expressed in the work of the church. Improved economic circumstances brought on by World War II, however, made the real difference. As the ward system improved economic conditions, careful attendance and tithing records were kept, creating more paperwork for church clerk R. D. Nesbitt. In the summer of 1941, the board hired a full-time secretary to assist the pastor and help the church clerk. Members also voted to construct an office for the pastor and the secretary in the church basement. Finally, the church was now able to pay Riley the $150 monthly salary that board members had wanted to offer him at the beginning of his pastorate.[70]

With a measure of financial stability restored, Riley's attention focused on responding to the church's youth. With help from the deacon, he appointed a director of young people's activities to create special programs for the church's youth.[71] On March 9, 1941, for the first time since Judkins's pastorate, Dexter Avenue held a Youth Day celebration, inviting Dr. A. N. McEwen III, grandson of the Dexter Avenue pastor who had led in building the present edifice on Dexter Avenue.[72] Similar to the Men's and Women's Day celebrations, Youth Day was not just a service of scriptures, prayers, and music led by young people, but was also an affirmation of African American youth. But, unlike the adult celebrations, this tradition emerged out of the new prosperity and hope that characterized life at the church. As in the days of the Judkins pastorate, church youth memorized poems and exposition and spoke before the congregation.[73]

Riley hoped to foster a deeper sense of piety among the church youth. Under his guidance and with the help of the director of young people's activities, Dexter Avenue's Baptist Training Union (BTU) adopted specific goals for 1941: first, to "cultivate the habit of praying daily in secret prayer and lead in public prayer"; second, reading their Bibles each day; third, speaking publicly for Christ and encouraging other Christians to "do as the Master would have them do"; fourth, to "influence sinners to accept Christ"; and fifth, to "contribute of their means spiritually and prepare themselves for special service." To enliven the BTU even further, members began sending representatives to state and national conventions. Riley's goal was to "create Christian youth today for tomorrow's challenges." Specifically, the new pastor was interested in assuring that church youth could move in the outside world comfortably.[74]

Riley also focused on enlivening the Sunday school. He made it clear that "every church member should feel it is his duty" to attend Sunday school regularly.[75] While Jacobs had emphasized improving the Sunday school, attendance and participation had diminished during the Gregory pastorate, and Sunday school teachers had ceased meeting with the pastor to discuss their lessons before teaching them. Riley reinstated this practice, setting aside each Thursday night to meet with the Sunday school instructors. Church members revived a regular format for the Sunday school; it began at 9:30 in the morning with a general assembly, followed by hymn singing and prayer and proceeding to thirty-minute Bible lessons.[76]

Another component of Riley's ministry—a holdover from his student days—was to promote interracial cooperation. Here he helped launch Dexter Avenue's return journey toward more social activism. Riley had been active in interracial affairs for many years. Each year he attended the Race Relations Congress. Dating back to the early 1930s, this organization, sponsored by the Federal Council of Churches of Christ in America, was an interracial and interdenominational religious group that met each year to discuss how relations among the races could be improved.[77] Riley believed that the nation was moving toward a racially integrated society, and the success of the endeavor rested upon the readiness of the nation's youth to embrace a new social order. At the church, Riley inaugurated an Interracial Day. Blacks and willing whites from Montgomery and Atlanta and usually associated with the YMCA gave talks on the nature and importance of racial cooperation.[78] African Americans B. R. Blazeal, dean of Morehouse College, and H. Council Trenholm, president of Alabama State University, and Reverend H. A. Brann, who was white, of Maxwell Field all addressed the audience on the topic "Interracial Goodwill and the World of Tomorrow."[79] Another part of this program involved a mass meeting of the NAACP at Dexter Avenue and featured Ella Baker, the NAACP's assistant field service representative, as the principal speaker.[80]

By 1941, the church was responding to some of the needs created by World War II. Alabama became one of the major training centers for U.S. airmen and soldiers because the mild weather afforded many more training days than harsher Northern climates. Northern Alabama was an excellent location for the war industry because of cheap Tennessee Valley Authority power and a surplus labor supply. Also, Alabama congressmen had President Franklin Delano Roosevelt's ear. At Dexter Avenue, several efforts were made to raise money for the war. Riley spearheaded the Committee on Warfare-Welfare Chest. Similar to the World War I organization once headed by Victor Tulane, this organization raised money for soldiers' dependent children. Riley held a dinner on the campus of Alabama State for church members who donated at least five dollars to this organization; board members purchased war bonds, and on one Sunday of each month the missions and benevolence offering was donated to the American Red Cross. Dexter Avenue sponsored several programs to entertain the soldiers in the area, and in August 1943 the church held a Soldiers' Day service to honor local soldiers. Some of the soldiers being trained in Montgomery regularly attended services at Dexter Avenue and participated in the life of the church. One soldier, a PFC William Starling from West Virginia, sang in the choir and was regularly featured in solo concerts at the church.[81]

Dexter Avenue, like most churches, supported the war, but Riley reminded members of the evils of war. In his 1943 Christmas sermon he told members that it was a tragedy to be "forced to witness Christmas in a time when the world seems to have been trying to destroy the very things which make Christmas sacred and real." Riley told the congregation that "there can be no Christmas without His [Christ's] spirit." He concluded his remarks with the hope that "Christmas in 1944 will find the veil of the world's evil corrected and the star that once shone out over the Bethlehem Plains many years ago will be the star of HOPE for all people."[82]

In March 1944, John H. Paterson, a captain of field artillery and recruiting, came to Dexter Avenue to ask African American women to join the Women's Army Corps. Paterson told the congregation that any woman "in good health and of good character" between the ages of twenty and forty-nine, with no children under the age of fourteen, and with at least two years of high school was invited to the local recruiting office. A few months earlier, a number of Dexter Avenue men were drafted and sent to Fort Benning for induction. Among them was clerk of the church R. D. Nesbitt, who was later not inducted because he was underweight. Later the same month, the Montgomery Civilian Defense Council requested that local churches engage in an evening of prayer and rededication, to be announced on the day of the Allied Forces' invasion of Europe.[83]

April 1944 brought an unexpected and unwelcome event that again challenged church leadership. Riley was offered—and accepted—the position of president of the American Baptist Theological Seminary in Nashville, Tennessee. This new opportunity, by all accounts, was an unsolicited surprise to Riley. He assured chagrined members that it was "with much regret that he was leaving them," and told the board that while he had been happy in his position at the church he believed he must "take full advantage of this chance to minister" in this new venue. He requested that the first Sunday in June 1944 be his official last Sunday as pastor but that he would be available to preach the remaining three Sundays in June as a guest minister. The board accepted this arrangement, and the first Sunday in July was set aside as a time in which his friends from the city and the church might show their appreciation for the service he had rendered. At the time, Riley was preparing six new deacons for ordination: C. C. Beverly, C. J. Dunn, Will McGhee, R. D. Nesbitt, and W. J. Wood.[84]

On Monday, June 3, 1944, members of Dexter Avenue held a banquet honoring Riley's efforts. They pointed out that Riley had met the church's need for strong leadership in a time of economic hardship by leading in the efforts that helped to bring about a return of the church's financial solvency. Riley had improve the church's youth ministry,[85] and (though the progress would be interrupted by the tumultuous pastorate that followed) he had helped a new generation of congregants and church leaders commit to making Dexter Avenue more accessible to its community and developing a renewed commitment to racial uplift.

In the summer of 1944, board members searched for a new pastor, and the church sent R. D. Nesbitt to the National Baptist Convention in Dallas.[86] While there, Nesbitt met and took special note of an "impressive man," Alfred Charles Livingston Arbouin, pastor of the First African Baptist Church in Brunswick, Georgia. Later Nesbitt would wish that he had asked himself why a man like Arbouin would be so willing to leave a historical church like First African Baptist, but for the moment he was "terribly struck by Arbouin's eloquence and credentials." Born in Jamaica and raised in the Episcopal Church, Arbouin joined the Baptist faith shortly after coming to the United States to begin his studies at Benedict College in Columbia, South Carolina.[87] He graduated with degrees in biology and theology before proceeding to law school at LaSalle University, studying psychotherapy at Columbia University, and completing his formal study with two years of training at the Jewish Theological Seminary in New York.[88]

It took the church almost a year and several interim ministers before the deacons and board agreed to offer the pulpit to Arbouin. In the intervening time, national events momentarily captured the attention of the church congregation. In the spring of 1945, Dexter Avenue joined the nation in mourning the death of President Franklin Delano Roosevelt. Like churches all over the country, Dexter Avenue held a special memorial service to honor the "beloved leader who had done so much for all Americans." H. Council Trenholm read a tribute to Roosevelt's life, and the service ended with the singing of "O God Our Help in Ages Past."[89]

Attention and energy quickly refocused on selecting a pastor. In May 1945, Deacon Will McGhee placed Arbouin's name before the official board, which voted unanimously to offer Arbouin the pastorate at a salary of $190 per month, along with the parsonage and a telephone. The official board invited Arbouin to address its members at the next meeting. Arbouin gave "a very fine talk," accepting the board's call "because Dexter Avenue and Montgomery offered the possibility of doing a greater service for the master." Arbouin explained, however, that he and his wife were currently paid $300 per month with a parsonage and a month's paid vacation. Board members told Arbouin the church could pay $225 per month, with the promise of a raise if offerings and tithes improved. Board members were pleased with Arbouin's "ready" and quick acceptance of the offer, but probably should have asked why Arbouin accepted so easily.[90]

When Arbouin arrived at Dexter Avenue, the church was financially solvent for the first time in many years, and board members were impressed that their new pastor presented them with a yearlong calendar of services including fund-raisers, the church's anniversary, and Women's, Men's, and Youth Day celebrations. Arbouin included in the church bulletin each Sunday a pastoral missive reminding members of their Christian duty to one another and to the community. "Give of your best," he implored, "to the master in love, prayers, interest, service and money." Initially, members were taken with their new pastor, who was reputed to be an outstanding "gospel preacher." Hopes and spirits soared, but they almost as quickly plummeted.[91]

Arbouin's pastorate was tumultuous and "mercifully brief." Within a year of the new pastor's arrival rumors circulated that he had more than one wife. At a board meeting in Arbouin's absence, a young woman showed up, claiming to be a former wife. Chafing at Arbouin's deception, board members called him in and demanded an explanation. Rather than apologize, Arbouin chastised them for accepting the word of a person they did not know and their lack of faith that he would have a reasonable explanation. What Arbouin told the board was not recorded, but his explanation assuaged, at least temporarily, the board's rage. Arbouin admonished the board not to "unduly" turn the membership against him. Of course, word traveled to the community, and church attendance and giving dropped precipitously. A few Sundays later Arbouin requested a vote of confidence among the congregation. As he had hoped, most supported his pastorate. There were those, however, who voted against him. Henrietta Gibbs addressed the congregation, sharing her belief that Arbouin was not fit for the pulpit. William Pettus, trying to keep the peace but sympathizing with the disgruntled

Gibbs, suggested that a church conference be called at a later date to allow time for emotions and passions to abate. Arbouin interrupted by starting to sing "Blest Be the Tie that Binds" to close the meeting.[92]

Perhaps feeling embarrassed by his public comeuppance, Arbouin would not let the incident pass. Later he included a biting note in the church bulletin titled "What I Owe My Minister," in which he wrote, "I owe him respect as the ambassador of God sent to teach me a better way of living than the selfish, sordid existence I might be guilty of ... the protection of kindly silence by refraining from repeating, in his presence, the slander of unkind gossip that would worry him." Messages in the church bulletin continued periodically with the same theme over the next year. Members of the congregation and board became outraged; board members C. C. Beverly, Will McGhee, and Henrietta Gibbs expressed bitter disapproval of what they believed was misuse of the church bulletin. Even the patient and always measured and courtly R. D. Nesbitt finally lost his patience. Arbouin defended his bulletin statements as a pastoral prerogative to encourage members to ever move toward improvement. But Gibbs would not be placated. She complained to Arbouin that his comments were "directed toward her and others who had some real concern about the state of his personal life." Arbouin assured Gibbs that his messages in the bulletin were intended to be instructive to the entire congregation. But clearly a rift had surfaced between the pastor and most of the board members.[93]

When it seemed that matters could not get much worse, they did. When Arbouin left for the convening of the National Baptist Convention in 1947, board members called in his wife, who had remained at home, to share with her their concerns over rumors that she was involved in a "flagrant flirtation" with a young airman at Maxwell Field. Rather than addressing the board's concerns, she raised her dress to reveal bruises on her shoulders and legs—Arbouin's work when he was not in the pulpit. At once confounded and horrified, the board agreed that its talented, well-trained pastor had to go. The board decided to recommend that the church declare the pulpit vacant.[94]

Upon Arbouin's return from the convention, board members confronted him and asked for his resignation. Hoping to resolve the matter quietly, the board offered to pay him two months salary in advance and allow him to continue living in the parsonage for sixty days. Arbouin would not have it; he reminded the board that the Baptist church was a democracy. Decisions require a majority vote of the church body. Board and auxiliaries do not, he insisted, have power to dismiss a minister. He demanded another vote of confidence at the end of the service the following Sunday. Board members acceded to

Arbouin's wish, believing their position would certainly be vindicated. After church, Arbouin asked "those who wanted to follow his leadership and retain him as their pastor to stand until counted." Of the 166 church members present that Sunday, 60 rose to their feet. In the face of sure defeat, Arbouin interrupted the process by refusing to ask for a count of those opposed to his continued leadership. Deacon chair W. J. Wood placed a motion before the congregation that the pulpit be declared vacant, and 106 members rose to their feet to give the board the majority vote it needed to oust Arbouin. Deacon C. T. Smiley tried to diffuse the tension; "in controversies of this kind" he told Arbouin, "the leader might be right or the people might be right, we however, are governed by the majority ... a Christian gentleman should recognize the rights of the majority." Arbouin declared that "he was accepting the decision of the church as evidenced by its vote, but as a Christian under protest." Arbouin contended that the influence of a certain group of board members swayed opinion away from him. He refused to leave, believing that Dexter Avenue's pride in its reputation in the community would prevent the board from airing what was sure to be a long, protracted and embarrassing scandal.[95]

Arbouin had miscalculated. Dexter Avenue board members, while they relied heavily on pastors for guidance and program development, always considered themselves the most important and enduring stabilizing force in church life. "Ministers come and go rather rapidly," explained R. D. Nesbitt. "We had a few board members who had been there since Judkins." Nesbitt's observation was especially true at Dexter Avenue, which in the first seventy years of its life had no fewer than fifteen different ministers. The board took Arbouin to court and called in National Baptist president D. V. Jemison to testify that Dexter Avenue had followed standard Baptist procedures in its dismissal of Arbouin. For his part, Arbouin argued that a civil court had no jurisdiction over church policy and procedures. The white judge sided with the board and ordered Arbouin to leave the pastorate. For Arbouin's final Sundays as pastor, the court ordered board members' complete silence when attending church. They were not permitted to open their mouths even to pray, greet, or sing the hymns at the service lest the ruling be rescinded. Edna King remembered that "the police showed up at services the next Sunday expecting trouble, but were told that there had never been violence at Dexter and that it would remain that way," and so they left.[96]

The months following Arbouin's removal from the pulpit were trying ones. Church members wanted a strong leader who would raise morale and help restore their faith in the institution of the church and the office of pastor. The experience with Arbouin had left them nervous about any new minister they might select. Slowly but steadily, the congregation began to recover from its "trial by fire." In the years to come, they not only made peace with the dire circumstances surrounding Arbouin's removal from the pastorate, but they reconciled with him and invited him back to preach at a church anniversary in the late 1960s.[97]

When R. C. Judkins had left the pastorate of Dexter Avenue in 1916, the church had entered its third generation of life as a vital and thriving religious institution; this growth and vigor continued until the late 1920s. The Jacobs pastorate challenged church members to become more professional and accountable in approaching their duties and responsibilities. By 1928, the church struggled under the severe strains brought on by the Great Depression, but even during the financially lean years, when it was difficult to retain a pastor, Dexter Avenue maintained its ministries (though at times they operated in a diminished capacity). Equally important, congregation members and leaders developed new traditions and rituals of spiritual uplift and moral affirmation with the inauguration of Men's, Women's, and Youth Day services. While financial conditions improved during and after World War II, morale and confidence among congregants fell because of the Arbouin pastorate.

Through the struggles of the two world wars, an economic depression, and a tumultuous pastorate, congregants at Dexter Avenue learned to function amid trying conditions. The near calamity and internal tumult of the interwar years, however, were a mere prologue to the dramatic events that, over the next twenty years, would propel Dexter Avenue into the national and international spotlight.

4

A PROPHET HATH BEEN AMONG
THEM, 1948–1953

And they, whether they will hear, or whether they will forbear
(for they are a rebellious house,) yet shall know that there hath
been a prophet among them.

—Ezekiel 2:5 AV

In August 1945, when U.S. Secretary of War Henry Stimson learned
that an atomic bomb had exploded in Nagasaki, Japan, he stated simply, "The world is changed." Most would agree that the events of World
War II profoundly changed the world and the United States; perhaps
even more remarkably, however, the war inaugurated a process of
economic, political, and social change in Alabama. The state's fledgling
economy boomed during the war years, affording new job opportunities for Alabama's African Americans. After a three-year struggle, the
National Association for the Advancement of Colored People persuaded
the U.S. Army Air Corps to accept black airmen, and an all-black unit
was created at the Tuskegee Institute. Moreover, Alabama whites initially embraced the Tuskegee airmen project until the contract to build
the new airfield was given to a black firm. Even so, change seemed to be

in the air. For a brief period, white residents of Alabama ceased to chafe at the mere mention of federal government aid and intervention, particularly in the economic life of the state. During the late 1940s and early 1950s, beyond embracing the federal government's Depression relief programs like the Tennessee Valley Authority, Alabama's congressional delegation (namely U.S. senators Lister Hill and John Sparkman) expanded the federal government's role in the state. Alabama accepted federal assistance to construct public housing, build hospitals, conduct medical research, provide free vaccinations for children, and aid small farmers.[1]

In 1947, Alabama elected a governor who was disposed toward racial tolerance. Because of his appeal to "common" people, Jim Folsom (nicknamed "Big Jim") was dubbed by some a twentieth-century Andrew Jackson. Interestingly, "blacks were especially prominent in the crowds" that celebrated Folsom's inauguration to the governorship. Their presence was symbolic of an improved economic status resulting from the war and maybe a renewed African American determination to participate in the political life of the state. Perhaps in the intoxicating optimism of the years immediately following World War II, white Alabamians believed that some change was not so bad.[2]

Moreover, it seemed that, by the early 1950s, many white Alabamians were possibly on the brink of embracing some aspects of liberalism. As this political philosophy became more closely associated with a racial tolerance that espoused integration, however, it met with a hasty demise among most whites in the state; their momentary inclination to consider change had never extended to race relations. In the 1944 case of *Smith v. Allwright* the U.S. Supreme Court outlawed white primaries. The 1946 state Democratic primary marked the first such primary in the twentieth century in which black Alabamians could legally vote. Anxious that large numbers of blacks might "infiltrate" the Democratic Party in Alabama, whites hastily erected a legal barrier. State legislator E. C. Boswell introduced an amendment requiring that prospective voters be able to read and write any article of the U.S. Constitution to the satisfaction of a registrar. In other words, the registrar would decide who could or could not vote. Boswell's explanation was, "After all, a small parrot could be taught to recite a section of our Constitution." Black leaders complained that even R. R. Moton (the president of the Tuskegee Institute) and H. Council Trenholm (the president of Alabama State University) had their voting fitness questioned by registrars. In 1949, it cost him politically, but governor Jim Folsom protested that "too many [blacks] have maliciously been denied the right to vote ... that is not democracy in any sense." Shortly thereafter, the amendment was declared unconstitutional. White Alabamians were still vexed at the mere mention of racial integration, and in 1951 amended the state constitution to require a voter to complete a questionnaire to the satisfaction of a registrar.[3]

Still, the 1940s brought heightened participation in civic life, and improved conditions for blacks in Montgomery. In fact, beginning in the late 1930s, for the first time, Alabama provided a publicly supported high school education for blacks. A black-owned newspaper, the *Alabama Tribune*, and a black radio station encouraged greater African American participation in city politics. Between 1949 and 1953, African Americans, among others, advocated for city leaders to reform the police department. Perhaps most remarkably, by the end of 1953, Montgomery had, for the first time since Reconstruction, seven black police officers—three women and four men.[4]

Even more encouraging to African Americans that a new day might finally be on the horizon was Folsom's speech on the occasion of the eighty-third anniversary of the black First Baptist Montgomery Church. Folsom declared, "I would say this about Civil Rights: Before we can charge the world … to lead a more democratic, righteous way of life for their peoples, we must practice what we preach … There is much to do here at home before we can claim a sound democracy for our people … we are making strides; but there are many hurdles yet to cross."[5] It seemed that the wheels of democracy might finally be turning for African Americans.

Yet, there was another reality every bit as powerful as the actualities giving African Americans hope. With few exceptions, white Alabamians were segregationists who vacillated between being moderate segregationists who wanted to maintain segregation indefinitely but sensed the inevitability of change and so focused their energies on slowing down the process of integration; intractable segregationists who were prepared to take any action short of violence to halt the march of integration; or violent segregationists who, though few in number, were willing to threaten, kill, bomb, incinerate, or engage in any kind of violence to preserve segregation. It was no surprise, then, that President Harry S. Truman's 1948 executive order ending segregation in the armed forces was unwelcome in Montgomery. This measure struck Montgomery segregationists particularly hard. Now it seemed that the institutions principally responsible for Montgomery's economic recovery from the Great Depression—Maxwell and Gunther Air Force Bases—would open the door to racial integration. The Montgomery City Council acted swiftly and definitively to prevent racial integration practices at the bases from spilling over into the city. It restricted interracial participation, making it illegal for blacks and whites to play checkers together or to share a taxi. And so in Montgomery, in many ways the more some things changed, the more other things remained the same. Whites saw to it that "the walls of segregation ... did not come tumbling down, like those of Jericho, after one mighty blast of trumpets.... every attack [on segregation was] met by counterattack to the very eye of surrender."[6]

Just after World War II many African American churches began to take on direct and confrontational approaches to demand the recognition of basic civil rights for all Americans. In some instances churches were shaken out of their complacency by dramatic events. In other cases a more active role in the demand for African Americans' civil rights was the product of rising expectations, improved economic conditions brought on by the war. In still other cases, dynamic religious leaders and individuals challenged the quiescent nature of some conservative black churches. Such was the case with Dexter Avenue Baptist Church. Here it is important to remember that Dexter Avenue had many traditions of protest that largely had lain dormant for more than a generation; and this was fine with most members. The reputation many members had worked hard to maintain—of an elite congregation that believed in democratic values and hard work as the road to progress—would soon be challenged by a messenger and his message.[7]

As Dexter Avenue Baptist Church struggled to recover from the Arbouin debacle, it turned for healing and creative leadership to a new pastor, Vernon Napoleon Johns. Much like John the Baptist, Vernon Johns was a portentous voice crying in the wilderness, challenging Dexter Avenue members to rethink their attitudes concerning the proper role of the church in the fight for racial justice. Johns fully acknowledged that the church had important traditions of protest that had brought a measure of success in the fight against racism, but he also believed these same approaches had debilitating limits for church members in their Christian walk and in their participation in civic life. This chapter reveals Vernon Johns's role in the painful transformation of a conservative Christian congregation from its fear and complacency. Johns challenged members to directly confront the white power structures that, despite members' abiding faith in democracy, denied them equal protection and, notwithstanding their hard work, refused them fair rewards. Johns insisted that in the struggle to improve themselves and the world members never lose sight of the church's mission and commitment to "walk in Christian love [and to support] an evangelical ministry and the spread of the Gospel."[8] In this chapter we shall meet a small group of laypersons who embraced Johns's message even though they had problems with his methods. This group formed the nucleus of Dexter Avenue leaders who would later assist Martin Luther King Jr. in the 1955 Montgomery Bus Boycott.

Just as much of the nation changed after World War II, so too did black churches. Most often these changes were continuations of processes begun during post–World War I migrations of African Americans. Attitudinal changes engendered by World War I had already challenged the idea of gradualism in demanding civil rights, but much of the impetus for a more militant movement was lost as African Americans struggled during the Great Depression. Thus, many pre–World War II African American churches held on to conservative attitudes toward racial integration. Gayraud Wilmore characterizes black churches during the interwar years as so overwhelmed by the demands of helping members cope with entrenched segregation and racism that they unwittingly lost much of their passion for racial solidarity and social change. Several historical analyses argue that the conciliatory approach to race relations enabled some forward movement, but by the end of the mid-1940s this approach was hindering more than helping. After World War II, however, many black Southern churches became poised to confront the nation directly and demand action without delay. How can we explain this transformation? The process of change within black churches was complex. Consensus took time, organization, and leadership to encourage small efforts already begun in the right direction. The change involved persuasive leaders who could motivate church members either satisfied with the status quo or too frightened to challenge the system. After 1945 many black churches were led by ministers who envisioned racial integration as essential in bringing about God's justice in the world.[9]

In many ways, Dexter Avenue Baptist Church epitomized the conservative African American church since it had historically appealed to African Americans who had experienced some measure of academic or economic success within the segregated world. The church was less anxious than many to consider a new, bold approach to fighting for civil rights. For years in Dexter Avenue's own accommodationist way, it had steadily fought for African American parity by modeling a middle-class decorum, believing that exemplary behavior might favorably incline white attitudes toward racial justice, and holding on to their faith in democratic institutions. Many of the church's pastors had preached racial pride, but they also had emphasized restraint and propriety. For the most part, African Americans remained relatively unmolested if they remembered their place in segregated Alabama.

They were keenly aware of the price to be paid for directly demanding equality. At the same time, however, church members were not oblivious to the postwar changes taking place in the nation and in Alabama. While always interested in improving conditions for African Americans, Dexter Avenue was also focused on its more traditional functions in providing a meaningful and effective ministry for the congregation and in maintaining a vital order of services and ministries. In accomplishing this goal, in 1948 church leaders believed that they should avoid controversy. Members of the congregation sought calm and healing, hoping to restore a large measure of security and to improve attendance and tithing.[10]

In their decision to call the Reverend Vernon Johns to the pastorate, Dexter Avenue members inaugurated a journey that would challenge them religiously and intellectually to take the next difficult step in answering the call to freedom—to directly confront Pharaoh. When Johns assumed the burden of leadership at Dexter Avenue, some were ready, perhaps even eager, for his message; most, however, were not. Johns was "an aggressive type who made no apologies for anything." Brilliant intellectually and profoundly gifted as an exhorter and preacher, he was committed to telling people what he believed they needed to hear, confident that "whether they hear or refuse to hear, they will know that there hath been a prophet among them."[11]

In late 1947, members at Dexter Avenue commenced the all-too-familiar process of searching for a new pastor. The Arbouin scandal had left some church members angry and demoralized. Attendance had dropped significantly, and so had tithing. T. H. Randall, who headed the pulpit committee, faced a difficult task: to help restore dignity and trust to the Dexter Avenue pulpit before too many members were lost, pastoral leadership needed to be secured quickly. At the same time, committee members were sharply aware that church morale could not withstand another scandal. Fueled by the conflicting imperatives of immediacy and caution, the selection committee began its search for new pastoral leadership. After Arbouin's dismissal, to maintain stability, board members had secured the Reverend B. J. Sims, a local minister, to serve as acting pastor. Nevertheless, for more than nine months the pulpit committee searched without success for the right man. Finally, in September 1948, two names were placed before the official board: one was Reverend C. H. Milton, who was immediately eliminated, and that left the name of one Vernon Johns.

Johns had been introduced to the Dexter Avenue community by his wife, Altona Trent Johns, who was working and living in Montgomery with their three youngest children. Altona Johns's pedigree fit Dexter's status-conscious congregation. The daughter of Livingstone College president William Trent, she had graduated summa cum laude from Atlanta University, obtained a master of arts degree from Columbia University, and was a pianist of some note. As a professor at Alabama State University, she passed along the name of her renowned husband to the Dexter Avenue deacons. They were immediately interested, but also determined to proceed with caution. Board members sought the counsel of their former pastor, Ralph Riley, for some insight into Johns's character. Riley assured his former board that Johns was a "remarkable preacher and an upright man."[12]

On September 7, 1948, when the official board met to take action on the pastor vacancy, R. D. Nesbitt spoke favorably of Johns, noting that he was the best preacher he had ever heard. J. T. Brooks, who had been in communication with Johns over the previous few weeks, concurred with Nesbitt's assessment. Essie Jette, head of the missionary society, raised concern about Johns as difficult and hot tempered. She also noted that Johns, even while a pastor, was reputed to accept numerous outside speaking engagements, leaving his Sunday morning pulpit vacant. Board members determined that securing Johns as a pastor was worth the risk. They noted that the deacon-pastor relationship at Dexter prevented ministers from having "kingly" authority. To assuage Jette's concern, one board member assured her that "if he was called he would do as we would tell him to." Having just run Arbouin out of town, board members had precedent from which to speak about their power and influence on their ministers. Johns, however, was unlike any minister they had encountered in the past.[13]

Confident that they could handle Johns's peculiarities and hoping that he would bring calm and healing to their congregation, board members voted to place the name of Vernon Napoleon Johns before the church. On September 12, 1948 at the end of services, officers of the Dexter Avenue official board asked members to remain for a few minutes. Even at this juncture, board members moved cautiously. They involved all church members, as closely as possible, in the ultimate decision to call Johns so that all would share in the responsibility should problems arise sometime later. After Johns's name was put before the church body, officers asked members to discuss the kind of investigation of Johns that should be conducted. Members asked the clerk to write letters to the deacons and members of Johns's last church. "Pending no questionable findings," church members voted to extend a call to Johns.[14]

After two weeks of investigation, church members officially offered Johns the pastorate. Church clerk R. D. Nesbitt wrote to Johns requesting a vita and photograph. Johns replied, "My dear Brother Nesbitt, I am enclosing some biographical notes for which you asked ... [but] regret that my cuts are not at home at present." Dexter Avenue Baptist Church now had as its pastor one of the most remarkable and highly acclaimed ministers in the black community. Vernon Johns was the Paul Bunyan of black preachers, the subject of numerous tall tales, many of them exaggerated but many of them true. He was also compared to the "royalty" of black preachers like Mordecai Johnson and Howard Thurman. His complicated early life and pastorates lend insight into the nature of the relationship that developed between pastor and congregation and the kind of ministry he established at Dexter Avenue.[15]

Vernon Johns was born in 1892 in Prince Edward County, Virginia, to Sallie Branch Price and the Reverend William Thomas Johns. The influences on Johns's life were numerous: his mother's passion and temperament, his father's preaching and peddling, his boyhood on a Virginia farm, his study of the Social Gospel with the professors he encountered at Oberlin College, and his marriage to Altona Trent. Johns was a hot-tempered, intellectually gifted man who loved the soil, preached a Social Gospel, sharply criticized what he judged as the vapid trappings of black middle-class propriety, and, above all else, did not suffer racial injustice gladly. It was Johns's mother who was perhaps the greatest influence on his character; in his later years Johns noted that his mother was "a great, towering influence" on him. Though she harbored typical motherly anxieties about the hostile society her African American son would face, she nevertheless willed that he should be a maverick—"a catalyst who might bring deliverance to less-endowed, fearful souls" in the fight for what he believed was right in the world. Johns claimed that he lived by his mother's credo: "If you ever see a good fight, get into it." Johns's sharp impatience with racial injustice pushed him beyond the maternal suggestion to get into a "good fight," often causing him to start a few "good fights" of his own.[16]

Willie Johns, his father, died when Vernon was young, but not before passing on to his son a passion for preaching and a love of the land. The elder Johns pastored Shiloh Baptist Church in nearby Buckingham County, Virginia, and worked his Darlington Heights farm during the week, growing an array of farm products. On weekends he loaded up a saddlebag full of fresh vegetables and Sayman soap to sell en route to his church. Like his father, Vernon Johns thought of himself as a preacher-plowboy and Virginia farmer. He would later preach to the Dexter Avenue congregation that there was virtue in tilling the soil, and that regardless of educational attainments, ultimately the soil allowed a person to retain some self-sufficiency. Johns often chastised church members for their "misplaced pride" in not working with their hands. He hoped to pass along to his congregation the important lesson he had learned from his father—that there is value and virtue in all honest work. Johns's paternal inheritance did not end with an appreciation for farming; it included as well a penchant for launching various business ventures in tandem with leading a church.[17]

Along with family influences, Johns's educational experiences shaped his life and influenced the ministry he established at Dexter Avenue. Johns accompanied his older sister, Jessie, to a one-room schoolhouse about four miles from the farm, and Johns was also self-taught. Eventually he entered Virginia Theological Seminary in Lynchburg, Virginia, for high-school-level courses. Closely associated with the Court Street Baptist Church, this school was established by the Virginia State Baptist Convention between 1884 and 1889. Johns was ultimately dismissed from the school for rebellious behavior, but not before encountering important people who changed his life—teachers who had graduated from Oberlin College in Ohio. Though Johns also attended Virginia Union University, his educational experiences at Oberlin College were more determinative in his life.[18]

Shortly after his expulsion from school in Lynchburg, Johns showed up at Oberlin College. Indignant that his application for admission was denied because his school lacked accreditation, Johns proved his intellectual mettle to Oberlin's dean, Edward Increase Bosworth, by translating passages of German and Greek. His performance earned him provisional student status, but by the end of the term Bosworth was so impressed by Johns's abilities that he saw to it that Johns found adequate work to support himself while completing his studies in the graduate Department of Theology.[19]

Johns credits professor George Fiske, however, as the "first to make me feel comfortable and at home in Ohio." As a student Johns flourished, making a favorable impression on his teachers. For his part, Fiske claimed that Johns was "the most efficient and capable young minister ... [who had earned a] splendid record of scholarship and ability." When a colleague asked Bosworth who his most promising student was Bosworth replied, "You don't know him, he's a Negro named Vernon Johns—the only student who ever frightened me out of my boots, when in class he raised a questioning hand, because I doubted my ability to answer correctly." Johns was further affirmed when his fellow students selected him to deliver the annual student oration at the memorial arch dedicated to Oberlin students killed in China's Boxer Rebellion. Beyond academics, Johns also found among the Oberlin community affirmation of himself as a person. As an alumnus he often closed letters to his former professors with affection and nostalgia ("Always remembering your great kindness and sympathy and the rich value of your instruction in the good old Oberlin days, I am faithfully yours").[20]

While at Oberlin, Johns received a thorough course in the social gospel from Bosworth. Briefly defined, the social gospel was the Christian philosophy developed toward the end of the nineteenth century that sought to apply the teachings of Jesus Christ to the problems of society. Initially, the specific problems addressed were the social challenges created by the industrialization and urbanization of America. In the summer of 1895, Oberlin College sponsored a conference on Christian sociology titled "The Causes and Proposed Remedies for Poverty" bringing in a host of speakers to address various social problems. Participants were representatives from the world of capital and advocates of labor and the working class: Jane Addams, railroad executive S. P. Bush, Clarence Darrow, Samuel Gompers, and James Sovereign. Between 1895 and 1917, the following social gospel advocates spoke at Oberlin: Robert LaFollotte, Florence Kelley, Walter Rauchenbusch, Lincoln Steffens, and Graham Taylor. More significant, Bosworth, Oberlin's professor of the New Testament, was one of the major proponents of this philosophy; his course titled "The Social Significance of the Teachings of Jesus" was required during Johns's student days. The ministry that Johns would later establish at Dexter Avenue echoed his training in the social gospel.[21]

After Oberlin, Johns continued his formal education at the University of Chicago. By this time he was preaching, but still unsure of his call to the ministry. He considered practicing law, and even won a scholarship to Western Reserve Law School. Only after a vivid dream did Johns have confidence in his religious calling. On the day he received notification that he had won a law school scholarship, he dreamt of being in a costume store trying on various types of suits and uniforms. Experiencing a level of discomfort with all others, only the minister's suit fit him perfectly. Johns awoke to find the doubts about his call to the ministry dispelled; still, he continued to involve himself in numerous ventures: farming, teaching, editing, and sales. Nevertheless, Johns began his professional life as a pastor of a small church in Painesville, Ohio, before returning to Virginia in late 1919, where he served as a teacher at his former school, the Virginia Theological Seminary, and a pastor at the Court Street Baptist Church. While Johns may have been happy in his dual roles as teacher and pastor, he was not content.[22]

In March 1920 he began his first business venture, the Southern Mercantile and Development Company. In a flyer for the business he quoted Harvard professor Albert Hart's claim that African Americans "produce more than sixty out of every hundred dollars … [but only get] one out of every hundred dollars." Johns's idea was to begin by manufacturing and selling shoes for the black population in Virginia. He calculated that there were seven hundred thousand blacks in the state and an average pair of shoes cost ten dollars so that if each person purchased one pair of shoes the company would gross an estimated seven million dollars in its first year of operation. Eventually Johns hoped to include other articles of clothing. He advertised shares for five dollars each, hoping to raise fifty thousand dollars, which, along with the aid of a wealthy investor, would be sufficient funds to get started. Johns shared his optimism with his Oberlin mentor, George Fiske: "We have in the management three Oberlin graduates, two Hillsdale men … one Phi Beta Kappa from Bowdoin along with some hard headed old conservatives who have considerable business experience." Fiske responded promptly, sending his support and confidence that Johns would "have real success in this venture for I do not in the least doubt there is a great field for it." Ever the teacher, in closing Fiske reminded Johns of his higher calling, "Are you still preaching occasionally in addition to this work?" Johns assured his mentor, "I am still preaching the Social Gospel," and closed nostalgically, "it is very, very pleasant to remember Oberlin." In spite of the well-wishes of his former teacher and Johns's momentary optimism, the business failed because of the withdrawal of an unnamed large investor. Some thirty years later Johns would create a very similar kind of business in Montgomery while pastoring Dexter Avenue Baptist Church.[23]

The demise of Johns's 1920 business venture left him far from idle; he had his ministry at the Court Street Baptist Church and his teaching at the Virginia Theological Seminary to challenge his talents and occupy his attention. Early in his pastorate at Court Street, Johns encountered a congregation critical of his ministry. With both pride and apprehension Johns described the Court Street congregation to George Fiske: "I am at present, pastor of the oldest and one of the largest colored churches in Virginia. I might add that it is frequently called the Ministers' Slaughter House! In fact, no pastor during the past forty years has been able to say, 'Lord now lettest thou thy servant depart in peace.'" Some members at Court Street complained to the church deacons that Johns's preaching was too erudite and lacked sufficient emotion, but Johns won over most of the deacons. In fact, on the occasion of his first pastoral anniversary, the deacons requested that Bosworth send encouraging words about his former student:

> Our pastor, Rev. V. N. Johns was once a student of yours. You can most likely imagine how one whose preaching is of his type will suffer in the estimation of masses of people so shortly removed from slavery…. We are preparing in connection with our pastor's Anniversary to make some sentiment in favor of real preaching [which most deacons believed Johns was doing]. Now our people attach great importance to the testimony of significant persons. Can you express favorable opinion as to the preaching of Mr. Johns or the possibilities which he showed as a preacher and Christian leader …?

The letter makes it obvious that the deacons supported Johns and that during Johns's first pastorate he learned to handle criticism. Even though members at Dexter Avenue Baptist Church would not criticize Johns for his preaching style, they would express serious misgivings concerning the volatile content of his sermons; having this experience with the Court Street Baptist Church gave Johns some prior practice handling disgruntled members of his flock.[24]

The tasks of pastoring and teaching left Johns with little time for socializing; still, he wrote Bosworth, complaining of his loneliness. Ostensibly, Johns wrote to share his hopes for the future of the Virginia Theological Seminary and to tell of the great camaraderie he was sharing with Oberlin alumni in the area: "The school is making great progress and there are so many Oberlinites on the faculty now that we are thinking of forming an Oberlin Club." Nonetheless, he lamented wistfully, "I believe I am the only member of the class who is single. I am beginning now to feel that I as well as my brother have a right to lead about a wife. If I weather the autumn and winter storms in the lonely voyaging, I shall put in port when summer returns. I hope for myself a peaceful harbor."[25]

Though Johns did not realize it, he had already met the woman who would be his wife and lifelong partner. In the summer of 1918, just after graduating from the theological school at Oberlin, Johns served as worship leader at the Southern Regional Girls Reserve of the Young Women's Christian Association held at Kittrell College in Kittrell, North Carolina. Fifteen-year-old Altona Trent from Atlanta was one of one hundred young delegates. She was in Johns's daily Bible class, and as it happened, served as pianist for the camp, playing hymns and spirituals Johns had selected the previous day. Johns and Trent left the meeting unaware that their futures would merge. Eight years later, in

August 1926—one year after Trent had completed college—she and Johns met again when she led a group of Girl Reserves to the Southern Regional Conference in Asheville, North Carolina. She recalled, "At the first evening meal Vernon and I were standing at tables at diagonal ends of the dining room. Instead of bowing our heads as we should have done to sing the grace ... Our eyes met and it was truly 'love at first sight.'"[26]

Indeed, 1926 was a vintage year for Johns. He was reunited with the woman he would marry, and he became the first African American minister to have a sermon, "Transfigured Moments," published in an annual book of sermons titled *Best Sermons*. In the introduction to Johns's sermon, editor Joseph Fort Newton noted, "Mr. Johns is the first colored preacher to appear in Best Sermons, and it is both an honor and a joy to bid him welcome, alike for his race and his genius." Newton favorably reviewed Johns's sermon, observing that it "lifts us into a higher air, above the fogs of passion and prejudice, where the ages answer antiphonally, telling us of the brotherhood of man in the life of God and Christ." This was an accomplishment that had eluded even the most prominent black minister of the day, Mordecai Johnson. Shortly after his publishing debut Johns proposed to his sweetheart, and on December 21, 1927, Trent and Johns married in a quiet ceremony at the home of her parents in Salisbury, North Carolina. Johns's marriage to Altona Trent thrust him into the circles of the black intellectual aristocracy, a world in which he certainly had the intellectual acumen and credentials to move fluently. He lacked, however, the inclination and temperament for what he saw as the banality of the black middle-class lifestyle. This would grow to be a problem, and it surfaced in several of the distinguished positions Johns attained, but most notably during his pastorate at Dexter Avenue Baptist Church.[27]

Johns's critique of black middle-class life combined various sentiments concerning how African Americans should participate in their own improvement and ultimately bring about the demise of racial discrimination in the world. Like W. E. B. Du Bois, Johns advocated education and intellectual attainment as indispensable to the struggle for civil rights. Concurrently, he agreed with Booker T. Washington that blacks must control a crucial part of the economic means of production; otherwise, educational attainment would garner little more than an erudite and refined group of second-class citizens. Above all else, Johns insisted that African Americans must have the kind of race pride promoted by Henry McNeal Turner and Marcus Garvey. A mélange of these beliefs and proclivities undergird Johns's critique of the black middle class.

Most important, however, is that Johns was an egalitarian. His egalitarianism was born not only of his religious beliefs but also of his attitude about and toward work. His concept of human equality emerged from his belief that human beings are created in the image of God and that all are generally capable of producing worthwhile work. He valued being educated, but he did not believe it made him a more valuable person than an uneducated person who performed manual labor. Johns had always performed some kind of manual labor, even while pursuing his education: at Virginia Seminary he milked cows and grew vegetables, at Virginia Union he cared for people's horses by manning the livery station, and while at Oberlin he made beds in the men's dormitories. Johns did not like the distance social class placed between people, and, in light of the discrimination most African Americans faced, he believed class division was particularly destructive to the acquisition of racial justice. These ideas and beliefs greatly influenced the kind of ministry Johns established at Dexter Avenue.[28]

Between 1927 and 1948, when Johns accepted the Dexter Avenue pulpit, the Johnses had six children—three sons and then three daughters—and Johns would hold a variety of jobs and positions, as director of the Baptist Educational Center in New York City; president of the Virginia Theological Seminary; pastor of several prominent churches, including Holy Trinity Church in Philadelphia and the First Baptist Church of Charleston, West Virginia, where he succeeded Mordecai Johnson. During these years there were sporadic periods of unemployment. For months he would be absent from his family, living a bohemian lifestyle, traveling about with his clothes in a paper sack, doing some itinerant preaching and selling books on the side. In such instances, his well-educated and employable wife probably provided most of the financial means to sustain the family.[29]

Living apart from his family on a farm in Farmville, Virginia, when he received the call to Dexter Avenue Baptist Church, Johns came to Alabama to share with church members his understanding of Christian love and justice and his notion of the church as God's instrument in society. Not since R. C. Judkins had a minister come to Dexter Avenue with such strong ideas about the role of the church in the struggle for equality. As Johns began his pastorate at Dexter Avenue, there was much that recommended him to the congregation but also much that gave them pause. On the one hand, many of Johns's ideas appealed to most Dexter Avenue members, and some members eventually embraced his message about the justice of God requiring that they directly confront the racial injustices against themselves and their working-class counterparts. Johns believed that the Gospel and the

Bible contained the most penetrating and moving justifications for racial solidarity and social change. On the other hand, his ambivalence and sometimes hostility about traditional black middle-class protest strategies in eliminating racism fueled and defined the challenges Johns proffered to the congregation. Johns's unconventional methods and unrestrained passion in preaching about Christian responsibility in the world not only offended some Dexter Avenue members' sense of propriety but also frightened them. Nevertheless, Johns held steadfast to both his message and his method; he could not or would not concern himself with decorum. Johns was, as he described himself in a letter to one of his Oberlin mentors, a "prophet and dreamer, leaving the more practical affairs to those who have more time and love for details."[30]

When Johns assumed the pastorate of Dexter Avenue, then, he was a man on a mission. Like many other Dexter Avenue pastors, he arrived with a vision for the church. He was a militant activist who believed that a Christian life must be a life of action and that the nation was long overdue on its debt of justice to African Americans. To these ends, Johns believed that "religion, education and home must find their justification in the practical, material and productive affairs of life, else all fail together." In other words, church, school, and family are sustained by the economic life of a nation, and if the relationship between all of these institutions is not sound, then all are ineffective. For African Americans, Johns believed this meant having a measure of economic self-sufficiency and reasonable access to economic means. These ideas formed the foundation of his ministry, which sought four ends: to persuade members that God often sent messages to the world through the humble and disavowed; to convince congregants of the natural relationship between "true" religion and social progress; to help congregants realize that self-sufficient economic development was indispensable to Christian living and in the struggle for racial equality; and, most important, that the dogma and doctrine of religion were futile, even immoral, without action. To achieve these goals, Johns harnessed the power of the pulpit, sharing his beliefs and passions with Dexter Avenue members in his Sunday morning sermons. Moreover, he demonstrated his message through his actions—for example, growing a garden in the backyard of the parsonage and bringing in fresh produce, roots and dirt still attached, to show church members and to sell to the public. Johns also founded a business, Montgomery Farm and City Enterprises. In seeking to accomplish the goals of his ministry Johns often found himself at odds with church members who wanted their minister to foster calm and stability in the cooperate church life; instead, he called congregants to a different challenge in their Christian lives, a call to see religion as "the very soul of protest against moral and social stagnation." Relations between Johns and Dexter Avenue began peacefully, but eventually Johns would leave amid controversy.[31]

October 1948 was a time of hope and optimism for Dexter Avenue Baptist Church and for Vernon Johns. The church had weathered turbulent and protracted internal struggles. It continued to function, but membership and tithing suffered. Now that the church had secured impressive new pastoral leadership things would surely improve. For Johns, his new position allowed him to reunite with his wife and children.

Relations between Johns and Dexter Avenue began harmoniously. Members noted in the church bulletin, "We are happy to have the pastor's family here—Mrs. Johns and four of the children. We welcome them to Dexter Avenue Baptist Church."[32] His first meeting with the official board opened with T. H. Randall leading the singing, and prayer by Alexander Campbell. W. J. Wood, the board chair, concluded the brief devotion by reading the fourth chapter of Matthew, which begins with a description of Christ's successfully enduring a period of temptation and trial before moving on to select his disciples and begin his ministry. This passage expressed the board's hope that Dexter Avenue's trials were now behind them. Johns was then officially introduced and complimented members on a "fine and inspiring devotional." He said he was delighted to receive their call to serve and was sure "this would be a time of mutual growth." He confessed his awareness of rumors that he was difficult, hot-tempered, and frequently left his pulpit vacant to accept outside speaking engagements. He assured the board that he would never leave the pulpit vacant and declared that in each of his past pastorates it was he who made the decision to leave, and that he was, later, welcomed back at all of them as a guest preacher. Church clerk R. D. Nesbitt noted in the minutes that the new pastor "had made a very beneficial talk to us" and the board was encouraged. The discussion then moved on to more practical matters like readying the furnished parsonage for the Johns family.[33]

The new pastor and the congregants noted that they had much in common, and members marveled at Johns's passionate, erudite, well-crafted sermons. He embraced the formal worship format of the church though he did enjoy eliciting an occasional responsive "Amen." At the time Johns arrived, he seemed comfortable with most of the infrastructure of the life of the church. He made no changes to the weekly ritual of church life. In addition to the regular eleven o'clock Sunday services, there was an active Sunday school, and prayer meetings on Wednesday nights and Sunday evenings. The Baptist Training Union was very active, and since the late 1930s, regularly had been sending representatives to state and national conventions. As well, the missionary society and the H. A. Loveless Working Club were busy with activities. Johns made one immediate change; he selected junior officers prepared to take over leadership positions on the boards of deacons and trustees in the future.[34]

The "honeymoon" between Johns and the Dexter Avenue congregation came to an abrupt halt one Sunday morning during the eleven o'clock worship service. Johns very much enjoyed traditional Baptist hymns, but he also delighted in spirituals, and this fact led to one of the first sources of tension. We already know that in its nascent years Dexter Avenue's founders, to distance themselves from the culture of slavery, did not include the singing of Negro spirituals in their formal Sunday morning services. They labeled spirituals sorrow songs of slavery and incompatible with emancipation. In the 1880s, however, a young group of African American students at Fisk University in Nashville, Tennessee, popularized these songs all over Europe and America. During the Harlem Renaissance famous African American musicians like Harry Burleigh revitalized these songs, creating new arrangements and musical scores for them; even so, spirituals were not regularly performed in many middle-class African American churches.[35]

At Dexter Avenue, organist Edna King, chorister J. T. Brooks, and most members of the congregation disagreed with Johns about the appropriate occasions for the singing of spirituals. Edna King intermittently had served as organist at Dexter Avenue since 1913, when R. C. Judkins had arranged for her to take organ lessons from the white organist at First Baptist, Montgomery. She continued to study music for many years, and cultivated very definite opinions about the appropriate kind of music for the eleven o'clock Sunday services. She explained, "I love all kinds of music, but you don't sing Amazing Grace at a party, and you don't sing informal music like spirituals at church on Sunday morning." In King's opinion, proper music for a church's most important service of the week should be traditional hymns and sacred pieces by classical artists such as Johann Sebastian Bach and George Frideric Handel. As for spirituals, King believed they were fine for Wednesday night or Sunday night prayer services and for special occasion services. Johns generally had no problems with the music at Dexter Avenue; no doubt, traveling as he did in circles that included members from prominent black churches, he had most likely heard of the reputation of the Dexter Avenue choir, famous for its elaborate music performances, especially at Christmastime. Even so, one Sunday morning Johns requested that King lead the congregation on the organ in a spiritual. To avoid outright disrespect for the pastor's request, King responded that she did not have the musical score for the spiritual Johns requested.[36]

Johns would not be circumvented, however politely. Later, at a church conference meeting, he asked J. T. Brooks, Esse Jette, and Joseph Nesbitt to select a new songbook, as the congregation was using songbooks purchased in 1912. A few weeks later Johns again beckoned Edna King to lead in a spiritual. This time she flatly refused, explaining that spirituals are simply not sung at Dexter Avenue on Sunday morning. A test of wills ensued: Johns continued to request and King sat still and silent. Johns's temper flared at what he believed to be outright insubordination and disrespect. In a fit of anger he slammed the Bible shut, left the pulpit, and stormed out of the church. R. D. Nesbitt chased after him, walked with him to the end of the street, and calmly appealed that if Johns did not return there would be "no one to give the people the word today." Nesbitt promised that the church deacons would see what could be done about the "music problem." Johns returned and the services proceeded. It is not clear if spirituals were ever sung at the eleven o'clock Sunday services at Dexter Avenue, but this incident was just a bellwether of clashes to come. In the midst of these struggles, Johns worked fervently to get his message across to Dexter Avenue members.[37]

For Johns, the refusal of the choir and church members to sing spirituals during the Sunday morning service was a sign of vanity and rigidity. More galling, he feared it indicated members might believe that because spirituals were African American artistic creations from humble origins, they were unworthy to be performed beside Bach cantatas, Handel's Water Music suite, or Baptist hymns. Johns was quick to point out to his congregation, "Many times over, God, the Spirit and Soul of Improvement, has been compelled to pass by the ... guardians of religious rites and records, the temples of the orthodox and the panderers of ceremonial to find in unwonted places the persons ... to become the messengers of eternal truth." Johns was anxious that relegating singing spirituals to special occasions created a faux distinction between middle-class African Americans at Dexter Avenue, and working-class or poor African Americans in the Montgomery community.[38]

Johns believed that the relative comfort of middle-class life in a segregated world had numbed church members' consciousness of the ubiquitous oppression of African Americans in America. He explained to congregants, "The 'proprietors' of the earth, who compass the destruction of many ... like to hear the disinherited repeating the deceitful formula, 'All is well,' but the servile movement of many lips does not make the false true, the diseased tissue of society healthy or fill the empty with good things."

Johns felt that the church members' position on spirituals reflected their belief that because they had achieved some measure of status within the sphere of racial segregation, things were right in the world, but he quickly warned members that "God is not in his heaven and much is wrong with the world." Johns often decried what he saw as members' misplaced vanity created by their elevated status. He reminded his congregation that frequently it was the ordinary and common that was transformed into greatness by God, that "On the Mount of Transfiguration there is no representative of wealth, social rank or official position." He told members that in the Christian community, all should feel equally valuable and essential in bringing God's message to the world.[39]

Johns offered Dexter Avenue members a new way to consider the purpose of religion and the church in the world. Religion and the church, he contended, involved much more than providing a comfortable place for members to model their fine clothes and sing polite hymns. "True religion," Johns preached, "provides humanity with both the revolutionary ideals and the revolutionary power which become the bone and sinews of progress." Johns claimed that "religion by its very nature is wedded to progress, albeit that which God joined together man sometimes puts asunder." In explaining what he meant by "progress," Johns chastised congregants, saying that the church was no place to develop rigid and static beliefs: "Churches and creeds, priests and preachers may halt in their tracks until they petrify and their influence becomes a stone wall in the way of progress, but Religion is not with them; it continues the march with God and the prophets, toiling in creative processes for the building of a finer world and a fairer humanity." An unapologetic advocate of the social gospel, Johns believed that religion should be actively making changes in the world and should be constantly involved in improving society.[40]

Johns was a man of action as well as words, evidenced in the third component of his Dexter Avenue ministry—his effort to help congregants realize that some self-sufficient economic development enhanced Christian living and was essential in the struggle for racial equality. In 1951, Johns established his business, Montgomery Farm and City Enterprises, which attempted to unite urban and rural African Americans in a joint venture. He set the stage for this business through both his preaching and his actions in the pulpit. To the great exasperation of Dexter Avenue members, one Sunday Johns showed up for church wearing shoes that had no shoe strings. When members pressed for an explanation he pronounced, "I'll start wearing them when Negroes start producing them." Edna King remembered, "[W]e did not know what to think ... Reverend Johns was brilliant and very well educated like all of our ministers, but he had some strange ways." Zelia Stephens Evans, who had arrived in Montgomery in 1949 to take a position at Alabama State University, agreed with King that "Johns would do whatever he had to get our attention." Johns admonished his African American congregation for its lack of land ownership. One Sunday he told them, "If you want to define perpetual motion, you give the average Negro a Cadillac and tell him to park on a piece of land that he owns." Johns's prodding his congregation toward economic self-sufficiency sometimes involved a "show and tell" from the pulpit. Zelia Evans recalled that Johns would often bring in from his garden fresh vegetables with the roots and red Alabama dirt still attached.[41]

Members politely tried to tolerate Johns's eccentricities, though he often transgressed their notions of propriety; and Johns sometimes pushed members beyond their tolerance. Perhaps recalling how his father would load up saddlebags with Sayman soap to sell en route to church, Johns began loading up the back of his truck with fresh vegetables, fish, and, whenever he could get them, Virginia cured hams to sell from the basement of the church on Sunday afternoons. Pushed past their limits, deacons and trustees called Johns into a meeting to tell him that they thought it was disrespectful to be selling from the church, and they requested that he refrain from such practices.[42]

It was a few months later, in August 1951, that Johns launched the Montgomery Farm and City Enterprises." In a circular titled "A Plea for Confidence and Cooperation" Johns explained that the business was "aimed at uniting rural production with urban distribution." It is not clear whether the entire church supported him in this effort, but at least two of the six-member board of directors, J. H. Gilchrist and T. H. Randall, were Dexter Avenue members. For Johns this business venture was tied to African Americans' Christian struggle to help bring about racial equality. He explained the interrelationship of business, religion, and justice in a sermon and in a business prospectus. He challenged members to consider this business venture for African Americans as similar to the wilderness experience of Jews formerly enslaved in Egypt. Just as the uncertain and untamed wilderness had ultimately meant freedom from Egyptian oppression, so too would black-owned businesses release African Americans from white oppression. Jews, Johns contended "learned the potentialities of uncrowded land," that the wilderness provided "standing ground, training ground, rallying ground ... living space and livelihood." The land was, he attempted to convince Montgomery's black community, "God's answer to a people's problem." Johns lamented, "The Negro has the only urban population that completely ignores the land." "Dirt," he concluded, "is basic to all culture."[43]

Johns's idea was to "bridge the costly gap between the Negro's city population and the rural sources of supply." His plan was to undersell local grocery stores and unite African Americans in an economic pursuit. There were a few black-owned businesses in Montgomery at the time. Victor Hugo Tulane's grocery store had closed some years earlier, though Ben Moore, who sat on the board of Johns's corporation, still owned a hotel and restaurant. As Johns had done with the business he had started in Lynchburg, Virginia, thirty years earlier, he began small, selling produce, dairy, and meat products, with the intention of later expanding to sell other items. But like the Lynchburg venture, Farm and City Enterprises eventually failed; however, Johns had already expressed his feelings about failure on the circular announcing the startup of the business: "If we try we may fail. Yes, but please listen! What has already happened if we don't try?" Johns had hoped to succeed, but it seemed just as important to alert people to possibilities and encourage them to dream and challenge them to act, even if success was unlikely. Dexter Avenue members never found the love of the soil Johns labored to impart to them. It would be years later before most realized Johns's implied message that some economic self-sufficiency would effectively challenge white oppression. He wanted them to see an alternative to buying into a system that gave them meager rewards for their work and precarious protection for their faith in the morality of democracy and civic life.[44]

Many Dexter Avenue members eventually responded more favorably, though not during Johns's pastorate, to another component of his ministry—that religious dogma and doctrine were useless without action. Johns argued that "the basis of an enduring civilization will not be Sound Doctrine but a certain kind of practice." Lifted from the pages of social gospel literature, Johns held that, "Christian civilization and a decent and sane and happy world, are not hindered in their advent or want of orthodox statements ... they are hindered for lack of heroic and kindly practices of the simple teachings of Jesus." Johns further explained, "An examination of our wills in their relation to the great questions of Brotherhood and Social Justice will more nearly reveal the presence or absence of God and religion, than can any measuring of ourselves by creeds." He also told his Dexter Avenue congregation, "The Master's difficulty now with religious leaders can be stated as He stated it two thousand years ago: 'They say, and do not.'"[45]

Johns tried to practice what he preached to his flock. He put himself and his family in mortal danger more than once by preaching incendiary sermons from the pulpit. In the 1940s, members had constructed a sign board in front of the church to advertise the topic of the Sunday sermon. On at least two occasions, Johns was dragged before local police for preaching provocative sermons. One was entitled, "Will There Be Segregation in Heaven?" Johns told the biblical story of Dives, the rich man who opened up his eyes in hell to see his servant, Lazarus, couched in the bosom of Abraham in heaven. Johns's answer to his homiletical interrogative was yes, but this segregation would place disavowed servants in heaven and their evil overseers in hell. Not satisfied merely to assign the privileged to hell, he went on to comment on Dives' arrogance. He told the congregation that, "even from the depths of hell Dives thought he still had the power to command that his servant, Lazarus, send for water to cool his parched tongue." There was little doubt who the Dives character represented and who was the servant in the sermon. Shortly after learning that white police officers had stopped a black man for speeding and beaten him unconscious, Johns preached a sermon even more vexing to the white community, "It is Safe to Murder Negroes in Montgomery." The Johns family received threatening phone calls, and a cross was burned in front of the church. Still, Johns proceeded to preach the sermon as he had planned. His actions led to a rather steady onslaught of threats to both his family and his church, but he would not relent in his challenges to segregation.[46]

Most members of the Dexter Avenue congregation believed Johns's message to be ahead of its time and his methods to be dangerous, and yet, even before he left, Johns would learn that a few members were trying to act on his message. In the fall of 1949, a group of Montgomery women, led by Dexter Avenue member and Alabama State English Department chair Dr. Mary Fair Burks, organized the Women's Political Council (WPC). Unlike the *Colored Alabamian*, this organization was not an arm of the church, though several of its members belonged to the Dexter Avenue congregation. The WPC was organized because Montgomery's League of Women Voters refused to admit black women. Initially the WPC did not challenge racial segregation per se, but contested inequalities within the system of segregation. Its credo was to inspire blacks "to live above mediocrity, to fight juvenile and adult delinquency ... and in general to improve the status of their group." Burks asserted that the women "agreed on a three-tier approach: first, political action, including voter registration and interviewing candidates for office; second, protest about abuses on city buses and use of taxpayer's money to operate segregated parks ... third, education, which involved teaching young high school students about democracy ... as well as teaching adults to read and write ... for voting." Similar to church and civic women's protest approaches during the late nineteenth century and early twentieth centuries, this organization began its protest through a letter-writing campaign to city officials. While the WPC began with rather genteel protests, over time it would become more militant. Perhaps most important, it helped form the nucleus and backbone for the direct-action protest that would later take place between 1955 and 1960.[47]

More than the challenges of Johns's message and ministry to members of Dexter Avenue, his behavior and temperament caused the most consternation and ultimately led to the membership accepting his resignation. Like his mother, Johns had little patience for what he called "protection for the fragile personality." Johns was blunt and acerbic regardless of the occasion or who might be insulted. This character trait proved a serious problem on at least three occasions. The first instance was a funeral at which Johns insulted the grieving family. Dexter Avenue had always revered its church fathers and the families who founded the church in 1877. Shortly after Johns arrived, one of the descendants of a Dexter Avenue first family, a young man with a reputation for being disorderly in the community, met with an untimely demise. More important to Johns than the man's standing in the community was his absence from the church in any capacity, but he agreed to perform this man's eulogy. In the presence of grieving relatives and guests, Johns began the service by walking down from the pulpit and asking the undertaker to open the coffin, exclaiming, "I would like to meet the man I am about to eulogize!" Family members were embarrassed and exasperated, but Johns was not fazed.

Indeed, Johns had little patience for members who attended church sporadically, regardless of their status. On another occasion, Johns stopped the Sunday morning service, declaring, "I want to pause here to give Dr. Trenholm a chance to get seated on his semi-annual visit to church." Trenholm had replaced his father as president of Alabama State University and his family had been members of the church since the turn of the century. Trenholm refused to return until Johns left the pulpit for good.

In what was perhaps the most provocative incident, Johns humiliated long time member Dr. R. T. Adair. Adair, a physician whose father had been one of the first African American physicians in Montgomery, had—in an act of domestic violence—shot his wife to death on suspicion of adultery. Perhaps it was because of the Adair family name and position that he was not arrested or taken to jail, but he did not escape the judgment of Johns. When Adair showed up for church, Johns declared, "We have a murderer in the house this morning and God said 'Thou shalt not kill.' Dr. Adair, you have committed a sin, and may God have mercy on your soul."[48]

Johns directly confronted anyone and anything he believed to be wrong. A proud man, Johns had no tolerance for what he believed to be polite, but often insincere, social graces that characterized both black and white middle-class culture. Shortly before he left his Dexter Avenue pulpit, Johns shared with the congregation an altercation he had had with one of the city's bus drivers. Johns told the congregation that he boarded a bus, sat in the "white" section and refused to vacate when ordered to do so. Johns explained that when the bus driver said, "Nigger, didn't you hear me tell you to get the hell out of that seat?" he stunned him by replying "and didn't you hear me tell you that I'm going to sit right god-damned here?" When the congregation gasped that Johns would repeat profanity from the pulpit, he told them, "I do not believe God was offended by the unauthorized use of his name [but probably said] 'I'd better keep an eye on that boy; he's going to do a lot for Christianity down South.'" Johns believed that being indirect or insincerely polite led to superficial if not fraudulent Christianity. He invented a term that he refused to define precisely, to refer to foolish vanity—*spinksterinkdum*—and he warned members at Dexter Avenue that they needed to avoid becoming "spinksterinkdum Negroes."[49]

Johns's temperament did little to help bring the calm and healing to the congregation that the board had so desperately wanted. The board's intermittent admonishments of what it judged as Johns's outrageous behavior fell on deaf ears. On one occasion the board called a meeting with Johns to "discuss the general conditions of the church" and what needed to be done to improve church morale and increase membership. Johns suggested that his behavior was not the culprit, but that the congregation was not welcoming. To prove his point, he told the congregation one Sunday that "'you don't even know each other's names,'" and he called on members to repeat new members' names. The lack of responses proved his point. Tithing and membership had increased briefly when Johns first arrived, but a year later it had begun a steady decline.[50]

Johns and the board could not agree on the problems that plagued the church. If the congregation made him particularly angry, Johns would resign, usually from the pulpit on Sunday or at the end of a particularly difficult meeting with the official board. On April 5, 1953, Johns told the congregation, "I want all the members to come out on next Sunday at which time I will make an announcement that I am sure will be of interest to all. Now tell those who are not here to be present." On April 12, Johns told the congregation that on the first Sunday in May, after he returned from his trip to Virginia, he would preach his farewell sermon. Johns realized that members harbored grave apprehension at the prospect of facing an unexpurgated Johns sermon. If he was leaving, whatever thin veneer of restraint inspired by continued fellowship with members would be gone. He quickly assured the congregation that "it would be the sweetest sermon" he had ever preached and that no one had "anything to fear." On May 3, Johns preached his farewell sermon in accordance with his earlier statement. After the service, T. H. Randall asked church members to remain to decide on a parting gift for Reverend and Mrs. Johns. Since Johns had "resigned" many times before, board members' wanted to make certain that he understood that they had accepted his resignation this time. They certainly wanted to avoid the debacle and controversy that had surrounded Arbouin's departure. On May 31, 1953, the deacons met in a special session. Board chair W. J. Wood asked that the pulpit be declared vacant. The motion carried unanimously. Then members of the official board passed the following resolutions:

> Whereas, inasmuch as the pastor, Rev. Vernon Johns, preached in accordance with his previous announcement, his farewell sermon, and
> Whereas, inasmuch as the members comprise the sovereign body of the church and have the right to act upon any fundamental action regarding contractual and other agreements ...
> Be it resolved, that the Board of Deacons accept this action of the pastor, Rev. Johns, as of May 3, 1953, ending his services as pastor, and thus vacating the pulpit and ....
> Be it further resolved, that this resolution be submitted to the church for final action.

This action was followed by a letter to Johns, who at the time was away in Farmville, Virginia. Nesbitt wrote Johns, "This letter comes to officially notify you that on Sunday June 7th, 1953 the membership of Dexter Avenue Baptist Church voted to accept the Farewell Sermon as preached by you on May 3, 1953 as terminating your service as its pastor." Nesbitt, who had been one of Johns's defenders, believing that much of what he had tried to explain to the membership about African Americans and economic self-sufficiency was something members badly needed to hear, could no longer stave off other board members' desire to seek alternative pastoral leadership.[51]

Members were able to prevent events from completely spiraling out of control, but Johns did leave in a fog of controversy. For reasons known only to Johns himself, he refused to move out of the parsonage when he learned that members had, indeed, accepted this particular resignation. It may have been that he was sixty-two years old and feared he would not find other work. Still, Johns remained in the parsonage until after board members had the gas, electricity, and water disconnected. Once again, Dexter Avenue members found themselves without a minister.[52]

By the summer of 1953, Johns had left Dexter Avenue and the Montgomery community, but he will never be forgotten.[53] Vernon Johns came to Dexter Avenue at a time in the church's history that was at once fortuitous and troubling. On the one hand it was a time when Dexter Avenue was being challenged to rethink its accommodationist approach in the struggle for blacks' civil rights and its notion of the church as God's instrument in the world. Concurrently, it was a time when members were trying to recover from years of controversy and unsteadiness. Profoundly influenced by the theology of the Social Gospel, Johns shared his belief that there was a nexus between religion and progress. He wanted the congregation to realize the great economic power it possessed if it would shun class divisions within the community and cooperate—rich and poor, urban and rural—in joint economic endeavors, developing a measure of economic self-sufficiency. Above all, Johns believed that a Christian life must be a life of action.

Of all the persons associated with Dexter Avenue Baptist Church, Martin Luther King Jr. would owe the most to Johns. Johns's message thoroughly schooled members in the principles of the Social Gospel. King noted that within "the Negro community [in Montgomery]" there was "indifference in the educated group" regarding the push for civil rights, but Vernon Johns had "never tired of keeping the problem [of racial discrimination] before the conscience of the community" and, furthermore, when others had feared to speak, Johns had dared to "stand with valor and determination."[54] To King and the civil rights movement's great advantage, the groundwork in readying a conservative Christian congregation to become a stable place to help steady and quiet King and others when the community was in tumultuous flux had been laid by a worthy forerunner. For whether members heard or refused to hear, indeed, there had been a prophet among them.

AFTERWORD

The Dexter Avenue pastorate was Vernon Johns's last tenure of pastoral leadership. For the next ten years, he preached at various prominent black churches and lectured at black colleges across the nation.[55] On May 16, 1965, at Howard University's Rankin Chapel, Johns preached his last sermon, "The Romance of Death," leaving his audience with these words:

> … No one ever saw anything buried about a person that was essentially personal. Everything that we put into caskets and bury belongs to objects in space … personality is not subject to the statistical laws of physicists….
>
> Instead of dreading death, let us reconcile ourselves to this strange statement: That unless a person comes to the place where he wants to die, he has been licked by life; because he has got to die, and if you have got to do something that you don't want to do and it's going to be the last thing that you do, then you've been licked…. let us learn … to approach our graves by living daily so that we can subordinate ourselves to the greatest things that come our way, and then the soul will finally throw off the body … without consequence.[56]

On June 11, 1965, a heart attack stilled the fiery and militant voice of the Reverend Vernon Napoleon Johns, a prophet and a dreamer who never passed up an opportunity to jump into a good fight.

5

THE SUBSTANCE OF THINGS HOPED FOR, 1954–1960

Now faith is the substance of things hoped for, the evidence of things not seen.

For by it the elders obtained a good report.

Through faith we understand that the worlds were framed by the word of God, so that things which are seen were not made of things which do appear.

—Hebrews 11:1–3 AV

By the 1950s, the U.S. Supreme Court had made considerable progress in chipping away at the precedents upholding state segregation practices. On May 17, 1954, in the case of *Brown v. Board of Education of Topeka, Kansas*, a unanimous bench rendered the decision that separate educational facilities were inherently unequal. It had been a long time coming. Largely the brainchild of Charles Hamilton Houston, one of the most eminent legal minds of the twentieth century, and successfully argued through the courts by his prized student Thurgood Marshall, *Brown* sounded the death knell for legally sanctioned racial discrimination in the United States. The *Birmingham World*, the most widely circulated black newspaper in Alabama, naively predicted that the cradle of the Confederacy would not strongly resist the forces of inevitable change. Not surprisingly, white newspapers in Alabama, though they called for calm, bitterly denounced the decision. Alabama governor George Persons declared that racial integration of Alabama's public schools was simply unthinkable.

Alabama whites' reaction to the historic *Brown* decision—though almost always trenchantly antagonistic—took many forms. First, feeble attempts to try to make separate equal surfaced. The gap between the salary of white state teachers and their black counterparts narrowed from a remarkable $222 to a nominal $6 per month. Like some other Southern states, the Alabama State Legislature gave local school boards the right to close any schools facing integration, arguing that the state did not have to provide education for all. There was a resurgence of Ku Klux Klan activity. The most powerful group of segregationists, however, did not associate itself with the Klan. The Alabama White Citizens Council, first organized in Dallas County, quickly spread all over the state. The Council operated on the premise that since whites controlled most of the money they could simply make it impossible for black integrationists to find jobs, obtain credit, or even renew a mortgage. White businesses that accepted integration were boycotted.[1]

Vernon Johns had predicted this very contingency. He had warned Dexter Avenue Baptist Church congregants to work toward some measure of economic self-sufficiency, so that they could be independent of total white control of their economic livelihood. Most at Dexter Avenue spurned Johns's message, but his young successor, Martin Luther King Jr. would have more success with them. This chapter examines the ministry that King established at Dexter Avenue and the circumstances that thrust this small, local congregation into the national and international spotlight so that it came to symbolize the struggle for freedom. Under King's leadership a few members of this church and numerous others in the Montgomery community challenged the nation to confront its denial—to a significant portion of its people—of equal access to the inalienable rights upon which America was founded: life, liberty, and the pursuit of happiness. From 1954 to 1960, in fulfilling the hopes of the Dexter Avenue congregation for a pastor who would bring a measure of healing, spiritual vitality, and moral leadership, Martin Luther King Jr. became "the substance of things hoped for."

For the members of Dexter Avenue Baptist Church, the summer of 1953 was entirely too much like the summer of 1947. Once again they were without a pastor, and yet again membership and tithing dwindled.

R. D. Nesbitt felt especially anxious about the low morale at the church. Since he had played an important role in bringing both Alfred Charles Livingston Arbouin and Vernon Napoleon Johns to the church as pastors, Nesbitt wondered whether church members' decision to make him chair of the pastoral search committee reflected continued faith in him or simply provided him with an opportunity to redeem himself. Utmost in the minds of Nesbitt, T. H. Randall, and the rest of the official board was that despite the painstaking care taken in calling Johns, still he had left amid controversy. With much trepidation the official board once again began an all-too-familiar process.[2]

The first few months of the search were disheartening, but late in the fall of 1953, things looked up. Walter R. McCall, a young minister and dean of men at Fort Valley State College in Fort Valley, Georgia, caught the attention of the search committee. Twice a classmate of Martin Luther King Jr., McCall had worked his way through Morehouse College in Atlanta and Crozer Seminary in Chester, Pennsylvania. In early November 1953, T. H. Randall invited McCall to preach a trial sermon, and board members were very impressed with his "poise, elocution, and skill." McCall was flattered, explaining, "I consider it [the pastorate] not because of self-aggrandizement, not for glory, nor for fame. But I consider it because it is a challenge whose task is momentous, which staggers my imagination and dwarfs my intellect … such a task places me at the mercy seat of God seeking his guidance and that of those who are seekers after truth." Board of deacons chair T. H. Randall was favorably disposed toward McCall, and, for a time, believed he had found the next man to lead Dexter Avenue. Nesbitt, too, thought McCall was a good choice, but along with other committee members believed that the search should continue. And so it did until an ordinary day's work for R. D. Nesbitt led to a rather extraordinary series of events, causing the official board to pause briefly in its pursuit of McCall.[3]

In December 1953, Robert Nesbitt was auditing the books for the Atlanta district office of the Pilgrim Life Insurance Company when he mentioned to W. C. Peden, the local manager, that Dexter Avenue was still searching for a pastor. Both longtime churchmen, Peden and Nesbitt often spoke of church matters to each other, so Peden was aware of all that had transpired between Johns and the Dexter Avenue congregation, and Nesbitt's determination to bring a noncontroversial pastor to the church. Nesbitt explained that the congregation had responded positively to Walter McCall, and that they planned to invite him for a second trial sermon. Even so, Nesbitt explained, the search committee wanted to be particularly careful before making a decision.

Suddenly, Peden had an idea. "I know of a young man," he told Nesbitt, "Mike King. He lives right here in Atlanta and is very impressive. He's in school in Boston, and his father is pastor of one of the most prominent colored churches in town, Ebenezer Baptist Church." Nesbitt nodded in recognition, having heard of Martin Luther King Sr. and remembering that Ebenezer Baptist Church was only two blocks north of the Atlanta branch office of the Pilgrim Insurance Company. Peden continued, "Bob, I think he is just the man for you." In stark contrast to his predecessor, Vernon Johns, whose proclivities made him an improbable choice to lead Dexter Avenue, the background of Martin Luther King Jr. made him a model choice for pastor of Dexter Avenue Baptist Church.[4]

When Martin Luther King Jr. assumed the pastorate of Dexter Avenue Baptist Church in 1954, black middle-class pedigree, church experience, and educational background converged to create a capable clergyman and a reluctant but ultimately willing institution with a historical moment pregnant with possibilities. King's life comported well with Dexter Avenue's embrace of notions about America's promise of progress and reward for hard work. In three generations the King family had risen from the depths of slavery to become part of Atlanta's black elite. Like Montgomery, Atlanta had a thriving black middle class that revolved around a host of black colleges, chief among them Atlanta University, Spelman College, and Morehouse College. There were numerous black-owned businesses along Auburn Avenue and a host of professional educators, doctors, and lawyers. King's maternal grandfather, the Reverend A. D. Williams—the son of a slave preacher named Willis Williams—had come to Atlanta in the 1880s and eventually graduated from Morehouse College. He was the second pastor of Ebenezer Baptist Church, which he transformed from a small fifty-member congregation into a thriving church and the spiritual home of much of Atlanta's well-to-do. Alberta Williams, the only child of A. D. and Jennie Celeste Parks Williams to survive infancy, was Martin Luther King Jr.'s mother.[5]

Martin Luther King Sr. was the son of sharecroppers James Albert and Delia Linsey King, and grew up in poverty. Ambitious but uneducated, Daddy King, as he later came to be affectionately called by many, came to Atlanta in 1920 hoping to improve himself. He enrolled in Bryant Academy intending simply to master the basic rudiments of knowledge, but an unassuming walk down Auburn Avenue changed his life. From afar he noticed a young woman who captured his attention. King soon learned Alberta Williams was not only distant from him in terms of physical space on that afternoon, but also in education and social class. Though they had never met, King had heard that Williams possessed "gracious manners, a captivating smile and scholarly manner." Traveling to Jonesboro, Georgia, to attend the Atlanta Missionary Baptist Association's annual convention, King confided to three of his friends that he intended to marry Alberta Williams. His friends responded with laughter, "calling out [his] name in disbelief," as she was the "daughter of one of Atlanta's most prominent and respected ministers" and he was just a "green country boy—fresh off the farm." Given the values and mores of the day, the Williams would likely have disapproved of King as a suitor for their only child. For her part, Alberta Williams planned to teach for some time before marrying.[6]

Undaunted by the challenge, King worked his way through Morehouse College while pursuing the hand of the woman he nicknamed Bunch. He later readily admitted, "I had no natural talent for study, and my learning came after long, long hours of going over and over and over the work until I was falling asleep saying lessons to myself." Overcoming the chasm of class difference that separated him from his sweetheart through acquiring a formal education, after a six-year courtship, Martin Luther King Sr. and Alberta Williams were married on Thanksgiving Day, 1926, at Ebenezer Baptist Church.[7]

Moving into an upstairs bedroom of the Williams's home promised the possibility of gradually beginning a new life together, yet the young couple's early married life was almost immediately fraught with dramatic change. King was pastoring two small Baptist churches and still working on his degree from Morehouse College, and within a year the couple had their first child, a daughter they named Willie Christine. On January 15, 1929, the Kings had their second child, Martin Luther King Jr.; a third child, A. D. King, was born a year later. Then, on March 21, 1931, the Reverend A. D. Williams died suddenly. The death of the family patriarch would affect more than just his immediate family. Under pressure from his mother-in-law, and acknowledging the debt he owed A. D. Williams because "some of the things I started off to do as a preacher he corrected," and because Williams had helped him "understand the larger implications involved in any churchman's responsibility to the community he served," Martin Luther King Sr. reluctantly succeeded his father-in-law to the Ebenezer Baptist Church pulpit.

Part of the legacy that Martin Luther King Jr. inherited from his grandfather and father was the idea that a minister must be responsible to his community. In the same yellow A-frame house on Auburn Avenue in which his mother was born, the younger King grew up couched in the heart of Atlanta's Auburn Avenue. He made special note of his father's position concerning the absolute authority of the pastor as the leader of the congregation and the way in which his father ruled over the finances of the church. People at Ebenezer did not complain or challenge Daddy King's authority because, while other churches around them were languishing during the Depression, Ebenezer was thriving. In fact, in 1934 the church sent the elder King on a month-long tour of the Middle East and Europe en route to the World Baptist Convention in Berlin, Germany. The younger King was also influenced by his father's participation in politics. In 1939, Daddy King started a voter registration campaign in Atlanta virtually on his own, leading hundreds of people to the courthouse to register to vote. As Daddy King explained, "Church wasn't simply Sunday morning.... It was more than a full-time job. In the act of faith, every minister became an advocate for justice. In the South, this meant an active involvement in changing the social order...."[8]

Along with family and church influences King was shaped by his education. There was never really any question that he would go to college, but what the King family did not anticipate was that, in 1944, Morehouse College would face declining enrollment because many eligible college men were fighting World War II in Europe or the Pacific Rim. For precocious young men like Martin Luther King Jr., these men's absences became opportunities to begin college early. King was fifteen years old at the time of his enrollment, and under president Benjamin Mays, Morehouse had undergone radical changes. Mays, the first African American president of the college, was also its first president with an earned doctorate. Born near Greenwood, South Carolina, Mays graduated Phi Beta Kappa from Bates College in Maine and then earned a Ph.D. from the University of Chicago. During his tenure, each Tuesday the entire student body gathered in the auditorium to listen to lectures on his travels. Since Mays occasionally lectured on India, it was most likely in this context that King first encountered the teachings of Mahatma Gandhi. Mays hoped to instill in all students "the idea that despite crippling circumscriptions" they "could accomplish whatever they set out to do." From the 1940s forward, in the black community, being a "Morehouse Man" gave a young man a special status.[9]

During King's time in college two important things happened for him. First, he experienced "a state of scepticism [sic]" in which he questioned religious beliefs passed on by his family. At thirteen, he had shocked his Sunday school class by doubting the bodily resurrection of Jesus Christ. Sunday School teachers, King complained, wanted him to accept "Biblical studies uncritically," which was "contrary to the very nature of" his being. King explained that at Morehouse "the shackles of fundamentalism were removed from my body." "This conflict," King contended, "continued until I studied a course in Bible in which I came to see that behind the legends and myths of the Book were many profound truths which one could not escape." It was only after he reconciled his religious skepticism that King considered a career in the ministry as a way to make a difference in the world.[10]

In explaining his personal reasons for his decision to study the Gospel, King stated, "My call to the ministry was quite different from most explanations I've heard. This decision came about in the summer of 1944 when I felt an inescapable urge to serve society. In short, I felt a sense of responsibility which I could not escape." In June 1947 King was licensed to preach and became associate pastor under his father at Ebenezer Baptist Church before being formally ordained to the Baptist ministry on February 18, 1948. In May 1948, King graduated from Morehouse College with a bachelor's degree in sociology on the same day that his sister Christine graduated from Spelman College. His father hoped that his son would join him as copastor of Ebenezer, but King wanted more education.[11]

In the fall, he left for Crozer Seminary in Chester, Pennsylvania, where a semester later he was joined by his college friend Walter McCall. While King had been a marginal student at Morehouse, he blossomed intellectually at Crozer. Much like Vernon Johns, King came into contact with the social gospel while in seminary; most likely it was in George Washington Davis's yearlong course, Christian Theology for Today, that King was formally introduced to Walter Rauschenbusch and the social implications of Christianity as they were understood at that time. During his Crozer years, the spark of interest ignited at Morehouse College by Benjamin Mays's Tuesday morning lectures on Ghandi ignited into a powerful blaze. One Sunday afternoon King went to Philadelphia to attend a lecture by Howard University president Mordecai Johnson on the life and teachings of Mahatma Gandhi. King recalled that Johnson's message "was so profound and electrifying that I left the meeting and bought a half-dozen books on Gandhi's life and works."[12]

King's Crozer education was supplemented by religious iconoclast Reverend J. Pius Barbour, editor of the *Baptist Voice*, a family friend, local minister, and the first Morehouse graduate to attend Crozer. Black students regularly met at the Barbour home for sumptuous meals and Socratic dialogues on theological subjects. King and Barbour debated the merits of various thinkers, including Immanuel Kant, Reinhold Niebuhr, and Paul Tillich. King was so taken with Niebuhr and Tillich that he would stay up all night reading. His intense intellectual pursuit of philosophy blossomed and he graduated as valedictorian of his class.

In the fall of 1951, he matriculated at Boston University for doctoral studies. While a student at BU, King met and married Coretta Scott, an Alabama native and student at the New England Conservatory of Music.[13]

Less than a year later, events brought King to a fortuitous day when he would meet with the chair of the committee charged to find a pastor. At the office of Pilgrim Life Insurance Company on that December afternoon in 1953, Peden's recommendation that Dexter Avenue consider King for the pastorate piqued Nesbitt's curiosity, and so he asked for a telephone number for King, who was home on winter break from graduate school. Nesbitt called King to ask when it would be convenient for them to talk about the vacancy at Dexter Avenue, and they set up an engagement for the following Friday. Nesbitt recalled ringing the doorbell punctually at two o'clock. Daddy King answered and led Nesbitt to the kitchen where the younger King was enjoying pork chops, his favorite meal. Nesbitt walked over and introduced himself, explaining that he was church clerk and chair of the search committee for a new pastor.[14]

Martin Luther King Jr. knew that Dexter Avenue was without a pastor. A month earlier, J. T. Brooks Sr., whose youngest child J. T. Brooks Jr. was King's classmate at Morehouse, had written a letter to both King and his parents telling them, "We are interested in having him [King] in the consideration for the pastorate of our church. The condition of our church treasury at present, however, does not seem to justify or make possible our bringing him down from Boston.... Please ascertain for me the earliest time that he does plan to come home." After receiving the forwarded letter from his parents, King penned his reply, "After carefully checking my schedule, I find that I will be in Atlanta on or before December 24, remaining through January 20, 1954. I will be available on the 2nd or 3rd Sunday in January, preferably the 2nd Sunday. Certainly I wish to express my appreciation to you for your kind consideration."

Shortly after King's reply to Brooks, however, for unknown reasons communication between King and Dexter Avenue broke down. One likely factor was the positive impression King's classmate Walter McCall had made on the congregation and especially on board of deacons chair T. H. Randall. For his part, King was very interested in preaching a trial sermon at the First Baptist Church in Chattanooga, Tennessee. Although the First Baptist congregation had drafted a letter to King three days after J. T. Brooks's letter, because it was sent directly to King's Boston address he probably received it first. At the time R. D. Nesbitt approached King, there had been a time lapse of almost a month since the earlier communication between King and Dexter Avenue.[15]

Even so, after talking with Peden, Nesbitt's interest in King was renewed. "We are currently without a pastor," he explained to King on that December afternoon, "and I wonder if you might be interested in the church." Before King could responded, Daddy King piped in, "Mike you don't want to go to that big nigger church. They'll do nothing but run you away." In the same breath, Daddy King recanted, telling his son, "Forget what I said because I don't intend to interfere with whatever you choose to do." Nesbitt, well aware of Dexter Avenue's reputation as the "difficult" church of Montgomery's elite but believing Daddy King's information to be outdated, calmly retorted, "Yes, the church has had a bad reputation so far as keeping a pastor, but most of those individuals [to whom Daddy King was referring] are dead now and the only one still living moved to Tuscaloosa with her daughter." Daddy King apologized, "Well, I'm sorry I said that." Nesbitt explained further, "Reverend King [Sr.], we have a different kind of congregation now." Daddy King paused, gave Nesbitt a long, hard stare, and then pronounced gruffly as he left the room, "Well, I'll let you and Mike talk." Nesbitt told the younger King, "Many of the members of Dexter Avenue, like yourself, are graduates of Morehouse College. You probably know J. T. Brooks and Franklin Taylor." King nodded in recognition.[16]

Still somewhat ambivalent, King wanted more time, explaining that he would "give it some consideration," but Nesbitt pressed for a commitment. "Let me give you a Sunday," Nesbitt implored. King explained that he was scheduled to preach a trial sermon January 17, 1954, in Chattanooga, and that if offered the call he wanted to be in a position to accept it. Nesbitt assured King that if the deacons at First Baptist were interested, they would give him time: "I've been dealing with Baptist churches for a long time, and I have been involved in the calling of several ministers. If the church is interested in you, you just tell them you're still praying over it and need to discuss it with your family and therefore need more time." Nesbitt persisted, "How about preaching for us on the next Sunday after your Chattanooga visit?" As it turned out, King was already committed to preaching elsewhere in Montgomery on the Sunday evening of January 24, 1954, so he agreed to preach a trial sermon at Dexter Avenue the morning of the same day.[17]

Nesbitt returned to Montgomery and shared his news with the rest of the search committee and the official board. He was so impressed with the young prospect that he wanted to make certain that King would find Dexter Avenue to be a friendly and welcoming church where things ran smoothly. Since the J. T. Brooks family knew the

Kings (Daddy King and Alberta as well as Martin Luther and Coretta) and their son had studied music at Morehouse College, Brooks was asked to host King and to write him a warm and welcoming letter. Brooks shared with King that the congregation was "glad that you can come to us for the fourth Sunday." "Plan a sermon which will not require too much dependence on a manuscript," Brooks suggested. He also requested that King send along, with a vita and photograph, the subject of his message and text since "it will help build up the attendance for the service … you know how congregations often are when they do not have a regular pastor." The plans were now set for King's trial sermon at Dexter Avenue.[18]

January 1954 was a very busy and pivotal time in the life of Martin Luther King Jr. Immediately after he arrived from his January 17 preaching engagement at First Baptist, Chattanooga, he began preparing for his January 24 trial sermon at Dexter Avenue. Taking J. T. Brooks's suggestion to heart, he spent the interim days memorizing his sermon. On the cool, wintry Saturday afternoon just before King set out for Montgomery, he received a telephone call. Vernon Johns was in Atlanta en route to a preaching engagement at First Baptist, Montgomery before continuing on to lecture at colleges in Louisiana, and he solicited a ride from King, who obliged. To pass the time on the journey from Atlanta to Montgomery, King turned on the radio and caught one of his favorite operas, Gaetano Donizetti's *Lucia di Lammermoor*. He listened attentively as they drove past the fertile farmlands of western Georgia and eastern Alabama. He hoped that the lovely music and peaceful, serene countryside were good signs. He had left Chattanooga ambivalent about how things had gone. He was not sure if perhaps he had not been too intellectual, too young, or too political, but he hoped that things would be better in Montgomery.[19]

As they journeyed, Vernon Johns said little to King about the people at Dexter Avenue. But as soon as they arrived at the home of Johns's hosts, Ralph and Jaunita Abernathy, Johns insisted that King come in and meet them. Acceding to the wishes of his elder, King entered the Abernathy home intending only to extend polite, cursory greetings and then be on his way. He explained that he was expected at the Brooks's home, but Juanita Abernathy extended a dinner invitation, and Johns urged him, "You better do it boy … I've eaten at both houses, and there's no comparison … Here you'll get the best meal you've ever had in your life." Abernathy remembered that King "laughed, threw up his hands and joined us at the dinner table." More important than the meal was the ensuing conversation about Dexter Avenue. Johns warned King that, should he receive the call, he must act quickly in establishing his program, giving the deacons as little opportunity as possible to challenge him. Abernathy agreed and added that "it was better in the long run to be a pastor than a prophet," by which he meant that King must see to it that he was very involved in all of the committees and organizations of the church. It was not enough, Abernathy told King, to just give inspiring words, but he must be an integral part of everything that went on in the life of the church.[20]

On his way to the Brooks's home King ran into an old college friend, Robert Williams, who upon graduating from Morehouse had gone to the Julliard School and the Union Seminary School of Sacred Music, both located in New York City. Now Williams was professor of music at Alabama State University in Montgomery. King explained that he was in town preaching a trial sermon at Dexter Avenue. Aware of King's phase of religious skepticism while they were undergraduates, Williams could not let the moment pass without teasing his friend about becoming a preacher, but it was probably his subsequent remark that resonated with King. Williams exclaimed, "They've got a lot of tough old buzzards in that church. But if anybody can pastor them, you can."[21]

Finally King arrived at the Brooks home, had a second meal, and spent the rest of Saturday evening poring over his sermon. Though he had preached many times prior and had served as associate pastor of his father's church for three summers, he was still very anxious about preaching for the people at Dexter Avenue. He told himself, "Keep Martin Luther King in the background and God in the foreground and everything will be all right." The next morning, after sharing breakfast with the Brooks family, he tuned in to the local radio station and caught the seven o'clock devotional. On the air was his newfound friend, the Reverend Ralph Abernathy. King called the radio station to tell Abernathy how much he had enjoyed dinner and what a fine sermon Abernathy had preached for the morning devotion. Now King was ready to face the surprisingly large audience gathered at Dexter Avenue to hear its new prospect. He preached a sermon titled "The Three Dimensions of a Complete Life," the three dimensions being love of self, love of others, and love of God. Members were impressed. Nesbitt claimed that after King's trial sermon, "I knew Peden was right when he said King was our man." Zelia Evans remembered that while the congregation took note of King's youth, "we were very favorably impressed. He articulated well, and he had a wonderful message." Mary Fair Burks, chair of the English Department at Alabama State University and head of the Women's Political Council, was taken with King, but exclaimed, "You mean that little boy is my pastor? He looks like he ought to be home with his mamma." Later, King rarely missed an opportunity to remind Burks of her initial reaction to him.[22]

That very afternoon Nesbitt, Randall, and members of the search committee met with King to begin preliminary negotiations. King forthrightly explained that he had other job options—two from colleges and one from a church up north—that he was considering. Dexter Avenue, too, had other options. Walter McCall was scheduled to preach a second trial sermon the very next Sunday. McCall already had intimated to Nesbitt when he learned that King was his contender—and it soon became obvious—that he could not compete with King. The day after King's trial sermon McCall wrote him to say, "If you are interested in getting that church, I would be glad to put in a plug for you." Whether he made this offer out of altruistic friendship or to save face, McCall believed that Dexter Avenue was the brass ring of pastorates. He told his friend, "Take it from me, this is a Great Church, Mike. Much honor will go to the man who gets it. Frankly, I have fallen in love with those people. Don't let anybody tell you that church is a hell raiser."[23]

King returned to Boston to discuss the matter with his wife, who was doubling her courses at the conservatory so that she could graduate in June. Initially Coretta Scott King was not enthusiastic: "I wanted to go back South someday ... but not yet. Selfishly, perhaps, I wanted to breathe the freer air and the richer cultural life of the north a while longer." King, too, was unsure about returning south, remembering that while in flight to Detroit to preach a trial sermon he had thought, "I have a chance to escape from the long night of segregation." Still, King wanted to devote his life to the black church and to the plight of African Americans. Coretta King remembered that "for several days we thought and talked and prayed over this decision." Feeling a powerful need to serve, the Kings finally decided "that in spite of the disadvantages and inevitable sacrifices, our greatest service could be rendered in our native South." And so they resigned themselves that should King get the call from Dexter Avenue, he would likely accept it.[24]

In March 1954 the official process of bringing in Martin Luther King Jr. to the Dexter Avenue pastorate began in earnest. R. D. Nesbitt drafted a letter to the "Honorable Board of Deacons, The Dexter Avenue Baptist Church" in which he told them, "After prolonged deliberations of the committee, it is the unanimous recommendation of the committee that we extend the call to the Reverend Martin Luther King, Co-Pastor of Ebenezer Baptist Church of Atlanta, Georgia." Nesbitt then began an almost weekly correspondence with King until the new pastoral candidate could meet with the official board. He telegraphed

King, "This is to advise that you have been extended by unanimous vote a call to the pastorate of the Dexter Avenue Baptist Church."

While King probably anticipated a positive response from Dexter Avenue, he was surprised to get a letter from another Morehouse classmate. It was Joseph C. Parker, who, just a few months earlier, had accepted a call to Hall Street Baptist Church in Montgomery. Parker wrote, "I certainly hope that you will accept this church. I have told them all along that you were the man for them." Parker advised his college friend, "Confidentially, I should like to give you a slight idea of what they agreed to offer you for a salary ... from $4,000.00 to $4,800.00." He warned King, "I should like to say that they have installed their officers and adopted their program for this year ... I felt that they should have waited. Nevertheless," Parker continued, "you can master the situation." Parker told King that their mutual friend Walter McCall had come back for a second sermon and "fell through." Conversely, Dexter Avenue "voted unanimously for you." Parker concluded, "I just wanted you to have some ideas about the Church in advance of your acceptance. But, please consider them." Parker's letter gave King a clearer sense of the parameters of negotiation.[26]

In March 1954 King wrote to Nesbitt and Dexter Avenue members, "Knowing the outstanding history of your great church, I feel distinctly honored by your call." Having to decline the date Nesbitt had suggested for a meeting with the board, King suggested the first Sunday in April. Nesbitt replied, "This is quite satisfactory with the board as we shall be happy to have you serve our Communion for us on that day ... we may wish to have you baptize about five candidates." Eager to begin his responsibilities, King answered, "I will be happy to serve communion on the First Sunday morning ... I am looking forward with great anticipation to a rich fellowship next Sunday." Coretta Scott King was too busy completing degree requirements to accompany her husband to Montgomery. King traveled alone and met with the deacons, worked out a tentative agreement, preached and served communion at the Sunday morning service, and baptized five candidates in the afternoon.[27]

The next day he returned to Boston to finish the residency requirements for his doctoral program and to outline the particulars of his acceptance of the pastorate. On April 14, 1954, King wrote to the members and officers, "After giving your call the most serious and prayerful consideration, I am very happy to say that I accept it." He insisted, however, upon three considerations: (1) that the parsonage be furnished completely; (2) that he be granted time to complete his work at Boston University, beginning his pastorate no later than September 1, 1954 (in the interval filling the pulpit at least once or twice per month, expecting the church to take care of traveling expenses); (3) a salary of $4,200 per year with an increase as the church progressed. Nesbitt and Randall asked members to stay after the service to vote on King's requests. Nesbitt reported to King that members agreed to the stipulations and, "We are looking forward anxiously to your being with us again for the first Sunday in May."[28]

Meanwhile, the unwelcome news that King had accepted the Dexter Avenue pulpit reached the King patriarch. Daddy King had been encouraged by his son's decision to return to the South, but upon learning that he had accepted the call to Dexter Avenue Daddy King was disappointed and apprehensive. Now that King Jr. was finally completing his education, his father had hoped that his young son would take his "rightful" place as the senior King's successor at Ebenezer Baptist Church. In fact, Daddy King used his influence to get Benjamin Mays to offer the younger King a professorship at Morehouse College. In tandem with the associate pastorate at Ebenezer, Daddy King thought this offer would be too good for his son to refuse. Also, despite R. D. Nesbitt's assurances, Daddy King's fears about Dexter Avenue did not abate; he told his son that "the notorious barons of Dexter would trample him ... [that] nothing but danger, humiliation and career disaster lay ahead in Montgomery." Young King's response was, "I'm going to be pastor and I'm going to run that church." At least for a short time, Dexter Avenue and King each found what it needed in the other. For members of Dexter Avenue, King was the leader who would bring a measure of healing and dynamic reorganization; for King, Dexter Avenue in many ways allowed him to briefly escape his father's hovering shadow, and at the same time, Dexter Avenue mirrored King's Atlanta milieu.[29]

In July, a month after graduating from the New England Conservatory of Music, Coretta Scott King came to Dexter Avenue. Hoping to share her husband's enthusiasm for his new venture but not a stranger to Alabama, she was apprehensive. When King rose to the pulpit during the Sunday morning service he said to his Dexter Avenue congregation, "I am going to ask Mrs. King to say a few words." Nervous but still wanting to make a good impression, Coretta King decided to abandon her prepared speech, opting instead to "tell members how pleased I was that they had called my husband to be their pastor and that I looked forward to living in their community and working with them.... I asked their prayers to help me become a good minister's wife." The warm reception Coretta King received at the church and the tour of the parsonage relieved many of her fears, and she came to feel "that Dexter Avenue was the kind of church where I could be comfortable and really useful."[30]

For the remainder of the summer, King returned to Boston alone to concentrate on his dissertation, while his wife temporarily moved to Atlanta with her in-laws. As he had agreed, he returned to Dexter Avenue to preach one Sunday each month. More significantly, however, he spent a portion of his time over the summer learning the names of congregation members, studying the programs and ministries that were currently functioning, and also writing to a few of his colleagues (pastors who had been his classmates at Morehouse, Crozer, or Boston University) to ask for their advice on the ideas he was formulating for his ministry at Dexter Avenue.

In September 1954, Martin Luther King Jr. and Coretta Scott King became permanent residents of Montgomery. Dexter Avenue members were happy finally to have their pastor in town. Perhaps remembering the advice that Vernon Johns had given him to act quickly, and also armed with the knowledge his college friend Joseph Parker had passed on that members had already created a church calendar for the year, King arrived to preach his first sermon as Dexter Avenue's resident pastor with a detailed, well-crafted vision for the future of the church. Very much his father's son, he began his "Recommendations to the Dexter Avenue Baptist Church for the Fiscal Year 1954–1955" with a preface meticulously and deliberately outlining his ideas concerning the authority of a pastor:

> When a minister is called to the pastorate of a church, the main presupposition is that he is vested with a degree of authority. The source of this authority is twofold. First of all, his authority originates with God. Inherent in the call itself is the presupposition that God directed that such a call be made. This fact makes it crystal clear that the pastor's authority is not merely humanly conferred, but divinely sanctioned.
>
> Secondly, the pastor's authority stems from the people themselves. Implied in the call is the unconditional willingness of the people to accept the pastor's leadership. This means that the leadership never ascends from the pew to the pulpit, but it invariably descends from the pulpit to the pew. This does not mean that the pastor is one before whom we must blindly and ignorantly genuflect, as if he were possessed of some infallible or superhuman attributes. Nor does it mean that the pastor should needlessly interfere with the deacons, trustees or workers or the various auxiliaries, assuming unnecessary dictatorial authority. But it does mean that the pastor is to be respected and accepted as the

central figure around which the policies and programs of the church revolve. He must never be considered a mere puppet for the whimsical and capricious mistreatment of those who wish to show their independence, and "use their liberty for a cloak of maliciousness." It is therefore indispensable to the progress of the church that the official board and membership cooperate fully with the leadership of the pastor.[31]

Here King articulated his position concerning the hierarchy of leadership in the church. He was not satisfied to leave so broad and general a vision for the church. On September 5, 1954 when King rose to the Dexter Avenue pulpit, he articulated three goals. First, he wanted to reverse the reputation of Dexter Avenue as a "silk-stocking church catering only to a certain social class" because, as he saw it, "worship at its best is a social experience with people of all levels of life coming together to realize their oneness and unity under God." Second, since many of the auxiliary programs were in a weakened state or had ceased altogether during the Johns years, King sought to broaden and revitalize them. Instilling in members a passion for serving the community would be the chief function of the Religious Education Committee and the Social and Political Action Committee. He also hoped to invigorate the missionary society to do more for the sick and needy. Additionally, King created a committee to provide scholarship money for worthy students, and he sought to create a Cultural Committee to support young, struggling artists by asking them to perform at the church. Third, King wanted to reorganize church finances in a way to assure financial solvency and growth. Whatever plans deacons and officials had made in his absence would have to fall in line with the following specific recommendations he laid out for the church, which ultimately amounted to a complete reorganization of church life, finances, and activities. As his father had done at Ebenezer in the 1930s, when financial strain temporarily forced its doors shut, King centralized control of the church around himself.[32] This was made abundantly clear by the thirty-two items presented to the membership, some of which are reproduced here:

1.   In order that every member of the church shall be identified with a smaller and more intimate fellowship of the church, clubs representing the twelve months of the year shall be organized. Each member of the church will automatically become a member of the club of the month in which he or she was born. Each month club shall choose its own officers.

Each club shall meet once per month, with the exception of the month for which the club is named. In the month for which the club is named, each club shall meet weekly. Each club shall be asked to make a special contribution to the church on the last Sunday of the month for which it is named. Also, on the Church Anniversary each club shall be asked to contribute at least one hundred dollars. All of the money raised by these clubs shall be placed in a fund known as the building fund. The work of these clubs shall be to supplement that of the Building Fund Committee.

2. That the church shall begin a four year renovation and expansion program. Immediate renovation for 1954–55 shall include: carpeting the main auditorium; public speaking system; electric cold water fountain; new pulpit furniture; Communion table; and painting the basement. Renovations for 1955–56 shall include: new pews; and a new heating and cooling system. Improvements for 1956–57 shall include: new baptistery, and a general improvement of the basement. The remaining year of this four year program shall be spent adding large sums of money to the Building Fund for the construction of a religious education building. It is hoped that by 1959 a religious education building will be under construction. Obviously many emergency renovations will arise which are not included in the present list.

3. That a Building Fund Committee be formed consisting of the following persons: Mr. J. H. Gilchrist and Mr. M. F. Moore, co-chairmen; the chairman of both boards [deacons and trustees]; the clerk of the church; the superintendent of the Sunday School; all members of the Finance Committee; Mrs. E. M. Arrington; Mrs. Thelma Anderson; Miss Verdie Davie; Mr. Roscoe Williams; Mr. R. W. Brown, Mr. J. T. Brooks and Dr W. D. Pettus. Dr. H. C. Trenholm shall serve as advisor to this committee. The responsibility of this committee shall be twofold: (1) To seek to determine the advisability of expanding on this particular spot; (2) To formulate a systematic approach to the problem of raising the necessary funds for expansion of the church plant. This committee shall be requested to report its results to the pastor within six months. After the findings of this committee shall have been reported, the trustees under the sanction of the church, will be on the lookout for the purchasing of property necessary for the expansion program.

4.   That a New Member Committee be formed consisting of the following persons: Mrs. B. P. Brewer, chairman; Mr. Julius Alexander, co-chairman; Mrs. R. E. Harris, Secretary; Mrs. Mary Morgan, Mrs. E. M. Arrington, Mr. Epreval Davie, Sr. and Mrs. J. T. Alexander.
The following shall be the duties of this committee:

a.   To welcome all new members into the church on the Sunday that they join.

b.   To interview all new members concerning their particular areas of interest in the church. If they have no particular interest, be sure to give them one. Place them in the particular department or circle of the church where they can exercise their maximum spiritual and intellectual potentialities. Also ascertain the month of the new member's birth, and assign him to his proper Month Club.

c.   Explain the financial system to each new member. See that each new member has a box of church envelopes.

d.   All names and vital statistics should be written plainly and turned over to the office secretary the following week in order that she may make an orderly transfer of such information to the permanent files of the church.

e.   Request the chairman of the deacon board to assign a sufficient number of deacons to visit all new members within a week after they have united with this church. The president of the Month Club receiving new members shall also be requested to make a visit of welcome or assign some qualified member of the club to do so.

5.   In order that there may be a reliable and orderly record of the church's origin, growth and future development, a Committee on the History of Dexter shall be organized consisting of the following persons: Mrs. Leila Barlowe, chairman; Mr. N. W. Walton, Mrs. Mary Moore, Mr. C. J. Dunn, Mr. John Fulgham. This committee shall be requested to present a summary of the history of Dexter each year at the church anniversary. This committee shall also be requested to keep on file at least three weekly church bulletins, and look into the possibility of having them bound at the end of each church year.

6.   A Scholarship Fund Committee shall be established consisting of the following persons: Mrs. Thelma Morris, chairman; Mr. P. M. Blair, co-chairman; Mrs. Ive Pettus, Dr. Edward Maxwell, and Dr. H. L. Van Dyke. It shall be the responsibility

of this committee to choose each year for a scholarship award the high school graduate of Dexter possessing the highest scholastic rating as well as unusual possibilities for service to humanity; one who has been actively engaged in some phase of church life and one who plans to attend college. The scholarship award for this year shall be one hundred dollars. The awards may be increased in proportion as the church may grow and prosper.

7. A Cultural Committee shall be established consisting of the following persons: Mr. J. T. Brooks, chairman; Mrs. Coretta King, co-chairman; Mrs. C. K. Taylor, Miss Agnes Jette, Mr. Cleveland Dennard, Miss Grace Jackson. This committee shall invite two big cultural events to Dexter per year, one in the spring and one in the fall. They should seek to make one a group event (a school or church chorus) and present an individual artist in the other. Such an undertaking will have a fourfold purpose:
   a. To lift the general cultural appreciation of our church and community
   b. To give encouragement to our school groups
   c. To give encouragement to promising artists
   d. To give financial aid to the church

8. In order to coordinate the efforts and aims of the musical units of the church a Department of Music shall be established. Mr. J. T. Brooks will serve as head of this department. The directors of all musical units shall be members. Other members will include: Miss Grace Jackson, Mrs. Coretta S. King, and Mrs. Edna King. The members of this department shall meet with the pastor once quarterly to discuss ways to implement the technical, artistic, and worship aims of the pastor.

9. In order to implement the program of religious education, a Board of Religious Education shall be organized. This board shall consist of the following members: Mrs. E. M. Arrington, chairman; Dr. W. E. Anderson, co-chairman; Mr. C. C. Beverly, Mrs. Jo Ann Robinson, Mrs. Sadie Brooks, Mrs. Queen Tarver, Miss Dean (Olivet), Mr. William Thompson, and Mr. Cleveland Dennard. The immediate work of this committee shall be to study the need for revitalization and reorganization of the B.T.U. and the Sunday School. Findings of this study are to be submitted to the pastor. This board will also plan for a two or three week Daily Vacation Bible School next summer. Obviously this should be one of the strongest boards in the church.

10.   A Social Service Committee shall be established consisting of the following persons: Miss Marguerite Moore, chairman; Mrs. Verdie Davie co-chairman; Mrs. Sallie Madison, Mrs. J. H. Gilchrist, Mrs. R. E. Harris, Mr. S. W. Wilson, Mr. Julius Alexander, Mrs. Mary Moore, Mrs. S. S. Austin. The duties of this committee shall be as follows: The care and visitation of the sick and needy. All appeals for help will come before this committee. This does not mean that the missionaries and deacons will be freed of their responsibility to visit the sick. It simply means that all financial aid to the sick and needy will be made through this committee by official checks of the Dexter Avenue Baptist Church. This system of helping the needy will discourage unprofessional practices, and prevent much duplication.

11.   Since the gospel of Jesus is a social gospel as well as a personal gospel seeking to save the whole man, a Social and Political Action Committee shall be established for the purpose of keeping the congregation intelligently informed concerning the social, political and economic situation. This committee shall keep before the congregation the importance of the N.A.A.C.P. The membership should unite with this great organization in a solid block. This committee shall also keep before the congregation the necessity of being registered voters. Every member of Dexter must be a registered voter. During elections, both state and national, this committee will sponsor forums and mass meetings to discuss the relative merits of candidates and the major issues involved. This committee shall consist of the following persons: Mrs. Mary Burks, chairman; Mrs. Jo Ann Robinson co-chairman; Dr. R. T. Adair, Mr. F. W. Taylor, Sr., Dr. W. D. Pettus, and Mr. Rufus Lewis.

12.   Mrs. W. E. Anderson and Mrs. Zelia Evans shall comprise a committee to reorganize a strong and dynamic Women's Council. All the women in the church will automatically become members of this organization. Although this organization will have the liberty to elect its own officers, the pastor is recommending that Mrs. Anderson and Mrs. Evans become president and Vice-president respectively, for the first year. Literature and suggestions for organization can be obtained from the pastor.

13.   Mr. P. M. Blair and Mr. J. H. Gilchrist shall comprise a committee to organize an active and dynamic Brotherhood. This organization will include every man in the church. Mr. Blair

and Mr. Gilchrist shall serve as president and Vice-president respectively at least for the first year. Literature and suggestions for organization can be obtained from the pastor.

14. Mr. Cleveland Dennard, Reverend John Porter, and Mrs. Athalstein Adair shall comprise a committee to organize a strong and functional Youth Council. This council will have three divisions (1) Children (2) Youth and (3) Young Adults. The organization of a Young Married Couples Club shall grow out of this Council. The pastor will meet with this committee to make suggestions.

. . .

17. That the following annual special days and events be enacted in the church calendar:
    a. Church Anniversary . . . . Second Sunday in December
    b. Youth Day . . . . Second Sunday in March
    c. Spring Lecture Series . . . . Week after Fourth Sunday in April
    d. Men's Day . . . . Second Sunday in July
    e. Women's Day . . . . Fourth Sunday in September

. . .

23. In order to revamp the financial system of the church, a Unified Budget Plan shall be established. This plan will do away with all rallies. Instead of giving haphazardly to this or that collection and to this and that auxiliary, the individual, through this method, pledges a simple weekly contribution to the Unified Budget of the church. At the beginning of the church year, each member will receive a pledge card on which he states the amount of his weekly pledge toward the overall budget of the church.

24. In order to implement the above financial plan as well as any business like plan, it is imperative that we have a Central Treasury. Therefore, I recommend that all money in the treasury of each auxiliary be turned over to the general church treasurer by November 1, 1954.

25. All bills shall be paid in checks.

26. All checks will be made out by the Financial Secretary.

27. No checks will be paid out without the O.K. of the pastor.

28. The honorarium for guest speakers will be left to the discretion of the pastor.

29.   In addition to the two check signers, there shall be a third signer in the person of the chairman of the Finance Committee.
30.   All money shall be deposited on the day that it is raised, and the deposit slip shall be returned to the church office on the following day so that an accurate record can be kept at all times of the money on hand.
31.   All money will be counted in the secretary's office in the basement of the church.
32.   An accurate record of receipts and disbursements as well as financial statement of each individual contributor shall be placed in the hands of every member at the end of each quarter of the church year.[33]

It is unclear how King found out so much about Dexter Avenue before he arrived. Ralph Abernathy and King's classmate Joseph Parker were among his informants, but he obviously had done his homework. He was able to assign all of the church leadership in the organizations he was proposing. Above all else we see in these recommendations King's determination to succeed as pastor by controlling the money, the leaders, and many of the church's activities. Any money spent had to have his approval. The Building Fund Committee was to formulate a systematic approach to fundraising and report back to the pastor. In fact, he subordinated all groups to his authority. The department of music, for example, had to "meet with the pastor ... to implement the ... worship aims of the pastor." He "recommended" the first president and vice president of both the Women's Council and the Brotherhood.

King provided a copy of his recommendations to all of the members and admonished them to take them home and hold them in prayerful and careful consideration. Zelia Evans remembered that "the church reacted quite positively. We were all very impressed that he already knew our names and knew the kinds of activities we were involved in at the church." Assigning members to the various committees gave them an automatic investment in the success or failure of the committee. As well, imitating his father's financial plan for Ebenezer Baptist Church was a wise move, since he already knew it could be successful. T. H. Randall, who initially had wanted to extend the call to Walter McCall and who, as chairman of the deacons ruled over church affairs (and, finally, whom Johns and Abernathy had warned King was one of the "difficult" members), approved of King's program. In fact, despite all of the warnings about the "Dexter barons" famous for "running off pastors," King's excellent education credentials and gracious manner led the deacons fully, even enthusiastically, to embrace his ambitious plan for

Dexter Avenue's future. In a letter to Walter McCall, King revelled, "Our work here is going very well. We are getting superb cooperation." McCall replied, "Be not deceived Mike, you are with a fine group of people. Therefore to know that they are cooperating is not surprising."[34]

Despite the confidence expressed in the letter to McCall, King wrote to Melvin Watson, a former mentor and dean of the Morehouse School of Religion and to Major J. Jones, a classmate from Boston University, for affirmation. Watson sent words of encouragement that he had "read with more than usual interest and satisfaction the recommendations made … to Dexter Avenue Baptist Church" and observed that, although recommendations 12 and 13 bordered on the repetitive, overall they reflected "clear evidence of careful thought." He further commended King, saying, "The manner in which they are put together deserves praise." Perhaps most gratifying to King, Watson wrote that "Dexter Avenue has displayed the depth of its yearning for a constructive program by the mood in which it accepted the recommendations." Watson reassured, "This is a favorable omen for your ministry in the Montgomery Community." A consummate teacher, Watson couched a caveat among the many accolades. "Organization," he admonished his former pupil, "is necessary for the advancing life of any institution. Religious institutions, however, have to be on their guard always against over-organization. Hectic activity in the church is not necessarily an indication that the cause of the Kingdom is being promoted."

King's classmate Major Jones concurred with Watson's positive response, noting, "I do not feel that there is anything I could say that you did not say in the act of speaking to the overall needs of the church." Yet Jones expressed concern that sometimes "when we organize any large group of people into many competing groups we have to be careful not to make each group the end of itself; each forgetting the whole." "Stating at the outset a group of aims and objectives around which all other things" could be integrated, Jones suggested, would circumvent this pitfall. King took all of these suggestions under advisement as he set out to make 1954–55 a good year for the church and himself. His first year, then, was consumed with establishing new activities, restoring the health of dysfunctional organizations and reviving old traditions.[35]

One goal King had omitted from the recommendations was that of strengthening ties between the church and both the local Montgomery-Antioch District [Baptist] Association and the National Baptist Convention. During his first week in town King met with and was elected recorder of the Montgomery-Antioch Baptist Association. On

September 6, the day after King delivered his recommendations, he left with his mother and father to attend the National Baptist Convention in St. Louis, Missouri. In August, the indefatigable Nannie Helen Burroughs, who intermittently had spoken at Dexter Avenue since 1908, invited King to deliver a speech, "The Vision of the World Made New," for the noonday speakers' forum. Moved by the reception to King's speech, Burroughs wrote, "The delegates were profoundly impressed. What your message did to their thinking and to their faith is 'bread cast upon the water' that will be seen day by day in their good works in their communities." King also joined the advisory council to the conventions' National Baptist Training Union Board. The King pastorate found Dexter Avenue increasing its participation in larger Baptist circles, especially in sending delegates to the BTU and the Sunday school conventions.[36]

These were days of optimism and belief that the many years of hoping and praying had finally brought Dexter Avenue the right minister. The grand program and fanfare to install their new pastor was indicative of members' expectation of a bright future. Not since the 1926 installation of Frank Jacobs had there been this level of excitement and activity. King's installation service fused together the past and present life of the young pastor and his new church. In fact, that late October day was one of reconciliation and exhilaration for King, as his old Atlanta world of Ebenezer came to meet and pass along its blessing to his new life at Dexter Avenue. All who attended received a glossy program detailing the order of the service and providing brief biographical sketches of Martin Luther King Jr. and Coretta Scott King. The program noted that King had "traveled extensively delivering the message of God" and that his young wife had favored "Boston audiences as guest soloist on many occasions and sang regularly at the historical Old South Church in Boston."[37]

As long had been the tradition for such occasions at Dexter Avenue, ministers from various churches in the community participated in the service. After an organ prelude, hymn, and an invocation, the Reverend W. J. Powell, representing the local African Methodist Episcopal Zion congregation, read the scripture. Next, King's old college friend and current informant J. C. Parker, pastor of Hall Street Baptist Church, introduced him to the crowd. Certainly among the things that must have meant the most to King was the fact that his father, Daddy King, gave the sermon. The thunderous baritone of Daddy King in ordination homily, however, was not the only voice from Atlanta to impart blessings on the young pastor. His mother, Alberta King, rendered the organ music for the service, and the entire choir from his home church performed for the celebration. More than one hundred members from Ebenezer came to see their favorite son vested as senior pastor. After all, this was Ebenezer's own Martin Luther King Jr., who even as he had saddened their spirits by leaving them had swelled their hearts with pride, having made such a fine mark for himself so early in his life.[38]

King was overwhelmed at the outpouring of love and support he felt from his home church. Later, he wrote to thank his home church and express his deepest gratitude: "I would like to take this way to express our deepest appreciation to you for the 'big way' in which you helped to make our recent installation a great success. Words cannot adequately express my gratitude, and I assure you that your tremendous response to this occasion shall be remembered so long as the cords of memory shall linger." He told them further, "All of this continues to prove to me that there is but one Ebenezer. Your generosity and big heartedness will always keep you in the forefront, and you will always stand as a symbol of what other churches ought to be." Finally, assuring the people and place that had lovingly nurtured him that they would always be a part of him, he wrote, "I want you to know Ebenezer, that I feel greatly indebted to you; and that whatever success I might achieve in my life's work you will have helped to make it possible." King maintained close ties with Ebenezer during the years he pastored at Dexter Avenue. One Sunday morning each year he and Daddy King exchanged pulpits.[39]

With bountiful energy and ambition, King sought to address the programs and issues laid out in his recommendations, but initially he focused on endearing himself to his parishioners, making the church financially solvent, offering more to the church's youth, and attempting to reinvigorate the special-occasion services. In the sobering days that followed the heady installation services, King returned to his arduous daily routine. He awoke at 5:30 and worked on his dissertation for three hours. Between 8:30 and 9:00 he had breakfast with his wife, and then it was off to Dexter Avenue. At church, he carried out varied tasks typical of many black pastors at the time: ministering to the spiritual needs of his congregation, sometimes in counseling sessions; serving as character witness, negotiating with whites on behalf of members; baptizing candidates; preparing sermons; overseeing the organizational life of the church; and conducting funerals. In fact, early in his pastorate, King endeared himself to longtime member Clyde Reynolds by beautifully eulogizing his mother, Francis H. Reynolds. The grateful son wrote to King, "You could not have delivered a better eulogy for my mother if you had been her pastor for 50 years. Thank you very much for a brilliant and comforting message, and a beautiful Christian funeral service." King was effective and moved through his many responsibilities with wisdom, sensitivity, and enthusiasm.[40]

King's charm helped make Dexter Avenue a warm and inviting place. Years earlier he had shared with his wife his desire to "adjust to 'Aunt Jane'"—that is, to treat the working-class and poor members with the same dignity and respect he afforded the more well-to-do. It was simply wrong, he told Corretta King, to patronize "good but less educated people." King developed a strong rapport with Dexter Avenue's less-sophisticated and uneducated members. A person with acumen and facility to communicate with a wide spectrum of people, King would ask the well-educated among his congregation "what they were doing," which was their cue to share with him their latest intellectual accomplishments, business feats, or excursions to exotic places. With the somewhat less sophisticated, he would query, "How are you?" and give them an opportunity to talk about themselves or their work. King's warmth proved to be a real asset both in his pastorate of Dexter Avenue and his leadership later in the civil rights movement. King wanted to create fellowship among Dexter Avenue members. He developed small groups of members to meet once a month for a meal and for fellowship. Each club sponsored a program for the entire church—a play, reading, or musical performance. Working together in close fellowship within the same small group over an extended period of time, King hoped, would foster in church members a close bond of Christian fellowship.[41]

King was anxious to invigorate the church's celebrations of special occasions: Women's Day, Youth Day, and Men's Day, the church's anniversary, and the spring lecture series. Like R. C. Judkins fifty years prior, King secured influential and talented speakers from the African American Baptist and academic communities. The first special-occasion program was very successful, financially. The board had already set aside October 4–10 as Women's Emphasis Week, culminating in Women's Day on October 10. With King's help, the membership was able to bring in Phoebe Burney, dean of women at Clark College of Atlanta University. King's role was important, but much of the preparation work had already been done. The Women's Day Committee, chaired by Jo Ann Robinson, had been working for months to create a memorable Women's Emphasis Week. Dr. Mary Fair Burks, as head of the publicity committee, saw to it that various activities were publicized in the local newspapers; as well, she wrote an ad for local churches to include in their bulletins. Meanwhile Dr. Zelia Evans and Thelma Austin Rice designed the program and laid out the order of worship for the October 10 culminating ceremony. Using King's new pledge system, the church raised an unprecedented amount of money. King bragged to Walter McCall, "Our Women's Day … was a tremendous success. Over $2,100.00 was raised."[42]

Rice went beyond just designing the program to also advising King concerning the budget and how best to get members to tithe; she would prove to be a great help to King both because of her math skills and her long history with Dexter Avenue. Rice had been born to Simuel and Henrietta Wade Austin in 1917. Her father was a deacon and her mother was a member of the missionary society during Judkins's ministry. Rice grew up in the Dexter Avenue congregation, and went to Alabama State University before getting graduate degrees in mathematics from the University of Kansas and the University of Minnesota. She returned to Montgomery in 1954 to head the math department at Alabama State. During his tenure, Rice was, for King, a font of information.

Encouraged by the Women's Day success, the board approved King's suggestion for the December church anniversary. Apologizing for the tardiness of the request, King penned a letter to Dr. Melvin Watson, dean of the School of Religion at Morehouse College, "Our Church Anniversary will be observed at the 11 o'clock service the 2nd Sunday in December, 1954. I would like to invite you to serve as our guest preacher for that occasion." Watson agreed. Also, Leila M. Barlowe, chair of the history committee, prepared a short history of the church to be included in the program. Barlowe began her history, "Great events and great men are immortalized by regular observances of anniversaries. And although in the making of history, the movement may be one of progression, it becomes necessary at intervals to take a backward glance in order to evaluate this progress. We foretell the future by pondering over the past." Including a brief history of the church on the inside of church anniversary programs thus became a regular part of Dexter Avenue celebrations, as King wanted concrete ways to measure and judge the church's progress. He had requested that the Committee on the History of Dexter Avenue keep three weekly church bulletins on file to be bound at the end of each church year. Like Women's Day, the church's anniversary raised a lot of money. Afterward Watson wrote a note to King: "I was thrilled by the church experience. It meant so much to me to see you in the Church functioning and to see the grand response the congregation is giving you. You are definitely off to a promising start, and I believe the Lord is with you."[43]

Another area King addressed early on was the youth ministry. On Sunday, January 16, 1955 the church organized the Baptist Youth Fellowship to address the spiritual needs of church members between six and thirty-five. This was to be a more extensive organization of church youth than was the BTU, which had consisted of youth between twelve and eighteen years of age. King wanted to organize youth "for effective service in all phases of the church and its activities ... to develop stewardship and fellowship ... and stimulate a devotion of all principles of Christian faith." Subdivided into three groups (ages six through twelve, thirteen through seventeen, and eighteen through thirty-five), the Baptist Youth Fellowship met every other Tuesday night to discuss issues of spirituality and to plan special activities. Each March, this organization's activities culminated in the celebration of Youth Day. For the first Youth Day venture, King invited his friend Walter McCall, telling him, "I would like to extend an invitation to you to preach the annual Youth Day sermon at the 11 o'clock service on the 2nd Sunday in March (13th) 1955. We are hoping that this will be a high day at Dexter and your presence as well as your message would add so much to the occasion." As part of the week's activities and in keeping with Dexter Avenue's goal to provide a forum for struggling black artists, on March 8, 1955, Coretta Scott King organized a "talent night" featuring local youth in the community. Also, following McCall's sermon, the Baptist Youth Fellowship held a symposium, "The Meaning of Integration for American Society." Along with the Social and Political Action Committee, we see here the preparation for the church's active participation in the civil rights movement.[44]

"To keep the members of this church and this community informed on the major doctrines and issues of the Christian faith," King revived the spring lecture series. He informed members that "we shall seek to bring some of our best theological and philosophical thinkers to this church and community." It was very important to King to select the right speaker to breathe new life into this previously abandoned tradition. While at Crozer, he had been very impressed with a minister and fellow alumnus, Samuel DeWitt Proctor, who guest lectured on Immanuel Kant. Proctor was a few years older than King, but King's graduate education at Crozer and at Boston University had mirrored Proctor's. Proctor had experience in both the church and the academic world, having pastored Pond Street Baptist Church in Providence, Rhode Island, and having been a professor of religion and ethics at Virginia Union University in Richmond, Virginia. King told Proctor, "In my recommendation to the church, I suggested that we have a Spring Lecture Series. I know of no one who is more qualified to initiate the series than you. So I am extending the invitation to you ..." Although King suggested that Proctor organize his talk around the theme "The Relevance of the New Testament to the Contemporary Situation," he assured him, "if you are more disirous [sic] of lecturing in another area, that would be acceptable." Conveniently committed to lecturing in Baton Rouge, Louisiana a week earlier, Proctor responded, "I am expecting to be with you on the 27th, 28th, and 29th of April." Like the Youth Day talk on integration, King wanted the lecture series to prompt members to become more aware and involved in the politics of their community, and to see a nexus between religious and civil life. In so doing, he was reviving an important tradition at Dexter Avenue dating back to the early twentieth century. Completely unaware of what lay ahead in the near future, King's efforts favorably disposed the church toward more active civic participation.[45]

Meanwhile, April 1955 found King at once anxious and joyful over more than just the upcoming spring lecture series. He noted in a personal letter to Samuel Proctor, "I am off to Boston now to take my final Exam. Please send up a prayer for me." Proctor sent his "Best wishes," stating, "As we say in Virginia, I am 'tickled to death' over this." On April 10, shortly after delivering his Easter sermon at Dexter Avenue, King left for Massachusetts. Five days later he delivered the final draft of his dissertation to his committee at Boston University, and on April 21 he successfully defended it. Upon returning home to Montgomery, King learned that he was going to be a father. Coretta King recalled, "Martin was, if anything happier about this than his degree." A few days later Samuel Proctor came to Montgomery and gave three lectures to inaugurate Dexter Avenue's first spring lecture series in more than thirty years.[46]

Later that year, in July, King invited his former college president, Benjamin Mays, to speak for the celebration of Men's Day. King wrote Mays, "I am seeking each year to bring some of the great preachers of our nation to Dexter Avenue Baptist Church for this occasion. I would like to extend to you an invitation…." He explained further, "I am seeking to make this a big event for our church and the community at large. Your presence as well as your message would mean so much to our church and to our community." Mays's enthusiastic acceptance capped off a busy year of special-occasion programming.[47]

R. D. Nesbitt asserted that the first year of King's pastorate was "remarkable." Zelia Evans and Thelma Austin Rice concurred, claiming that members were hopeful and looking for a bright future. The comments of the many guest speakers, complimenting King on his relationship with the congregation, confirmed members' contention that the first year was a success. Members and pastor had achieved more than they believed was possible. Happily and proudly King summarized the year in his annual report, noting, "we have much to be proud of. The horizons in the life of Dexter were greatly extended in 1954–55 … for Dexter it is blessed history." Financially, he further stated, "Receipts from all sources have exceeded twenty-two thousand dollars ... we have given generously for benevolent purposes, missions and education ... one thousand dollars has been paid into the building fund, and our debt ... has been totally liquidated." King pointed out several improvements to the physical structure of the church and the revitalization of organizations and traditions, and that "special days through the church year have been tremendously successful ... we have been able to bring to Dexter some of the great minds and pulpiteers of our nation" and "various auxiliaries of the church are alive and growing stronger." King was particularly proud of the Board of Religious Education, which, for the first time in the church's history, conducted a daily vacation Bible school in the summer. As King told members, "in my little way and with my stumbling words, I would like to express my deepest appreciation to each of you." At the annual church dinner held to celebrate the year's accomplishments and discuss the pastor's recommendations for the next year, King told members, "Those noble great yesterdays must inspire us to work courageously for more noble tomorrows."

In October 1955, Dexter Avenue Baptist Church and Martin Luther King Jr. entered their second year as congregation and pastor. Again, King began the year with a set of recommendations. Having firmly and successfully established his authority the first year, the 1955–56 recommendations were truncated to five:

1. In order to increase the membership of the church as well as extend the spiritual influence of the church throughout the community, a serious evangelistic campaign shall be carried out by twenty-five evangelistic teams, each consisting of a captain and at least three of the members. Each team shall be urged to bring at least five new members within the church year.... The pastor shall serve as general chairman of this campaign.

2. In order to further strengthen the spiritual life of the church, the regular mid-week prayer services shall be rejuvenated. Each week some organization from the church shall be called on to lead the prayer service.... The prayer service shall be each Wednesday at 7:45 going thru 8:30.

3. The Men's Brotherhood shall be reorganized with Mr. J. H. Gilchrist serving as chairman. This organization will include every man in the church.

4. The Youth Council, as set up last year, shall be dissolved. All youth work shall grow out of the missionary society. The youth shall be divided into four groups: Sunshine Band Circle (boys and girls, ages 5–9); Crusaders (9–14); Red Circle

(14–18); Young Matrons League (19–35). [This last was for young women only; at age 19 men would become members of the Men's Brotherhood.]

5. That persons who join the church on Sundays shall no longer be voted in the church from the floor. As soon as a person joins the church, the chairman of the Deacon Board and the clerk of the church shall take him to the pastor's study in the first unit of the church and interview him concerning how he wishes to join [through baptism or a letter confirming good standing in another church]. The person or persons joining shall wait in the study to be interviewed by the New Member Committee.

These recommendations sought primarily to refine the massive number of programs that had been organized during the 1954–55 year. Adding midweek prayer services to the revitalization of "special days" represented a reestablishment of a calendar of weekly and yearly services that had not existed since the pastorate of Reverend Ralph Riley. More important, King helped restore the rhythms of church life.

A few weeks later, the church celebrated another Women's Day. Dr. Lynette Saine Bickers, an associate professor of education at Atlanta University, spoke and again the church raised a large sum of money. In November, the entire Dexter Avenue family celebrated the birth of the first King child, Yolanda Denise (nicknamed Yoki). The flurry of effort and activity in the first year represented a shoring up of the foundations of Dexter Avenue church life. Beyond anything either King or the Dexter Avenue congregation imagined, the next two weeks would bring them face to face with a historical moment that not only changed King and the church, but the nation and the world forever. A stable day-to-day life at the church took on even greater significance when attention turned toward directly confronting racism in the Montgomery community. Just before members celebrated the annual church anniversary on the second Sunday in December, unexpected circumstances disturbed the serenity and calm but not the productivity of life at Dexter Avenue. These events thrust King and the church into the national and international spotlight.[48]

On December 1, 1955, Mrs. Rosa L. Parks, a local seamstress at the Montgomery Fair Company, boarded a bus in front of the Empire Theater, located on Dexter Avenue. In keeping with Section 11, Chapter 6 of the Montgomery City Code, twenty-six black passengers were seated from the rear forward, and ten white passengers were seated from the front backward. Parks sat down in the first seat behind the section reserved for whites. The bus was now full save only standing room in the black section. The bus stopped and two white Montgomerians boarded. Shortly thereafter, Montgomery City Bus Lines driver J. F. Blake ordered Parks and three other black passengers to move back to accommodate the white passengers. Quietly, Rosa Parks refused to yield her seat. Blake left the bus and called police, who arrested Parks. A 381-day bus boycott ensued that contributed significantly to the passage of the 1957 Civil Rights Bill prohibiting racial discrimination in public conveyances. The boycott had been a long time coming, and Parks's arrest represented the coalescing of numerous other events and the brave actions of many other men and women, among them fifteen-year-old Claudette Colvin, whose arrest for refusing to surrender her seat on a Montgomery bus antedated Parks's by more than nine months.[49]

Essentially, Dexter Avenue Baptist Church was involved in the Montgomery Bus Boycott in three ways: (1) through the direct participation of some of its members—namely, Mary Fair Burks, Rufus Lewis, and Jo Ann Robinson; (2) through the use of the church facility for the crucial meeting where religious and civic leaders committed to boycott the city buses; and (3) through the leadership of its pastor Martin Luther King Jr., who became the leader in helping inspire and sustain demonstrators during this long and ultimately successful protest. The activism of some Dexter Avenue Baptist Church members against the discriminatory practices of the bus lines antedates the beginning of the boycott by several years. In 1949, in protest to their exclusion from the Montgomery League of Women Voters, Dr. Mary Fair Burks had founded the Women's Political Council (WPC).

The WPC was not a part of the church, but many of its members and early presidents were members of the congregation, such as Sadie Brooks, Jewel Lewis, Thelma Austin Rice, and Jo Ann Robinson. Most of the women were professors at Alabama State University. A native Alabamian and Dexter Avenue member since 1939, Burks served as president of this group, which was organized to fight racial discrimination and injustice in the Montgomery community. In 1949, Jo Ann Robinson moved to Montgomery from Mary Allen College in Crockett, Texas, to take a position teaching English at Alabama State. Soon after her arrival she became an active member at Dexter Avenue Baptist Church, and in 1952, Robinson succeeded Jewel Lewis as president of the WPC.[50]

For years, African Americans complained about the Montgomery City Bus Lines' discrimination toward African Americans. In protest, Vernon Johns had forbidden his school-age children to ride the buses.

Particularly appalling was the "floating line" that required blacks to surrender their seats to whites if the white section in the front of the bus filled up. Attempts to appeal to the bus company usually resulted in a glib response that it should not be blamed for state and city ordinances that it did not pass. The bus company discriminated against blacks in other ways; for example, on its routes in the white communities, buses usually stopped at every city block while they stopped only every four blocks in the black neighborhoods. But most egregious was the contemptuous behavior on the part of bus drivers, which Robinson experienced firsthand shortly after she moved to town.[51]

Robinson recalled, "I was as happy as I had ever been in my life that Saturday before Christmas in December 1949." En route to Dannelly Airfield to catch a flight to visit family in Cleveland, Ohio, Robinson boarded an almost empty bus and took a fifth row seat. "If you can sit in the fifth row from the front of the other buses in Montgomery, suppose you get off and ride one of them!" exclaimed the bus driver. Deep in thought about her upcoming holiday, Robinson initially did not move. Suddenly the driver stopped the bus, left his seat, and stood over her with his hand poised to strike and yelled, "Get up from there!" Dazed, frightened, and humiliated, Robinson leapt from her seat and stumbled off the bus. Her shame prevented her from telling anyone else and she admits, "I thanked God none of my students was on that bus." She remembers weeping all the way to Cleveland and during much of the holiday. Later, when humiliation turned to anger, she resolved that she would take some action.[52]

In 1952, when Robinson became WPC president, more than thirty complaints against the bus company recently had been brought to the council. Two members of the WPC, Sadie Brooks and Zolena Price, had already availed themselves to speak at a public hearing on the bus company's petition to increase fares. Price and Brooks urged the city commission to model its bus segregation seating policy after the one used in Mobile. In this plan, rather than having certain seats set aside for whites' exclusive use and blacks' exclusive use, blacks would be seated from the back forward and whites from the front backward. The dividing line would be readjusted only as passengers exited the bus and their seats became available. This way African Americans would not have to stand while empty seats went unused. Nothing came of the request. Later, Robinson and Burks requested and were granted an audience with Montgomery Mayor W. A. Gayle and city commissioners George Cleere and Dave Birmingham. Gayle and the commissioners were very agreeable—especially Birmingham, a liberal who favored integration—but nothing came of that meeting either. Then in May

1954, Robinson wrote a letter to Mayor Gayle calmly outlining black grievances but alerting him to a mounting crisis:

> The Women's Political Council is very grateful to you and the City Commissioners for the hearing you allowed our representative during the month of March, 1954 … the Council asked for:
>
> 1. A city law that would make it possible for Negroes to sit from back toward front, and whites from front toward back until all the seats are taken.
> 2. That Negroes not be asked or forced to pay fare at front and go to the rear of the bus to enter.
> 3. That busses stop at every corner in residential sections occupied by Negroes as they do in communities where whites reside.

As Robinson informed Gayle, "There has been talk from twenty-five or more local organizations of planning a city-wide boycott of busses," but, "we Sir, do not yet feel that forceful measures are necessary in bargaining for a convenience which is right for all bus passengers." Robinson warned, "Please consider this plea, and if possible, act favorably upon it, for even now plans are being made to ride less, or not at all, on our busses. We do not want this."[53]

Along with Robinson, Dexter Avenue member Rufus Lewis was involved in community activities. Born in 1907, Lewis came to Montgomery in 1935 to coach the Alabama State football team, and also served as the assistant librarian. During the 1940s, Lewis inherited an interest in one of the local black funeral homes, Ross-Clayton, and soon became a successful businessman in the community. At the end of World War II, Lewis was hired to direct a job training skills program sponsored by Montgomery's public schools and the U.S. Veterans Administration to provide returning veterans with job training skills. As well, Lewis worked to develop blacks' sense of civic pride and entitlement to the rights of full citizenship and organized the Citizens' Steering Committee to help black veterans become registered voters. He had been a close ally of Vernon Johns, especially having supported Johns in his business ventures. Like Robinson, Lewis was a member of the Social and Political Action Committee at Dexter Avenue. In this capacity, he worked to keep members abreast of the activities of the National Association for the Advancement of Colored People (NAACP) and encouraged congregants to vote. Robinson and Lewis were both outraged that Rosa Parks was arrested.[54]

After Parks's arrest, she was taken to the police station, booked, fingerprinted, and incarcerated. She called her mother, who initially panicked but calmed down after she learned that Parks "hadn't been physically manhandled." Parks's mother called Clifford and Virginia Durr and E. D. Nixon for help. Alabama natives, the Durrs were a patrician family among the few racially progressives whites living in Montgomery in the 1950s. Clifford Durr was an attorney and had advised and availed his law library to attorney Fred Gray during the trial of Claudette Colvin. His wife Virginia was an activist in her own right. She had led a campaign to end poll taxes in Virginia during the 1930s. Both were personal friends of Rosa Parks. Nixon, too, was an Alabama native. He worked as a Pullman porter and was a committed union man. For well over twenty years he had served as president of the Alabama branch of A. Philip Randolph's Brotherhood of Sleeping Car Porters, and also as president of the Montgomery branch of the NAACP. More important, in the Montgomery community Nixon was the person many African Americans called whenever they were in trouble with the law. He knew every policeman and every judge, and he had gone on the bond of countless black defendants. Notably, Rufus Lewis's civic groups had catered mostly to well-educated, middle-class blacks living in south Montgomery near Alabama State. But Nixon was the undeniable voice of working-class and poor blacks living in the western section of town. The boycott, and to some extent King's leadership, bridged the class divide—at least for a time.

The same evening Parks was arrested, Nixon called Jo Ann Robinson who, with other members of the WPC and a few trusted students spent the night's balance mimeographing and distributing a flyer that encouraged African Americans to boycott the city bus lines. Nixon also called Ralph Abernathy, pastor of First Baptist, Montgomery, and then Martin Luther King Jr.; he suggested that they call a meeting to talk about the possibility of boycotting the buses. They called local ministers and civic leaders and settled on meeting the following night, December 2. On the unseasonably warm winter night more than forty persons gathered at the invitation of King in the basement of Dexter Avenue Baptist Church. Nixon, who had remarkable organizational experience and skills, was the logical choice to lead the meeting, but he was absent, having left town earlier for his regular railroad run; this left Reverend L. Roy Bennett, president of the Interdenominational Ministerial Alliance, to chair the meeting. A period of confusion and heated disagreement ensued. King remembered, "It looked … as though the movement had come to an end before it began." Eventually calmed, ministers unanimously endorsed the idea to boycott the buses. The ministers also decided to hold a citywide mass meeting on the night of Monday, December 5. Because of its size and central location,

Holt Street Baptist Church was the choice for the central meeting site. To provide alternative modes of transportation to boycotting bus riders, the ministers persuaded the black taxi companies to carry passengers for the current bus fare of ten cents. King and Abernathy remained in the Dexter Avenue basement, after the other ministers left, to revise Robinson's leaflet to include an announcement of the Monday night meeting.[55]

The next day the bus boycott unwittingly got an advertising boost from an unsolicited source. When a white employer was given the leaflet for the boycott from her maid, she promptly called the *Montgomery Advertiser*, which printed an article on the front page of its afternoon edition, "Negroes Urging Bus Boycott." On the morning of December 4, 1955, members at Dexter Avenue gathered for the eleven o'clock service amid heightened whisperings about recent events. King began the service with his usual entreaty: "Whosoever thou art that worshipest in this church, enter it not without the spirit of reverence, and leave it not without a prayer to God for thyself, for those who minister, and for those who worship here." Following the organ prelude, choir processional and invocation, King rose to the pulpit and preached a sermon titled "Why Does God Hide Himself?" After the sermon, King told his members of the planned boycott of the city buses and of the mass meeting the next night at Holt Street Baptist Church. Dexter Avenue members supported their pastor, but they did not realize they were at the ingress of a great historical moment.[56]

The next day, King and other black ministers felt encouraged by the support for the boycott and for the mass meeting that night. To the great joy and exuberance of much of the African American community, it appeared that nearly 100 percent of black Montgomerians refrained from riding the city buses. At 9:30 that morning Rosa Parks was found guilty of violating segregation laws, and was fined ten dollars plus court costs for a total of fourteen dollars. Parks's attorney, Fred Gray, appealed the case. At three o'clock that day, L. Roy Bennett called a meeting of several ministers and civic leaders to make specific plans for the mass meeting. At this meeting an organization was created to run the boycott, the Montgomery Improvement Association (MIA), and Rufus Lewis nominated Martin Luther King Jr. as its first president.[57]

King rushed home from the planning meeting with only twenty minutes to prepare for what he later described as "the most decisive speech of my life." Forced to park four blocks away from the church because of the thousands of blacks who thronged for the meeting, it took King fifteen minutes to move through the crowd. He rose to the pulpit, told everyone the story of what had happened to Rosa Parks and briefly relayed other insults and abuses blacks had endured while riding city buses. King told the audience, "We are going to work together. Right here in Montgomery, when the history books are written in the future somebody will have to say 'There lived a race of people, a black people, fleecy locks and black complexion, a people who had the moral courage to stand up for their rights. And thereby they injected a new meaning into the veins of history and of civilization.'"

King used this opportunity to clarify what he judged was an egregious misinterpretation of the meaning of the boycott by the *Montgomery Advertiser* and others in the white community. In its initial coverage of the boycott the paper dubbed it "a campaign modeled along the lines of the White Citizens Council program." Mayor Gayle and city commissioners Clyde King and Frank Parks all joined the White Citizens Council in protest to the boycott. After learning this, King told the audience, he was "forced for the first time to think seriously on the nature of the boycott. Initially, he had "uncritically accepted this method as our best course of action." The query raised for King was, "Is it true that we would be following the course of some of the White Citizens Councils?" But then, remembering Henry David Thoreau's essay "Civil Disobedience," King concluded, "We can no longer lend our cooperation to an evil system. He who accepts evil without protesting against it is really cooperating with it." Living righteously and being true to one's conscience and to God, King insisted, demanded noncooperation with an immoral and corrupt system. The bus boycott, as defined by King and ultimately embraced by the participants, was "an act of massive non-cooperation." This definition, along with the idea of loving one's enemies and refusing to return violence with violence, defined much, but not all, of the civil rights activity between December 1955 and August 1963.[58]

At the conclusion of King's speech, Ralph Abernathy placed before the gathering a resolution extending the boycott until conditions changed. Standing up with thunderous applause the crowd overwhelmingly consented. Greatly moved, King later explained, "I realized that this speech had evoked more response than any speech or sermon I had delivered, and yet it was virtually unprepared. I came to see for the first time what the older preachers meant when they said 'Open your mouth and God will speak for you.'" In order to encourage one another, those present at the mass meeting committed to meeting once a week at different churches for a status report on the boycott and to pray and sing hymns in Christian fellowship.[59]

Most of the members of Dexter Avenue were not active in the bus boycott movement, but the overwhelming majority of the church membership strongly supported its pastor. Congregants of Dexter Avenue followed the example of Coretta King who, when her husband told her he had accepted the presidency of the Montgomery Improvement Association responded, "You know that whatever you do, you have my backing." In addition to the involvement of Mary Burks, Rufus Lewis, and Jo Ann Robinson, J. T. Brooks, the reserved musical aesthete at Dexter Avenue, often played the organ at the Monday night mass meetings of the protesters. The Social and Political Action Committee used the incident of the bus boycott to make real the Social Gospel activism King was preaching from the pulpit. This organization, also headed by Jo Ann Robinson, saw to it that church members were registered to vote, and they were responsible for putting into the church bulletin announcements reminding members to pay their poll taxes. They also provided members information on the positions of candidates running for election.[60]

Since the pastorate of Vernon Johns, members' hearts and minds at Dexter Avenue had favorably inclined toward the church's participation in the social activism of the civil rights movement. When King was arrested for driving thirty miles per hour in a twenty-five-mile-per-hour speed zone, the entire board of deacons, most of them the very same ones who had chastised Vernon Johns for arguing with a bus driver, came to the jail to make certain that King was released unharmed. On another of the many occasions when King was arrested, he received solace from members of the church's January club. Club president Thelma Austin Rice told King, "There comes a time in the life of each individual when he or she faces trying moments.... Realizing these circumstances, we ... share with you our favorite sources of comfort, hope and sense of direction." Rice sent King a collection of poems, biblical quotes, and printed prayers.

King's decision to accept leadership of the boycott protest rendered his family and church members vulnerable to violence. By mid-January, King and other boycott participants were receiving thirty to forty threatening phone calls each day. Both threats and good wishes, in the form of letters and postcards, flooded the church mail.[61]

On Sunday, January 29, King told Dexter members that he and his wife were getting so many menacing phone calls at night that they were leaving the phone off the hook. In fact, at King's request, a Dexter Avenue member Mary Lucy Williams agreed to stay with Coretta and Yoki when King was out at night. The very next evening the King home was bombed. No one was hurt, but the threat of violence was now a reality. After this incident, Dexter Avenue church men volunteered to guard King's home in three-hour shifts from eight at night until eight in the morning. Members also decided that it was not safe for King to be driving, and insisted upon escorting him on most of his daily errands.[62]

King was always cautious and concerned for his family, but he and other leaders in Montgomery whose homes and churches fell victim to violence refused to be deterred. Their patience, along with the sustained determination of 50,000 African Americans who chose "tired feet over a weary spirit," was ultimately rewarded. In November 1956 the U.S. Supreme Court affirmed the decision of a U.S. District Court declaring Alabama's state and local laws requiring segregation on buses to be unconstitutional. Even though the victory was now sure, members of the MIA voted to continue to boycott buses until an official order arrived in Montgomery from Washington requiring the desegregation of the buses. On December 20, 1956, the Supreme Court order reached Montgomery, and Mayor W. A. Gayle announced that the city would obey the ruling.

The success of the Montgomery Bus Boycott inspired protests in other parts of the South, in Birmingham and Mobile, Alabama; Atlanta, Georgia; and Tallahassee, Florida. King reasoned that all of the movements should be coordinated, believing that combining efforts would be a way to be more effective and comprehensive. On January 10 and 11, in Atlanta, the Southern Christian Leadership Conference (SCLC) was created to coordinate the burgeoning civil rights movement. On the actual morning of the organizational meeting of the SCLC, Juanita Abernathy, wife of Ralph Abernathy, sent word that there had been a series of bombings in Montgomery, so King rushed home to encourage calm. In his absence Coretta King opened the Atlanta meeting and took nominations for officers; Martin Luther King Jr. was elected president. King's leadership of the bus boycott and the SCLC created an interesting phenomenon. On the one hand it did not significantly disturb the tranquility or the productivity of life within the Dexter Avenue parish—a testament to how effectively church life was organized. Concomitantly, however, it brought the struggles of the community and nation more acutely into the walls of the church.[63]

In the midst of the boycott activities, all of the ministries at Dexter Avenue, including the auxiliaries and the special series, moved along with continued success. Six days after the December 5 mass meeting, former Dexter Avenue pastor Ralph Riley, now president of the American Baptist Theological Seminary in Nashville, Tennessee, came to town to preach for the church's anniversary. Riley commented on the pride he felt seeing his former congregation's bold stand against racism.

Appreciative of his support, King informed Riley, "your message meant so much to the people of Dexter."[64] King added to Riley's messages of encouragement, preaching the next Sunday his own sermon of optimism, "Our God is Able."[65]

For many reasons Martin Luther King Jr. was beloved by his Dexter Avenue congregation, but chief among them was his preaching skill. King is considered among the greatest ministers of the twentieth century.[66] His sermons reveal an important objective of his Dexter Avenue ministry: like Vernon Johns before him he wanted the congregants active both inside and outside of the church, and he fervently hoped they believed that love was the basis of Christianity and therefore should be the foundation of all Christian actions, including protest. King often preached to members of his faith on the virtue of "redemptive suffering," that ultimately good triumphs over evil. The Bible, King stated, "affirms the reality of evil in glaring terms…. But we need not stop with the glaring examples of the Bible to establish the reality of evil; we need only to look out into the wide arena of everyday life." He continued, "Many years ago the Negro was thrown into the Egypt of segregation, and his great struggle has been to free himself from the crippling restrictions and paralyzing effects of this vicious system." King pointed out, however, that African Americans' struggle would not simply be about discrimination. "In our own struggle for freedom and justice in this country we have gradually seen the death of evil…. There is a Red Sea in history that ultimately comes to carry the forces of goodness to victory, and that same Red Sea closes in to bring doom and destruction to the forces of evil."[67]

King shared with the Dexter Avenue congregation his belief that the problem of evil in the world stemmed from people's self-centeredness—a quality, he would tell his congregation, that knew no bounds of race or social class. In his sermon "Conquering Self-Centeredness" he told the congregation, "There is but one humanity. All are interrelated, parts of one great whole. Aiding a fellow human is merely aiding a small division of one's own larger spiritual self. Hurting another only hurts one's self." King often promoted ideas of social justice and non-violent protests in his sermonizing to the Dexter Avenue congregation. In November 1956, several months into the Montgomery Bus Boycott, perhaps as a means to encourage himself as well as other members of the congregation, King preached the sermon "Paul's Letter to American Christians." He told the Dexter Avenue audience, "Always be sure that you struggle with Christian methods and Christian weapons. Never succumb to the temptation of becoming bitter. As you press on for justice, be sure to move with dignity and discipline, using only the weapon of love."

King told members, "In your struggle for justice, let your oppressor know that you are not attempting to defeat or humiliate him or even to pay him back for injustices.... Let him know that you are merely seeking justice for him as well as for yourself. Let him know that the festering sore of segregation debilitates the white man as well as the Negro." Concluding, King explained the quality he considered basic to the Christian faith and how he believed God worked in history: "So the greatest of all virtues is love. It is here that we find the true meaning of the Christian faith.... The great event on Calvary signifies more than a meaningless drama that took place on the stage of history. It is the telescope through which we look out into the long vista of eternity and see the love of God breaking forth into time." Like other pastors before him, King sought to create a congregation of compassionate, active Christians.[68]

Church life thrived at Dexter Avenue, and in 1956 the membership wanted to extend the life of the church within the larger community. The church began publishing a church newspaper. The *Dexter Echo*, first edited by George Jones, hoped to keep current and past Dexter Avenue members (the paper was mailed to former members living out of town) informed of issues and activities at the church. Published biweekly, this four-to-six-page paper usually contained an editorial by a church member that dealt with the social, political, and economic circumstances of Alabama and of the world. For example, one publication included a Christmas message by Dr. Reva Allman, then head of the Board of Religious Education. Allman wrote, "[A]s we say 'Peace on Earth, good will to men' we find ourselves separated from this holy concept by a chasm so deep it shocks the imagination ... in many localities of our world there is little Peace." Allman continued, "[S]till the voice of freedom cries in the wilderness not only in the remote corners ... but also at home in Alabama. Peoples of the world living in the bogs and quagmires of poverty are searching for that bright star of hope for Christianity lived and for the realization of brotherhood." In addition to the editorials, the subsequent pages included reviews of previously held occasions or discussions of upcoming events. The latter section of the paper, "Doings of Dexterites," updated the church community on the personal activities of its members. All of this was part of King's program to create strong bonds among the members of the Dexter Avenue congregation.[69]

Despite the heavy demand on King's time as he continued to lead the bus boycott, he and Dexter Avenue remained committed to the special-programs agenda he had revived during the first year of his pastorate. King had promised to use the spring lecture series to "bring in some of our best theological and philosophical thinkers to the church and community." Sometimes this included persons who challenged his point of view. In 1956, Dexter Avenue members brought in one such person—King's seminary mentor J. Pius Barbour. Barbour and King respected one another's points of view and Barbour did not disdain King's nonviolent approach of religious protest. Still, Barbour often took it upon himself to challenge King's point of view. He once wrote to King, "The trouble with you fellows from Universities is: You think there is only one type in the world ... the Socratic ... history records Attila the Hun as well as Jesus; Stalin as well as Paul. And by the way I never heard of Atilla drinking Hemlock or Stalin going to the cross. Don't believe the mess about the Penn [sic] is mightier than the sword. Give me the Sword." A release announcing Barbour's arrival promised that the lectures would be "of educational as well as religious value to both youth and adult ... so be sure to hear this dynamic literary genius...." Although the content of these lectures is not available, the titles give some indication of their essence. Barbour began the series with a Sunday sermon, "Can You Change a Social Order without Violence?" In the course of the next four days this sermon was followed by four lectures: "Christ and Obedience"; "Caesar or Christ"; "Caiaphas or Christ"; and finally "Christ." These titles suggest that Barbour examined issues of compliance, and conformity, versus violence, and the state versus the church. Renowned for telling good stories and an amateur philosopher, the provocative pastor reveled in discomforting audiences. At the same time, he fully supported the efforts of King and the bus boycott; in fact, when he learned King's house had been bombed he sent a telegram, "Stand by your Ground. We are praying for you. Calvary Baptist Church, Crozer Seminary Boys."[70]

In 1958, Dexter Avenue invited Dr. Clarence Jordan, of Americus, Georgia, for the spring lecture series. A white religious visionary and progressive, Jordan was born and educated in early-twentieth-century Georgia during the apex of racism, but came to believe that Christianity demanded the recognition of racial equality. In 1942, he established Koinonia Farm as an experiment in Christian communal living that would "give flesh as well as voice to the basic ideas of peace and love." Jordan delivered three speeches: "The Church and the Kingdom," "The Church as a Revolutionary World Order," and "The Church in God's Plan." In these lectures he expressed his belief that "a failure to read the Bible with a sense of participation and imagination helped explain the great distance that separated the ideas of the New Testament from the activities of twentieth-century churches." Jordan told the Dexter

Avenue audience that in Christ the walls of culture, race, and status come down. Exposing the congregation and larger Montgomery community to Jordan's attempts to create a beloved community as well as Barbour's intellectual challenge to his ideas on nonviolence were part of King's effort to foster a dynamic and a thoughtful Christian community. He wanted members to embrace his beliefs, but in the manner that he had as a young Sunday school student, he wanted members to engage ideas critically.[71]

Men's Day also continued with much success, and like earlier Men's Days, this was not just an occasion to impart spiritual and intellectual nourishment to the congregation but also a day in which African American manhood was affirmed. King explained, "Men's Day has been conceived at Dexter as an effort to stimulate further the religion of the church family and the community by offering an opportunity for the men of the congregation to assume certain types of responsibility. It offers an opportunity for the presentation of some outstanding personality to point up some fresh point of view." Men's Day speakers included (from King's seminary days) Dr. William H. Gray of Bright Hope Baptist Church, Philadelphia, and Dr. Arthur D. Gray, president of Talladega College, in 1958. And on July 12, 1959, all of the men of the church, led by King, proceeded into the sanctuary as the congregation sang "God of Our Fathers" and Reverend Samuel W. Williams, pastor of Friendship Baptist Church in Atlanta, spoke on his civil rights activity in Atlanta. Commiserating with Dexter Avenue members' activism in the Montgomery Bus Boycott, Williams told of his success in a transportation case against the city of Atlanta. That evening the men performed a religious drama, "And Now Faith Is the Substance," depicting the lives of some of the "Great Men of the Old Testament," ranging from Abraham and Moses to Solomon and Isaiah. In addition to celebrating men's presence in the church, on these "special days" King always, like Daddy King had at Ebenezer, asked all of the men of the church to pledge a set amount of money.[72]

In the same way that Men's Day celebrated the men of the church at Dexter Avenue, so too did Women's Day feature, affirm, and celebrate women. The church recognized that "[t]he role of women has never been an easy one. But the great pressures of the twentieth century brought about by social changes, economic upheavals, and educational reappraisals have catapulted woman into a role more difficult today than before." The purpose of Women's Day was "to take time out of the regular routine to pay homage to woman." In 1957, former Dexter Avenue member Dr. Henrietta Gibbs (now living in Tuscaloosa with her daughter) was the guest. Gibbs, the first African American woman to cast a ballot in Alabama, paid tribute to Mary Fair Burks, Thelma Austin Rice, Jo Ann Robinson, and others who were politically active and civically involved much in the tradition she had set earlier in the century. In fact, Gibbs spoke on "Civic Activity and the Church," telling of her efforts with Cornelia Bowen to establish a reform school for wayward teens.[73]

The next year's speaker was Daisy Bates, president of the Little Rock, Arkansas, NAACP. In 1957, under Bates's leadership, nine black students had integrated Central High School in Little Rock. Mary Fair Burks, who directed publicity for special events, called Bates "an unusual woman of dedication and courage. She has been described rightly as 'The First Lady of Arkansas.'" On October 12, 1958, Thelma Austin Rice opened the service with a reading on women. Following a hymn, Jo Ann Robinson introduced Bates before a standing-room-only crowd. Her talk, "It Might as Well Be Today as Tomorrow," addressed the urgency and importance of civil rights activity and the perils and high price that had already been paid because so many African Americans had embraced a "gradual" approach to demanding their rights. She began by paying tribute to Dexter Avenue's pastor, repeating what she had mentioned to him in an earlier correspondence: "You, Dr. King, are an inspiration to us that all is not lost in our quest for a 'brighter day.'" Bates told those gathered that the integration of Central High school "has made several things obvious. We must fight along with children involved in school integration suits. Negro Professional people must participate in the fight. We must develop local leaders who have the courage of their convictions and are willing to make the necessary sacrifices. We can't grow weary." As Robinson summarized the occasion in the *Dexter Echo*, "Women's Day at Dexter Avenue achieved its goal of recognizing Christian womanhood and at the same time unifying the church family into an even closer bond of fellowship."[74]

Along with Women's Day and Men's Day and despite continued activity in the civil rights movement, Dexter Avenue members still managed to celebrate church anniversaries. In 1956, Vernon Johns returned as the featured speaker for the church's seventy-ninth anniversary. Seeing some of the church members involved in protest gave Johns a certain degree of satisfaction. The message he had once attempted to convey was one that some members now realized they both needed to hear and to heed. Church historian Leila M. Barlowe noted in her description of Johns, "Through his teachings and his precepts, he aroused not only the Dexter family but hundreds of citizens of Montgomery." During his ministry he "emphasized the concept of human fellowship that would know no narrow racial, religious or national boundaries." Another Dexter member admitted that, "Johns was just what we needed at that time—a shot and a shock that would irritate us out of our complacency with the sheer audacity of his practical ... religious philosophy and the daring eloquence of a Jeremiah." Church members would long remember this day of celebration and reconciliation with their former pastor, a day that made extraordinarily evident the transformation in consciousness that had taken place since the pastorate of Vernon Johns.[75]

The year 1957 brought about some changes in the celebration of the church anniversary. Beginning the Thursday night before the Sunday anniversary celebration, members organized a three-day symposium on the theme "The Role of the Church in Solving Problems." On the first night there was a panel discussion; participants included: Reverend Raymond Harvey, pastor of Greenwood Baptist Church in Tuskegee, Jo Ann Robinson, representing the Alabama State University faculty; and Robert E. Graetz, a white minister who pastored a local black church, Trinity Lutheran. On Friday night, at an anniversary banquet, Theodore Alexander, a former church member who had relocated to Atlanta, paid tribute to Dexter Avenue's reputation as a difficult church. He said, "Dexter is a unique church—controversial, Christian, courageous.... It has developed its trends and evolved its pattern of action based upon its own convictions, with full consciousness of its shortcomings ... it has earned the justifiable allegation of being a difficult and often a controversial church." Alexander suggested that these were the very qualities that made Dexter Avenue great. For the Sunday service, Dr. Mordecai Johnson, president of Howard University and the speaker who inspired King to learn more about Mahatma Gandhi, gave the featured address. These programs helped keep before members' consciousness the work being done and the work still needing to be done to bring about civil rights and the vision many members had of how Christians could improve society. We also see here, in these difficult but still hopeful days, evidence for many members that democratic institutions were moral and could be, with persistent effort, radically improved.[76]

In many ways the church had changed, but it was still very conscious of its status in the community as the church of Montgomery's black elite. This reality was clearly borne out in the music program. The music ministry flourished during the King years. As it turned out, there was an abundance of musical talent among people in the congregation at that time: J. T. Brooks, a professor of music at Alabama State, was the director of music. Ralph Simpson, who taught organ and piano at Alabama State, was Brooks's assistant; Althea Thompson Thomas, a music teacher at Booker T. Washington High School, was the organist. Edna King was around intermittently, having taken leave from her responsibilities at the church to care for her ailing mother. Coretta Scott King and Robert Williams both held advanced degrees in music from impressive conservatories and had given concerts nationally and at the church. Music was taken very seriously during these years, and members of the audience were expected to understand some of the basic facts about the music they would sing each Sunday.

In fact, Ralph Simpson, assistant director of music, wrote a piece for the *Dexter Echo* instructing members in the basic art of hymn singing. In "Some Facts of Good Hymn-Singing," Simpson explained that "hymn-singing plays a major role in all musical parts of the Sunday service.... Worship is dependent largely upon the extent to which the congregation supports this area." He assured the Dexter audience that while they were doing a fine job, they needed to learn more: always allow the organ to set the tempo, do not lag on the first word, let go of the last word, and look forward rather than down at hymnals to get the proper projection. In addition to getting instruction in singing from time to time, there were also numerous concerts and musical performances during King's tenure as pastor. At least twice, King arranged for his mother, who directed music at Ebenezer Baptist Church, to bring its choir to Dexter Avenue for a concert. In 1956, Coretta King gave a solo recital in which she performed both classical pieces and spirituals. In 1958, the missionary society sponsored Altona Trent Johns, wife of Vernon Johns, in a piano recital. The next year, accompanied on piano by Ralph Simpson, Robert Williams performed the aria from the opera *Tosca* as well as some spirituals that he had arranged. The Dexter Avenue choir also thrived during these years, singing both for the Sunday services at Dexter Avenue and on special occasions for other churches in the Montgomery area. The music ministry blossomed, but in the emphasis on formal music and proper hymn singing were still echoes of issues related to Johns's critique about the church's refusal to allow spirituals during Sunday worship. As well, it was likely intimidating to less-educated people to see instructions in the bulletin about singing hymns. It is true King tried to make Dexter Avenue more welcoming, but it is also true that traditions persisted that marked the church as overly formal.[77]

Since it was important to King to establish a comprehensive ministry—one that would address all aspects of people's lives—he also wanted to broaden their horizons. Along with the observance of "special days," the cultural committee, cochaired by J. T. Brooks and Coretta Scott King, presented an array of cultural activities as a regular part of the ministry provided to the congregation: travelogues, a film series, book review discussions, and visits from guest speakers. Among the highlights of these activities was the travelogue that King and his wife presented to the church upon their return from Africa. In 1957, president-elect Kwame Nkrumah, having learned of King and the Montgomery Bus Boycott through a story in *Time* magazine, invited the Kings to attend Ghana's Independence Day Celebrations. When it looked as though money was going to prevent them from making the trip, Dexter Avenue gave them $2,500, a substantial amount equivalent to half of King's yearly salary. Upon their return, King shared with the congregation his impressions of West Africa and Ghana. He began with a short geography lesson, naming some of the countries and giving some population statistics, and then gave a brief history of the Gold Coast (Ghana) as a colony of Great Britain. He told his audience, "The thing that impressed me more than anything else was the fact that Nkrumah walked into the Independence Day ceremonies with his other ministers who had been in prison with him … not with crowns … but with prison caps and the coats they had lived with for all of the months that they had been in prison." Two years later the Kings also shared with the Dexter Avenue congregation via travelogue their trip to the Holy Land and to India. Just as King's college life had been greatly enriched by Benjamin Mays's Tuesday-morning travelogues, so did he hope to broaden the horizons of church members, to make them more aware of the world and to give them a greater sense of what he meant when he preached that all people are interconnected. Also important was that Dexter Avenue's name, reputation, and fame traveled around the world along with King.[78]

Also part of the cultural events programs was the film series put on by the women's missionary society. Under the direction of Elizabeth Arrington, the missionary society sponsored religious films for both the youth and adults of the congregation. The society hoped to achieve several goals. Some films, like *The Voice in the Wilderness*, exposed the congregation to Christianity in foreign nations and to the efforts of missionaries there. Other films, like *The Blind Beggar* and *Holy Night*, promoted the idea of Christian service and responsibility to others. After viewing the films, those gathered discussed them and their applications to their lives. Arrington hoped that the films "helped Dr. King by making the congregation easier to preach to." In addition to the film series sponsored by the missionary society, once each quarter the Women's Council sponsored book-review teas. In November 1957, Dr. Ralph Bryson, Dexter Avenue member and Alabama State English Department faculty member, reviewed

Gwendolyn Brooks's *A Street in Bronzeville*. In August 1958, Jo Ann Robinson led a discussion of E. Franklin Frazier's *The Black Bourgeoisie*. These discussions were a means for interested members to read and discuss both literary and sociological works. In this way, the church was becoming a place for religious, political, and cultural instruction and enrichment.[79]

Among the highlights of the events sponsored by the cultural committee was to bring to Dexter Avenue Kaka Kalelkar, a graduate of the University of Bombay, but—more notably—an assistant to the late Mahatma Gandhi and member of India's Upper House of Parliament. In August 1958, Kalelkar spoke at the morning service on the problem of race relations in the world. "The human heart is the greatest force in the world, and the unity of the human heart is what the world needs," Kalelkar began. He continued, "If it were possible to reconstruct the human heart, then we could reconstruct human society, and human freedom and liberty would triumph." Kalelkar concluded, "Nonviolence is the law of life. God has given every man the strength of 'soul force' and despite racial or religious or economic or class differences, the application of 'soul force' must result in local, national and international peace, freedom and liberty." The Dexter Avenue audience was very impressed with Kalelkar. Zelia Evans noted that "we all listened carefully to his every word." King hoped to create among Dexter Avenue members a dual commitment—to participate in the ministries within the church, and to serve the larger Montgomery community—and members did just that. Dr. Reva Allman, Mary Burks, Dr. Zelia Evans, Rufus Lewis, R. D. Nesbitt, T. H. Randall, Thelma Austin Rice, Jo Ann Robinson, and many other Dexter Avenue members spoke at local high school graduations and civic clubs, and at functions at other local churches throughout Alabama as well as the Southeast and the Midwest.[80]

Despite King's great success in maintaining the ministries at Dexter Avenue, by 1958, his celebrity in conjunction with the burgeoning activity of the civil rights movement left him precious little time to attend to his responsibilities at the church. In a spirit of gratitude, King thanked Dexter Avenue members for their "willingness to share [him] with the nation." "Through force of circumstance," King continued, "I was catapulted into the leadership of a movement which has succeeded in capturing the imagination of people all over this nation and the world." King explained, "Little did I know on that brisk afternoon in December, 1956, when I accepted the presidency of the Montgomery Improvement Association that I was accepting the presidency of an organization whose influence would rise to international propositions."

All of this activity began to take its toll on King both personally and professionally at the church.[81]

Eventually Dexter Avenue's needs became more than King could meet, so on January 6, 1958, the distressed pastor called a meeting of the official board. "The matter I need to discuss tonight," King began "is of a personal nature, and I doubt that a solution can be reached, but the time has come where we must talk about it. The demands on my time have tripled, and I can't continue to carry on under the present load," he lamented. He quickly reassured the board that he did not have any plans to leave Montgomery at this time, that in fact, he felt the need to stay, but if so he would need some assistance. King asked for an assistant pastor, to act as a director of religious education, and also a personal secretary since the church secretary was overwhelmed by his correspondence alone. King's need for assistance was so great that he was willing to take a cut in salary for the current year to help free up funds.

Sympathetic and supportive of its pastor, the board acceded to King's request. They appointed a committee to devise ways various members of the church could assist in some pastoral responsibilities. Later that year, King and the board took other steps to assist him. They appointed Dr. Zelia Evans and J. H. Gilchrist to cochair a coordinating council to oversee church auxiliaries and organizations. At an annual church conference, members agreed to provide King with a "visitor" to assist with visitation of the sick and those in need of spiritual counseling. This person, King stated, should be a longtime church member, someone thoroughly familiar with the Bible as well as the life and history of Dexter Avenue. The board appointed, and the church voted to place, T. H. Randall in this position.[82]

Still, outside demands rendered King less and less available for his pastoral duties. In the 1958–59 church year, he filled the Dexter Avenue pulpit only twenty-eight Sundays. In tandem with numerous speaking engagements around the country, for more than three years King had been commuting weekly between SCLC headquarters in Atlanta, and his home in Montgomery. Nevertheless, Dexter Avenue members found it hard to consider his leaving them. They would tell him, "Dr. King we don't ever want you to leave us." "We realized," however, recalled Thelma Austin Rice, "that it was selfish to want to keep him at Dexter when the whole nation needed him desperately." Meanwhile, King was assailed by guilt, knowing that he was not spending a sufficient amount of time pastoring his church.[83]

On Sunday, November 29, 1959, King requested Dexter Avenue members to stay after church for a short conference. "For four years now," King began "I've been trying to do what should be done by six persons." Overcome with emotion, he paused briefly. "I have been praying a lot about this," he finally continued. "I have prayed with my wife. I have prayed in my office with friends. Regrettably, the answer is always the same. The time has come when I must leave Dexter." Though some Dexter Avenue members were aware that King was going to make this announcement, there was still an audible gasp among the congregation. King continued, "I hate to leave Dexter because of lots of things I want to do that I had planned, but did not have time to do." Sharing what he now believed to be his urgent call, King told the congregation, "I must leave and free those of us who are in vulnerable positions." "Therefore," King finally declared, "I submit my resignation to become effective the 4th Sunday in January." As Coretta King recounted, "We loved the congregation and they loved us. They wanted Martin to stay, and though we knew we must move on, we shared their feeling." Emotions ran high at the service; even so, the motion put before the church body to accept King's resignation passed. An emotional and tearful King and Dexter Avenue congregation rose together to sing the benediction:

> Blest be the tie that binds
> Our hearts in Christian Love
> The fellowship of kindred minds
> Is like to that above.[84]

For the next two months, King continued to carry out his duties as usual. One of the officers of the SCLC, Reverend C. K. Steele, spoke at the last anniversary the church would celebrate with King as its pastor. On the last Sunday in January, exactly six years to the day that Martin Luther King Jr. came to Dexter Avenue Baptist Church to preach his trial sermon, he preached his final sermon as its full-time pastor. Regret and disappointment gave way to wistful resignation. His farewell Sunday service was as joyful as his resignation Sunday had been tearful. "We were all so grateful," recalled Zelia Evans, "that he was able to be with us." The church planned a "This Is your Life" ceremony for King and invited King's parents, brother, and sister and Coretta King's parents. No doubt Daddy King must have reflected upon his earlier pronouncement that King's decision to pastor Dexter Avenue would bring him career disaster. As King and his wife Coretta stood joyfully, proud of their accomplishments at Dexter Avenue, the church presented them with an engraved tea service.

The next day the Montgomery Improvement Association held a city-wide testimonial for them. King, the church, and the larger Montgomery community had been through much together. "It was as though we had a whole life time with Dr. King and his wife," said Thelma Austin Rice. Rice's statement is apt, for together Dexter Avenue and Martin Luther King Jr. had both come into their own. The man and the institution had grown in ways neither could have anticipated. For the last four years King and the Dexter Avenue congregation had borne one another's burdens. The congregation had done everything in its power to keep the King family as safe as possible. The congregation was sorely saddened when, in a 1958 book signing, King was stabbed, and they rejoiced and celebrated his return to the pulpit three months later. In 1958, when the Alabama press began to sharply criticize King, Dexter Avenue members wrote editorials in his defense, expressing their belief that King and his work were "a symbol of the way democracy should work and how it should be practiced. He is providing the kind of leadership Alabama needs in these changing times." King returned their feeling when he told them in an annual message, "I can not begin to thank you with words. I can only say that there are strong torrents of gratitude flowing from the depths of my heart which can never be captured by the thin vessels of words." In his 1958 account of the Montgomery Bus Boycott, *Stride Toward Freedom: The Montgomery Story*, King brought not only notoriety to himself and the Montgomery community, but to Dexter Avenue as well. After the MIA testimonial, Martin Luther King Jr., his wife, Coretta Scott King, and their two children, Yolanda and Martin Luther III, moved to Atlanta, where King dedicated his time to the SCLC and the growing civil rights movement. Perhaps as a means to avoid abandoning totally his call to the ministry, King assumed the position of assistant pastor of Ebenezer Baptist Church; Daddy King finally had his son at his side.[85]

With Martin Luther King Jr., the church had gotten a measure of internal peace and contentment they had been seeking for more than a generation. It was a time of extraordinary success: the ministries and auxiliaries of the church flourished; there was also remarkable financial solvency and growth. The church generously supported Baptist missions and Baptist colleges, especially Selma University (which past members of the church had been instrumental in founding) and Morehouse College (King's alma mater); in addition, the church gave one-hundred-dollar scholarships each year to high school seniors planning to enroll in college. Both the church and parsonage were renovated, the church with new carpet, pulpit furniture, and gas heaters, and the parsonage with new furniture. The Board of Religious Education, headed by J. T. Alexander and Reva Allman, developed a Sunday school program that had record attendance. The missionary society and the Young Matrons Circle grew, as did the youth ministry. King's "special days" programs also experienced success and growth. Along with the Women's Day, Men's Day, Youth Day, and church Anniversary celebrations, King had revived the spring lecture series, which at the time he came to Dexter Avenue had been defunct for more than thirty years. The Cultural Committee enriched the life of the church through films, book clubs, and speakers. The music program thrived as well, both through congregational singing and the various concerts and recitals that become part of the ritual life of Dexter Avenue.

There are some interesting parallels between Martin Luther King Jr.'s programs and successes at Dexter Avenue and those of turn-of-the-century Dexter Avenue pastor R. C. Judkins. Both men had very clear visions for the ministries they wanted to establish and very specific programs that were the product of theological points of view they had developed through their religious experiences and educational training. Both men had a passion for justice and an unshakable belief that the black church could be used as an effective instrument with which to bring about God's justice in the world.[86]

In addition to the rich organizational and auxiliary life during the King pastorate, there was also Dexter Avenue's role in the burgeoning civil rights movement. The Social and Political Action Committee, and the extraordinary commitment of people like Mary Fair Burks, Rufus Lewis, and Jo Ann Robinson represented Dexter Avenue in the struggle against racial discrimination in Montgomery, in Alabama, and in the nation. In many ways, the presence of Martin Luther King Jr. and Coretta Scott King took Dexter Avenue Baptist Church to the height of its hopes and dreams. Ironically, even as King was able to bring about a measure of healing, moral and spiritual leadership, and—indeed—growth in the Dexter Avenue ministry, concurrently, this growth was fraught with violence and danger as it intersected with the larger African American protest for freedom and equality. Even so, during the King pastorate, Dexter Avenue exploded with creativity and activity. In leaving the Dexter Avenue Baptist Church and its larger community with a hope and a vitality far beyond anything they had known in the past, Martin Luther King Jr. indeed was the substance of things hoped for.

6

STILL, A PLENTIFUL HARVEST, 1960–1977

The harvest is plentiful, but the laborers are few; pray therefore the Lord of the harvest to send out laborers into his harvest.

—Matthew 910:37–38 RSV

Life in the United States between 1960 and 1977 was characterized at once by extraordinary hope and utter despair. The tension of optimism and anxiety formed an appropriate backdrop for a time fraught with exacting progress and change as well as immense turmoil and tumult. This generation was a season for all things: the U.S. Congress passed two important civil rights bills; women challenged traditional gender assumptions and roles; the government declared war on poverty; youth protest against the Vietnam War tore the nation apart; assassins murdered four national leaders; and a U.S. president was forced out of office in shame amid scandal. By the time Martin Luther King Jr. left the pastorate of Dexter Avenue Baptist Church, the mid-twentieth-century civil rights movement had proffered a formidable challenge to America's comprehensive system of racial discrimination. Nevertheless, more would have to be done to eliminate the entrenched and insidious oppression of blacks created by over three hundred years of enslavement and another one hundred years of legalized discrimination.

This oppression was imbued in all areas of life: economically, blacks had been relegated to the dirtiest and lowest-paying jobs in towns and cities; politically, such measures as the all-white primaries, poll taxes, and grandfather clauses prevented the majority of blacks from participating in the political process; socially, blacks were denied personal freedoms routinely enjoyed by most other Americans and were forced to use substandard public toilets, drinking facilities, waiting rooms, parks, and schools; psychologically, blacks were consigned to inferior status by whites' practice of refusing to use common terms of politeness and respect such as Mr. and Mrs. when referring to African Americans.[1]

Even so, the Montgomery Bus Boycott had successfully inspired protests all over the nation. There were sit-ins, marches, and freedom rides. In Alabama, black voter registration between 1960 and 1965 increased from 66,000 to 113,000 and by 1969 to almost 300,000. Additionally, Judge Frank M. Johnson Jr., whom president Dwight D. Eisenhower appointed a federal judge of the District Court of the Middle District of Alabama, launched a judicial assault on segregation. Still, unlike many other Southern states, Alabama never elected a New South or progressive reform governor. Race continued to be a crucial factor greatly influencing the political and economic development of the state. As these issues and struggles challenged the nation and the state of Alabama, Dexter Avenue Baptist Church sought to refine and enhance its ministry as it entered its centennial generation.[2]

It would be an exaggeration to suggest that African American churches unanimously supported civil rights activism, but the civil rights movement was, indeed, anchored in black churches.[3] As institutional centers for the movement, churches provided a mass base, economic independence for movement leadership, and financial resources to support protest activities. There were, however, other voices of protest. Malcolm X, the eloquent voice of black Muslims until 1964, first called for black separatism, but later advocated unity among all people. Moreover, both the Congress of Racial Equality and the Student Nonviolent Coordinating Committee, though influenced by and connected with King, were generally considered more militant organizations both in terms of their demands and approaches. Nonetheless, King and his Christian-based, church-anchored nonviolent protest remained preeminent in African Americans' struggle for freedom.[4]

In the last chapter of *Stride Toward Freedom: The Montgomery Story,* King, reflecting upon the success of the Montgomery Bus Boycott, posed the question, Where do we go from here? The year-long protest had been difficult. It had engendered unparalleled unity and enthusiasm among Montgomery's black community; it had also garnered sympathy, admiration, and support from persons all over the world for the cause of racial equality. Likewise, the resignation of King from the pastorate of Dexter Avenue Baptist Church created a similar scenario for members of the church. King's pastorate had generated extraordinary activity, commitment, and growth, and upon his departure church members found themselves asking, Where do we go from here? Although King's pastorate consummated years of foment in the church's history, members realized that the work of the church was far from over—that the harvest was still plentiful, that they must continue to "fight the good fight." In the years between 1960 and 1977 under the leadership of G. Murray Branch, Robert Dickerson, and Herbert Hoover Eaton, members of Dexter Avenue Baptist Church sought to find an effective balance between the church's mission as a religious institution committed to evangelizing for the cause of Christian salvation and its function as an institution symbolizing the fight for equality. While these missions were not mutually exclusive, they were sometimes in conflict. This chapter examines life at Dexter Avenue Baptist Church as it continued to define its spiritual mission in the world during the 1960s and 1970s as well as its decision to become a memorial symbol to honor the life of the Reverend Dr. Martin Luther King Jr. and the struggle for human equality.[5]

On January 3, 1960, Martin Luther King Jr. presided over his last church meeting as pastor of Dexter Avenue Baptist Church, and members inaugurated the search for a new pastor. Resolved in his decision to leave Dexter Avenue, King nonetheless felt some responsibility in helping search for new leadership. He presented a list of five possible replacements: Dr. Samuel Gandy, dean of the chapel at Dillard University in New Orleans, Louisiana; Dr. Charles Morton, a professor of religion and philosophy at Dillard University; the Reverend Charles Butler, pastor of the Metropolitan Baptist Church in Detroit, Michigan; the Reverend Earl Lawson, pastor of the First Baptist Church in Maulden, Massachusetts; and the Reverend Kelly Miller Smith, pastor of the First Baptist Church in Nashville, Tennessee. Aware of the profound loyalty most members felt for him and their disappointment over his resignation, King suggested that they could best honor that loyalty by giving their full cooperation to his successor. To that end, he encouraged members to create a six-month budget, believing that the church would probably have another minister at the end of that six months who would want to set up new programs without the restraints of a budget created before he arrived. Finally, King implored members to continue paying their tithes and maintain their high level of active participation in the life of the church. As a last order of business, Elizabeth Arrington requested that the deacon board be called into session and that a pulpit committee be appointed. On February 2, 1960, chair of the board of deacons T. H. Randall convened the official board. This time J. T. Alexander chaired the search committee and the search officially began.[6]

Much about this search mirrored the many past searches for a pastor, but this time internal and external circumstances created real differences from other recent searches. In many ways, King's departure signaled the close of an age. He had presided over arguably the most productive and dynamic six years of the church's recent history, and this was marked by record participation in church life and in membership involvement in various auxiliaries and organizations. The church was now internationally acclaimed as a symbol of freedom in Western society and in parts of Africa and Asia; it was no longer floundering from economic hardship or agitated by controversy; in sum, the church was operating from a point of strength.[7]

Dexter Avenue was used to ministers coming and going, but for the first time, almost overnight, the church would also lose a group of active leaders and influential members. King's departure, in conjunction with these losses, indeed marked the end of an age. It is true that many congregational leaders—J. T. Alexander, Reva Allman, Elizabeth Arrington, Zelia Evans, Rufus Lewis, R. D. Nesbitt, T. H. Randall, and Thelma Austin Rice—remained. But several Dexter Avenue members lost their employment because of their participation in the civil rights movement. On February 19, 1960, an aging and distressed H. Council Trenholm, the president of Alabama State University, was called before the Alabama State Board of Education, which demanded that he give an account of the behavior and activity of faculty members and students active in the Montgomery Bus Boycott and subsequent desegregation protests. Trenholm tried to convince the board members that his major goal was "the cause of Negro education" and not civil rights protests. The board members concluded, however, that Trenholm lacked either the will or the skill to "control his students and faculty," and he was given an unsolicited and indefinite leave of absence. Shortly thereafter, he retired. Meanwhile, state officials targeted certain Alabama State faculty members by sending in daily evaluators to their classrooms for several weeks. To the board evaluators' frustration, they found no legitimate grounds on which to terminate identified faculty members' employment, but the psychological pressure of the daily evaluations and the years of struggle for civil rights soon took their toll. On the last day of the spring semester of 1960, several exhausted and harassed Alabama State professors, some of whom had taught there for over thirty years, resigned and eventually left Montgomery. Among them were Mary Fair Burks, Jo Ann Robinson, Ralph Simpson, and Robert Williams, all of whom were actively involved in the auxiliary and organizational life of Dexter Avenue. These absences were felt immediately and, not surprisingly, the Social and Political Action Committee became defunct and remained so for almost three years.[8]

How and where would members find a new pastor to maintain a dynamic church life and provide wise counsel to help Dexter Avenue balance its spiritual and evangelical mission with its social and political activities? Early in the search, members learned that none of the pastors that King suggested were available. In the interim, the search committee used guest preachers to fill the pulpit, and several months passed before there was a viable candidate for the pastorate. During this time, the organizational life of Dexter Avenue began to suffer, and the church was not able to celebrate some of its "special" days, most notably Men's Day and the spring lecture series. The church's predicament changed, however, during late spring of 1960 when Dr. Daniel W. Wynn, chaplain at the Tuskegee Institute and the acquaintance of several Dexter Avenue members, suggested that the pulpit committee consider Herbert Eaton, a young man he had met in Washington, D.C. At the time, Eaton was the assistant dean in the School of Religion at Howard University. As in the past, the pulpit committee moved with caution, but it soon came to believe that, indeed, Eaton was the new leader for whom they were searching.[9]

On August 15, 1960, the pulpit committee convened a meeting of the official board, and it approved that the name of Herbert Eaton be placed before the church. Two weeks later, Dexter Avenue members were requested to gather for their quarterly church conference. After a short devotion, T. H. Randall noted that Dexter Avenue "has been without a pastor since February and that the church is at a low ebb." Randall continued, "we now have a very strong candidate in consideration." Randall placed Eaton's name before the congregation and read from the strong letters of recommendation the pulpit committee had received on Eaton's behalf. D. G. Hill, dean of the School of Religion at Howard University and Eaton's immediate supervisor, described him as "a very earnest, dependable, industrious and studious young man."[10]

More meaningful to Dexter Avenue members was that Allan Knight, a professor of applied Christianity at Boston University and a former instructor of Martin Luther King Jr., wrote to the board, "I can not imagine a better solution to your problem of replacing Martin Luther King at Dexter Avenue than to call Herb Eaton. He is not only well trained but has a natural, fine disposition." Impressed and hopeful, members voted overwhelmingly to issue Herbert Eaton a call to the Dexter Avenue pastorate. They were delighted with Eaton's quick and affirmative response.[11]

In addition to his strong letters of support, Eaton's background made him a good match for Dexter Avenue. Herbert Hoover Eaton was born in Creedmoor, North Carolina, and received his formal education at North Carolina Central University, Howard University, and Boston University. A veteran of the Korean War, he came to the Dexter Avenue pastorate with experience in church service as an associate pastor and, in university life, having served as a chaplain and director of the Student Christian Association at Howard University. Members hoped that Eaton would bring dynamic spiritual and intellectual leadership to the church. Like King, prior to coming to Dexter Avenue, Eaton had never pastored a church, but unlike King, Eaton did not have his summer months free to plan his church program and memorize the names of his congregation. Still, he came to Dexter Avenue with a very definite vision for the kind of ministry he wanted to establish. He was interested in broadening and revising the religious education program in order to improve Sunday school instruction and to include a course of study for new church members and newly ordained deacons. Eaton also hoped to establish a closer and more effective relationship between the church and its youth.[12]

On September 19, 1960, Eaton had his first official meeting with the board as pastor; the meeting began on a positive note. Chair of the board of deacons T. H. Randall, before turning the meeting over to the pastor-elect, implored officers to give "the new pastor their full cooperation and to talk up the pastor rather than talk him down." Eaton pledged to spend time personally with each church member and to work very hard with all groups to build a better church. His first suggestion to the board won them over. He began, "I believe that it is important that the pastor and the board be on one accord as much as possible, but especially on Sunday mornings. Realistically," Eaton continued, "the nature of church work and the strong personalities often involved in leadership" made it impossible not to have disagreements from time to time, "but I believe that the pastor and the board must be of one mind during Sunday morning worship services." To facilitate harmonious relations, Eaton suggested that, beginning the very next Sunday, deacons meet in his office fifteen minutes before the start of service for prayer to lay aside whatever ill-feelings or conflicts might be present. Pastors, deacons, and the board would thus be in agreement while leading the Sunday morning worship service. Board members all endorsed this new practice; in fact, it remains a tradition at Dexter Avenue.[13]

The calm and harmony that characterized the first part of these meetings, however, soon gave way to tension and discomfort as board members and pastor tackled a sensitive issue. Herbert Eaton was the only unmarried man called to the pastorate. A few board members were anxious about Eaton "entertaining women at the parsonage." To thwart rumors, and, no doubt, avoid "reliving the Arbouin controversies," some suggested that Eaton live with a church member in a rented room or an apartment. The new pastor took a hard and firm stand; "I intend to live in the parsonage," he insisted, and asserted further, "If I am not strong enough to protect myself from a moral standpoint, then I am not fit for the ministry. I assure all that you will not hear anything about me from a moral standpoint." In the uncomfortable silence that followed he assured the board that he held "marriage in the highest regard and had no intention of living as a bachelor." All present assured him that he had their full confidence. But this was not the only issue causing tension between board members and their new pastor. Eaton himself used this opportunity to raise a second prickly issue. Well aware of the strong relationship that had existed between King and Dexter Avenue, and mindful of several church members' involvement in the civil rights movement, Eaton took this opportunity to ensure that members understood he was his own person with his own ideas about the kind of Christian ministry he would lead. He announced, "I am Herbert Hoover Eaton and will only fill the shoes of Herbert Hoover Eaton. I shall work with all community activities but my first obligation is to my church." Again, board members assured Eaton that he had been called for what he had to offer and "not for any resemblances to past ministers." Still, Eaton could not completely escape King's shadow. He eventually served on the board of the Montgomery Improvement Association and this board meeting, like so many others over the years, ended the ritual power tug-of-war between the Dexter Avenue "barons" and the incumbent minister.[14]

Indeed, members fully embraced their new pastor, but they did have to make some adjustments to Eaton's subdued style and tastes. As in the past, members planned an elaborate pastoral installation service, but Eaton gently objected, explaining, "I appreciate the thought and effort," but also that he did not personally "attach too much importance to such occasions." Eaton asked Elizabeth Arrington and T. H. Randall to cochair a committee to plan for his installation service.

Honoring the young minister's request, on November 13, 1960, Dexter Avenue held a simple pastoral installation service in which Dr. Daniel G. Hill, dean of the School of Religion at Howard University, gave the ordination sermon and the Dexter Avenue Choir, under the direction of J. T. Brooks, provided the music. As had been the tradition since the installation of Reverend Charles Arbouin in 1945, M. C. Cleveland of Day Street Baptist Church gave the formal charge to Eaton. Pastor Eaton and the Dexter Avenue congregation now had moved beyond the joyful but awkward process of forging a new working relationship together. Eaton wrote, in a personal note to members, "I wish to thank you again for the wonderful way in which you have cooperated with the program of our church since I have been with you."[15]

The first area of church life that Eaton addressed was that of religious education. He reevaluated the church's Board of Religious Education and in addition to the Sunday school and vacation Bible school added various fellowship organizations under its purview, including the youth's, men's, and women's groups and the missionary society. The new Board of Religious Education was also asked to examine the quality of literature used by the Sunday school, to clarify the responsibilities of various educational groups at the church and finally to develop new and more effective methods of religious instruction. Eaton was particularly interested in Dexter Avenue improving its "religious education in a downtown church," to provide a more effective ministry to Montgomery's African Americans living in the western part of the city, Montgomery's African American working-class neighborhood. Eaton sought the assistance of Josephine Kyles, who was director of religious education for the National Council of Churches in Washington, D.C. Kyles had, importantly, established programs that effectively addressed the needs of inner-city African Americans. Eaton arranged for her to conduct a workshop at the home of R. D. Nesbitt for the heads of various Dexter Avenue organizations. Eaton and others present agreed that Zelia Evans was the obvious choice to head the Board of Religious Education: in more than ten years as a member of Dexter Avenue, she had served in numerous leadership positions and, more important, Evans had been a teacher for more than thirty years and was now director of the Early Childhood Education Center at Alabama State University.[16]

The first task was to draft a document explaining the purposes, policies, and procedures of the board. Evans began, "No one person ... can adequately administer all features of the total desirable educational program of a modern church [nor] know the most effective methods to meet all [educational] needs." A Board of Religious Education, Evans continued, would offer a "wide representation" and provide for the kind of "exchange of ideas and experience" that would ultimately allow a greater chance for members to receive effective training in Christian education. Under Evans's leadership, the board "determined the policies and planned the total program for all educational functions of the church." Various subcommittees were formed to supervise specific projects and activities of the board. Evans's ultimate goal was to provide an effective means of training members of Dexter Avenue in spiritual, intellectual, moral, and character-building activities. The church began a tutoring program that targeted children living in the inner city. For a few years, supplemental instruction was provided for these children, none of whom belonged to Dexter Avenue, and beyond the tutoring program, there were no other gestures made toward bringing this population within Dexter Avenue's walls.[17]

Eaton combined his goals for education with his desire to revise the administration of the church. He believed training and education were key elements in helping church members make an effective commitment to Christianity. He set up a rigorous program of training for new deacons and for new church members. Like Frank Jacobs, who led Dexter Avenue during the 1920s, Eaton wanted to ensure deacons understood the gravity of their position and that they should be thoroughly schooled in Baptist doctrine, polity, and practices; as a result, prospective deacons attended class once a week for almost eighteen months. Using two texts—William McNutt's *Polity and Practice in Baptist Churches*, and Robert G. Torbet's *A History of the Baptist Practice in Baptist Churches*—and a series of more than thirty lectures, Eaton required those studying for ordination for the deaconate to complete his course, The Baptist Deacon. Here we see again a shoring up of one of the founding principles of the Dexter Avenue ministry, the same emphasis on education as crucial to a mature and effective Christian faith.[18]

The first group of deacons trained by Eaton included Severne Frazier, Robert Jones, Jerome Morris, Amos Person, Lucius Smiley, and Robert Williams. Just prior to their ordination ceremony, Eaton charged the new deacons as follows: (1) that fighting with the preacher should be avoided, and yet that they owed the pastor no special loyalty but must always vote their conscience in church matters; (2) that accepting the designation of deacon was a lifetime commitment, and that their ministry was an extension of the pastor's ministry; therefore, they must never say no to the interests of the church; (3) that seeking to be ambassadors of goodwill meant avoiding any activity that might bring shame on the church. Particularly pleased that his new deacons were thoroughly schooled in Baptist doctrine and polity, Eaton reminded them that they had the power to build the church up or to tear it down.[19]

As he had been formally trained in pastoral counseling at Philadelphia State Hospital, above and beyond all other goals Eaton worked to establish a close personal relationship between himself and all of the members of Dexter Avenue. He set up a system of pastoral visitations to get to know all members personally at times when there was no crisis or special event. Beginning with members who were sick and homebound, Eaton arranged to have dinner and spend a portion of an evening with each church family. Additionally, he reached out to the Dexter Avenue youth who were away at college. He penned a personal letter to college students, and wrote a letter as well to their chaplains, asking them to help look out for students' spiritual well-being. In so doing Eaton was able to provide emotional and spiritual support for Dexter Avenue members during their college years while strengthening the bond between the church and its young people.[20]

A few years into his ministry Eaton preached to the congregation, "Let us dare to believe that through our united constructive effort in the rebuilding of Dexter, God will do miraculous things for us—bring us together, restoring our hope, reviewing our spirits, reviving us in ways that we may not now be aware of. In addition we will have the joy of knowing that we are workers together with God...." Eaton's ministry promoted togetherness among the congregation by continuing to celebrate monthly club fellowship dinners. Moreover, continuing to celebrate the "special" days gave chuch's members an opportunity to work together. As in the past, Dexter Avenue brought in notable members of the African American community to serve as guest speakers for these occasions. Among them were Samuel Gandy, who at the time he spoke in 1961 was Dean of Dillard University in New Orleans; former pastor Martin Luther King Jr.; Wyatt Tee Walker, who was working with King in the Southern Christian Leadership Conference; and James DeOtis Roberts, a professor of religion at Howard University.[21]

Eaton also worked to improve financial conditions at the church. He believed that members would be motivated to give more if they could be convinced to invest in long-term planning. He asked Thelma Austin Rice, to chair a committee of Christian stewardship whose goal was "to inform the church as to the full meaning of Christian Stewardship, and to seek ways of developing more tithers." To introduce the program, Rice edited a newsletter that included a pastoral message: "Every man according as he purposeth in his heart, so let him give; not grudgingly, or of necessity; for God loveth a cheerful giver." With other committee members, Eaton and Rice created the Finance Forward Program in which they projected the needs of the church into the immediate future and then asked members to give according to their abilities. For two years, Rice and the stewardship Committee members studied and analyzed the giving habits of church members; Rice also designed a lesson on stewardship to be taught in all Sunday school classes. Although these financial drives fell just short of the goal of having all members tithe 10 percent of their incomes, sufficient money was raised to keep the church solvent. The experience gave the congregation its first real experience in long-range financial planning. Having a stewardship program in place was particularly helpful a few years later, when members began planning for Dexter Avenue's centennial celebration.[22]

Eaton's primary goal was to leave Dexter Avenue Baptist Church more united and working more smoothly than when he arrived. More important was the fact that aside from all of the programs, organizations, and celebrations, the church had been stable for almost ten years. Now it needed to do everything possible to maintain a comparable level of soundness. This led pastor and members to ask an important question: Recognizing the inevitability of change, how could the congregation maintain an effective and growing ministry, even in those inevitable times when it would be without pastoral leadership? Eaton concluded that church members should write a new constitution outlining the various processes and operating procedures. In the previous thirty years there had been attempts to write a new constitution, but each time attention was soon diverted by more urgent needs. To begin the process Eaton approached the church leadership, which endorsed the idea of the church drawing up an official constitution. On February 3, 1964, in a specially called church meeting, the pastor and official board presented the idea to the membership and created a committee of seven to complete the task. In less than a year, the committee completed a draft of what eventually became the official church constitution. In its preamble, the Dexter Avenue Constitution states the common theological beliefs that bind together the Dexter Avenue community: "We the members of the Dexter Avenue Baptist Church, affirm our belief in the faith of the Baptist Church. We recognize that our Church is a body of baptized believers in Christ, Our Lord and Savior. We further recognize that the steps of repentance, confession, and surrender lead to church membership and a Christian life." The new church covenant included the criteria for membership in the church and in its many organizations and auxiliaries. Equally important, it defined the responsibilities of the pastor, deacons, and all church offices. The constitution clarified and explained procedures, hoping to prevent confusion and misunderstanding in the absence of a pastor.[23]

The church constitution, formally adopted by a standing vote on December 20, 1964, was the last project Eaton directed as pastor of Dexter Avenue. On November 15, 1964, he asked the membership to remain for a brief meeting after the morning service. He informed them that he had received a call from Kenwood United Church of Christ in Chicago, and that he believed it "offered a wider growth for him." As well, Eaton explained to members that he "felt a need for more challenge to reach his potential as a religious leader." With regrets, the membership accepted Eaton's resignation.[24]

On January 10, 1965, Eaton preached his farewell sermon at Dexter Avenue. He explained to members that he was pleased with his work at Dexter Avenue and was grateful for the marvelous working relationship that had developed with the congregation, but that it was time to move on. Eaton told the Dexter Avenue audience, "I have fought the good fight, I have finished my course, I have kept the faith…." He continued, "No church fights in the literal sense. No ill will was generated … rather, creative struggles or encounters which have been a healthy and necessary part of our growth as a church." Imparting a simple blessing, "the Father of us all continue to bless and keep you as we continue to do his work in the area of our calling," on January 10, Eaton officially left the pastorate of Dexter Avenue Baptist Church.[25]

Dexter Avenue was indeed running more smoothly than when Eaton had arrived. He had effectively filled the church's need for guidance and direction, and, true to his word, he had emphasized life within Dexter Avenue's walls. Under his watch the church had revitalized its board of religious education, developed new training programs for members and deacons, and written a new constitution. The church continued modest outreach to the local community, largely through benevolence and tutoring programs for local youth. Eaton set up a ministry that addressed several components of church life, from administration and education to finance and close personal ties between pastor and congregation. Furthermore, at the end of Eaton's tenure as pastor, members had come to believe that the church was moving in the right direction, providing an effective ministry for its members and the local community.

Shortly after the announcement of Eaton's resignation, the official board met to complete two tasks: first, to discuss the failing health of chair of the board of deacons and Dexter "baron" T. H. Randall, who had become gravely ill in recent months; and second, to appoint a new pulpit committee. Board members acknowledged the "excellent leadership [Randall] had provided for more than thirty years"; they were hopeful that he might be able to return to his post at a later date. Soon, however, they were informed that the outlook for Randall's health was extremely grave and that they should proceed in electing a new chairman of the board of deacons. In the first order of business deacons elected a more subdued, less contentious member, W. J. Wood, to succeed Randall. Next, board members appointed J. T. Alexander to chair a pulpit committee consisting of Elizabeth Arrington, R. D. Nesbitt, F. W. Taylor, and W. J. Wood, and once again the search for new pastoral leadership began. The constitution, though not officially ratified, did help to keep church affairs running along smoothly after Eaton left. Deacons facilitated the training and education of new members; Deacons J. T. Alexander and Robert F. Jones taught a course "instructing new members in what it means to be a Baptist" for the ten members Eaton had baptized in his last official act as pastor.[26]

Members of the pulpit committee, busy searching for a new pastor, combined new and traditional search methods. To expedite the current inquiry and narrow the pool, the pulpit committee created and sent out to potential candidates a ministerial appraisal form. This nineteen-question form addressed several areas: a few of the questions concerned the minister's approach to preaching, such as whether he used notes in delivering a sermon; other questions focused on the minister's administrative talents—his planning and organizational skills and his fundraising abilities. One question illustrative of how much Dexter Avenue had been changed by the pastorates of Vernon Johns, Martin Luther King Jr., and members active in the civil rights movement asked candidates to address their ability to "apply the gospel to social, economic and industrial problems." The form was designed to expedite the process of looking for a minister, but more important, it represented a more professional approach in seeking pastoral leadership. It suggested that church leaders now had a more precise idea of the kind of leadership they were seeking in a pastor. Still, the search committee did not abandon its traditional method of seeking out possible candidates—word of mouth. In the January 1965, members of the pulpit committee wrote a letter to Morehouse College president Benjamin Mays, seeking his suggestion to replace Eaton. Mays gave the pulpit committee the name of G. Murray Branch, who at the time was a professor at the Interdenominational Theological Center (ITC) in Atlanta.

Members invited Branch to fill the pulpit as a guest speaker on the first Sunday of March 1965. Contacting people like Mays or Samuel

Gandy at Howard University was motivated by the practical need to find a new pastor, but we must also understand such outreach as a means to maintain contact with larger African American middle-class circles and to keep the Dexter Avenue pastorate among the more highly sought-after positions.[27]

Branch spoke the same Sunday that a Selma-to-Montgomery march was to begin. The march, regarded by some historians as the last civil-rights-movement effort before the movement split into competing and often warring factions, was a campaign to secure voting rights for blacks living in Selma, one of Alabama's reputedly most racists towns. Like so many other efforts, the march evoked violent and deadly resistance, but refusing to be deterred, marchers walked on. As a means of maintaining some involvement in the civil rights movement, church members permitted Dexter Avenue to be used by former pastor Martin Luther King Jr. and other marchers as a kind of penultimate space for rest and refreshment before concluding the march on the steps of the Alabama state capitol building.[28]

Meanwhile, members of the pulpit committee continued working to find a new pastor. They noted that Branch had given "a fine talk as guest preacher ... and rated higher than other prospects on the ministerial appraisal form." As usual, the committee took several months to investigate its new prospect, but by November, committee members were ready to recommend that Dexter Avenue extend a call to Branch. When approached, Branch explained to J. T. Alexander that, while he was interested in the pastorate, he wanted to be able to continue to teach part time at the ITC.[29]

The idea that a Dexter Avenue pastor would have a part-time teaching commitment was new for members, and it met with strong opposition from a vocal minority. While it was common for a Dexter Avenue pastor to occasionally teach a night course at Selma University, no other pastor had regular outside employment. For his part, Branch was willing to commute weekly; he would spend Thursday evening through Monday night in Montgomery, and return to Atlanta early Tuesday morning to teach at the ITC and remain there through Thursday afternoon. Branch also explained that he would not be able to assume full responsibilities of the pastorate until the close of the ITC school year in the spring of 1966.[30] Some board members remained concerned over such arrangements, but all voted to move ahead.

Following the morning service on November 29, 1965, when Branch's name was placed before the church for approval, one member of the board stated that he simply did not believe that Branch "had the church's interest at heart ... that his loyalty would always be divided."

J. T. Alexander tried to calm the opposition by explaining that Branch had agreed to put Dexter Avenue first in the case of competing needs, and Alexander also reminded members of how favorably many of them had spoken to him regarding Branch's deportment and preaching style. In the spirit of compromise, one Dexter member suggested that they postpone voting for Branch for a few weeks until the church had celebrated its anniversary. Alexander persisted; he reminded members that Dexter Avenue had been without a pastor for a year, and that a delay in action might result in losing a good man. Persuaded by Alexander's appeal, members voted seventy-six to five in favor of Branch becoming their next pastor. The very next day chair of the board of deacons W. J. Wood informed Branch that Dexter Avenue had voted to extend a call to the pastorate. Branch responded, "It is an honor to be called to any church, but especially to a church with Dexter's rich history and present high potential." Even after Branch had been contacted, a few board members and some congregants argued that they had been pressured into voting before they were ready. So that Branch could feel he was not "invited to Dexter through the back door" they suggested that another vote be taken. Confident of the result, on January 9, 1966, Alexander again asked members to remain. Another vote was taken, eighty-four to six to call Branch.[31]

Murray Branch's approach to Christianity was both intellectual and spiritual. His overarching focus would be to push members to celebrate their past but to keep their eyes focused forward on the work still to be done. The ministry he established at Dexter Avenue was influenced by his background and educational experiences. Born in Prince Edward County, Virginia, in 1914, Branch—like several other Dexter Avenue pastors—received his undergraduate degree from Virginia Union University. He received his divinity degree from Andover Newton Theological Seminary, a master of arts degree in Old Testament studies from Drew University, and then won a Ford Foundation Fellowship for one year's study at Hebrew Union College Rabbinical School in Cincinnati. Beyond his educational training and experience Branch was also influenced by the job he held as field secretary for the student division of the Southern division of the Young Men's Christian Association (YMCA), and thus was particularly interested in the relationship between the church and youth. Unlike King or Eaton, Branch came to Dexter Avenue having led large churches: the Peoples' Baptist Church in Portsmouth, New Hampshire, and First Baptist Church in Madison, New Jersey. These experiences caused Branch to create a ministry at Dexter Avenue that emphasized adult Bible study (especially among older adults who had stopped coming to Sunday school), more initiative from congregants in crafting a vision for the church, and an increased voice and participation of youth in the church's decisions.

On February 7, 1966, Branch and the official board met for the first time. After the traditional prayer and song, the meeting was turned over to the new pastor-elect. Branch explained his leadership style and shared with members what he considered to be the most important component of church life. "I like a democratic approach to leadership, and I don't like to make any decision without input from the deacons and whatever specific church organization that might be affected by my decision," Branch began. He told deacons that he had come to Dexter Avenue with no overall program for the church because he believed that "the beginning of any program is with the deacons first" and that moreover "an overall program belongs to the church and must come from the will and initiative of the church leadership." Not yet familiar with all of the organizations and boards of the church, Branch suggested that all leadership should remain unchanged, at least for a time. Members of the official board expressed their approval of Branch's approach to the pastorate and told him that "he could expect the full support" of church members. Branch responded that he was "very pleased with the church and felt that if we all worked together things would happen at Dexter." Here it is important to understand that Branch could be more casual and open with the deacons and members of the board because of his age and experience, a luxury that both King and Eaton had lacked; as well, Vernon Johns by nature and temperament had not been willing to be so "democratic" in his approach.[32]

Although the new pastor had no overall program for Dexter Avenue, he had definite ideas for changes. Building on Eaton's work, he told members that "in order to lead a successful church program, the leadership must know the Bible both in their minds and in their hearts and have achieved a level of spiritual growth to enable them to provide effective direction and inspired guidance for the church." He reminded members that "studying the Bible must be a lifelong pursuit, and the higher church position one held, the more extensive his or her study and training of Biblical scripture should be." Branch appealed to adult church members to improve their Sunday school attendance. He encouraged all church members to study diligently by continuing the deacon and new-member training courses that Eaton had developed. He added, however, a new course in the Old Testament to the curriculum and requested that the Board of Religious Education conduct leadership workshops and, as soon as possible, start a church library.[33]

Initially, the changes that Branch had in mind for Dexter Avenue, like those of Herbert Eaton, focused largely on internal issues. Branch noted that the church's constitution had helped the congregation continue along smoothly in the absence of a pastor. He was particularly impressed with the strong Board of Religious Education, which had kept most of the church auxiliary life active. He noted as well that the stewardship committee had done a fine job of encouraging members to tithe. Yet Branch wanted to refine the constitution, more in line with his idea that the church—especially a Baptist church—should be a democratic institution, and suggested two amendments. First, he believed that "the enemy of any democracy is allowing power to concentrate in the hands of one or two people." To guard against any individual of the church garnering excessive power, Branch suggested that the church constitution limit the number of years the chairman of the deacons could serve to three consecutive years. Chair of the board of deacons Wood had shared with Branch the difficult time getting the deacons who had been under T. H. Randall for so long to embrace a new leader. Second, perhaps as a result of his many years of experience with the YMCA, Branch believed that the voices and opinions of young people needed to be heard in the church. Accordingly, he requested that church leaders rethink their requirement that church members must be the age of twenty-one before they would be able to vote on church issues. While Dexter Avenue members amended the constitution to limit the term of the deacon chair, they remained unwilling to change the age requirement for voting.[34]

Another area of church life that Branch tried to reform was members' relationships to one another. At one of his first church meetings, Branch queried, "Do you take the church covenant seriously?" Were church members willing to abide by a pledge to "walk together in Christian love ... and to exhort and stir up each other unto every good word and work; to guard each other's reputation?" No specific act at the church had prompted Branch's questions, but this move was not new: Johns, one Sunday after services, had challenged members to call each other's names; King had developed monthly dinner meetings of those with birthdays in the same month; Eaton had visited members and encouraged them to visit one another. Still, Branch's angle was slightly different. He wanted to foster intergenerational relationships, believing it was a good way for young people to learn about how leadership functions in the church. He also wanted older church members to be personally invested in the young and "understand that they still had much to learn from the young." Branch established a yearly dinner to honor graduates at all levels of educational achievement (high school, college, and graduate school) along with members who were retiring. He believed that both recent graduates and retirees could have an interesting dialogue with one another. And so each year the church brought together the different generations of members for a common fellowship. These occasions combined the giving of scholarships to help with future goals and the giving of certificates to recognize years of service to the church and community.[35]

Later, at a meeting of the official board, Branch reminded deacons that many years prior, the church membership had been divided into districts and each church deacon personally oversaw the spiritual welfare of persons living in his assigned district. Branch requested that each deacon personally contact members in his district to encourage them to attend church and special-occasion programs. Personal contact, Branch assured his deacons, would make all the difference. Finally, he suggested that church members offer the use of the church station wagon to pick up members who had problems with transportation to services. One board member's suggestion that they explore Branch's suggestion in greater detail later ended the meeting.[36]

Branch's efforts to nourish a close relationship among Dexter Avenue members did not end with the current members of the church but sought to include former members as well. During Branch's pastorate, the church made a special effort to bring in former Dexter Avenue members as guest speakers for the special-occasion days. Branch had members list the names of all of the former Dexter Avenue members they could remember, including students at Alabama State University who attended Dexter Avenue regularly during their college years. These people received personal invitations to Men's, Women's, and Youth Day ceremonies and especially church anniversary celebrations. Adding his personal touch to help unite Dexter Avenue members past and present, Branch reinstated the practice of sending an annual Christmas letter; this had not been done at Dexter Avenue since the pastorate of Ralph Riley in the early 1940s. In the letter, Branch briefly reviewed the church year, noting particularly those who had died in the past year, and those who had married or become parents. In this missive, Branch admonished members that "the year is now ending.... What has been done has been done.... The future is before us, and only those opportunities we appropriate with gratitude and expectation can cultivate us and discipline us to make us grow." This letter and the many other activities were part of Branch's program to nurture close personal relationships at Dexter Avenue and encourage members to live within their covenant to one another.[37]

Between 1966 and 1972, the church's celebrations of special occasions proceeded as they had in the past. The church continued to bring in speakers for the Men's and Women's Day celebrations. Youth

Day celebrations became more entertaining and instructive. Church youth brought in well-known speakers, like attorney Maynard Jackson, who gave a speech at Dexter Avenue in 1969, "Youth Involvement: A Must for Today's Church." He challenged Dexter Avenue youth "to love and to 'fight the good fight' through an examined life." In addition to a morning speaker, church youth sponsored afternoon activities such as dialogues and debates on current topics; examples include, "Should Church Youth Be Seen and Not Heard?" "Bridging the Generation Gap through Religion," "Understand Me—Walk a Mile in My Shoes," and "We've Only Just Begun." These topics portrayed Dexter Avenue youth struggling to apply the Christianity of their elders to the current issues they were facing.[38]

While the leadership and direction provided by Branch focused much of Dexter Avenue's attention on affairs within the church, members still struggled to find the right balance between its spiritual mission and its social and political activism. This tension surfaced at a church conference members had to discuss the spring lecture series and annual revival. In early 1968, Branch queried church members about their poor attendance at the previous year's spring lecture series and revivals. Initially, members were silent. Branch then asked if the spring calendar was too full. If so, he suggested that rather than having both a spring lecture series and spring revival each year, the church could hold the series and revivals on alternate years. Branch noted that membership and church attendance were also beginning to lag, and wanted members to consider what kinds of things could be done to improve this situation.[39]

Soon it became evident that the diminished attendance at special services and regular church services was about more than busy schedules. Rather, some members felt that Dexter Avenue was "losing its enthusiasm" for social activism. They noted particular problems attracting and keeping young people. The lecture series, contended one church member, should always deal with socially relevant subjects and "must be aimed at school age and college students." Another church member countered, however, that the lecture series "should be conducted for all members of Dexter." Dexter Avenue trustee Levi Watkins asserted that congregants were missing the real issue in the life of the church. Watkins explained that he was proud of Dexter Avenue's role in social protest, but that the church had been involved in social action to the point that it was now detrimental to the spiritual and evangelistic roles of the church. "We need," declared Watkins, "an old-fashioned revival as a means of adding new members and reaffirming Dexter Avenue's influence through the ministry of Evangelism." Branch was sympathetic to Watkins's concerns, but explained to the church that both the revival and lecture series were important and had their place in an active church. Branch challenged the board of deacons to plan a revival for the fall that could achieve both goals, but the church conference ended with no tangible resolutions to the conflict.[40]

At the same time that some voices were strongly advocating that the church needed to expend more energy addressing its evangelical mission, an unforeseen event diverted church members' attention toward a new mission. On Thursday evening, April 4, 1968, in Memphis, Tennessee, the Reverend Dr. Martin Luther King Jr. was assassinated. Only thirty-nine years old, King had given direction and leadership to one of the largest and sociohumanitarian movements in the history of America. Also significant, as its pastor, King had helped to transform Dexter Avenue Baptist Church into a more active congregation. Members of Dexter Avenue were stunned, hurt, and frightened. Upon hearing the news some members gathered to pray and comfort one another.[41]

On Saturday, April 6, the members of Dexter Avenue along with many others in the Montgomery community held a memorial service at noon in the sanctuary. Reverend Branch officiated, and Thelma Austin Rice wrote one of the official Resolutions from Dexter Avenue:

> Whereas, we share with the rest of the world the tragedy of the removal from our midst, in a physical sense our beloved twentieth pastor, DOCTOR MARTIN LUTHER KING, JR—the foremost champion of non-violence in the twentieth century as the most powerful positive approach to the problems of all men regardless of race, color or creed,
>
> Be it resolved that the tragedy of his death at the hands of an assassin in Memphis, Tennessee on April 4, 1968 will not deter us for one moment from our goal to make America truly "the land of the free and the home of the brave" as we embrace more firmly the tenets of non-violence in our efforts; to the end that we shall remove from America its sickness of racism, poverty and other conditions which make for demeaning discrimination among God's greatest creation —MAN.
>
> We extend to his family that which gives us here at Dexter some comfort. Inasmuch as Doctor King was truly an instrument of God's will, his body is dead, but the God he served still lives. Therefore, Doctor King lives. The work he carried forward will live as God lives and the cause will go on. "The Lord gave and the Lord hath taken away; blessed be the name of the Lord."[42]

Among the many ways that the church sought to honor King's life, members resolved to "embrace more firmly the tenets of non-violence in our efforts; to the end that we shall remove from America its sickness of racism and other conditions which make for demeaning discrimination among God's greatest creation—MAN."

King's death profoundly affected the members of Dexter Avenue Baptist Church, and at a very pivotal time in its history. On April 29, 1968, the official board met formally to discuss a matter members had been discussing among themselves privately ever since they learned of King's demise: what could the church do to honor King's life and contribution? Board members suggested and church members later agreed to make the church a "national shrine" to King's civil rights activity. Though they did not realize it at the time, this decision forever altered the direction of the church. On the one hand, it led to opportunities that members heretofore had not envisioned. Conversely, it placed a burden and responsibility on this religious organization that members found rather difficult to fulfill. The changes that the memorial brought to the church came slowly over a period of the next few years.[43]

Immediately following their decision, members of Dexter Avenue simply continued about the usual work of the church; the profundity of their recent decision was initially obscured by the urgency of day-to-day and week-to-week church activities and responsibilities. Rather than discussing exactly how and when the church should honor its slain former pastor, the board moved on to discuss the problem the church was having with deacons missing church on the Sundays for which they were assigned to serve communion. Branch suggested devising a schedule well in advance that included substitutes in the event of absences. Next, members postponed taking any action on a report that there was discontentment among choir members that needed investigation; board members closed the meeting with prayer.[44]

As the 1970s progressed, Dexter Avenue, prompted by Branch, began planning for the church's centennial celebration, which would come in 1977. In the course of making these arrangements they also began formally to incorporate into the church's mission the notion of memorializing the church in King's honor. But changes had already begun to take place in outsiders' perceptions of Dexter Avenue before the church did anything formally to identify itself as a memorial. Members noticed that more and more tourists coming to Montgomery were stopping in to visit "Dr. King's church." Members placed a guest book in the church basement for visitors to sign, and also they voted to create and sell souvenirs.[45]

It had been Murray Branch's intention to remain pastor of Dexter Avenue at least until they celebrated their centennial. For six years, he had commuted weekly between Dexter Avenue in Montgomery and the ITC in Atlanta. By the spring of 1972, the strain become too much for the fifty-eight-year-old pastor. But more important, he lacked the time to do many of the things he had planned. Above all else, he became frustrated that church membership continued to decline and that board members' interest was tepid at best. He came to believe that congregants, especially some deacons, were adopting an attitude that belonging to Dexter Avenue was "more of an honor than it was a responsibility to work." To be sure, there was still a small nucleus of church people working very hard, but Branch believed that more members should be actively involved at the church. Frustration gave way to resolution when on June 2, 1972, Branch submitted his resignation.

When Branch came to Dexter Avenue, the church was running smoothly. He had hoped to refine many of the programs earlier ministers, especially King and Eaton, had established. He emphasized rigorous study and training as part of church members' responsibility to themselves as well as to the church. During Branch's tenure as pastor, the church's board of religious education effectively oversaw a variety of training and instructive church programs and organizations. Moreover, he pushed for members to go beyond current programs, to take initiative in creating a more dynamic church life. He failed in this particular area. In his final message to Dexter Avenue, Branch told the church members that he hoped they realized "Dexter Avenue was at a pivotal point in its history as it continued to search for balance and excellence in its ministry." His valediction, "Christ's Mission and Ours," told members to "look again, at Christ's mission and His ministry to come to a deeper clarity of what your mission ought to be." Ever the teacher, Branch left members five directives for defining their Christian duty; they should (1) create a community in which to invite others to share; (2) consistently propagate the legacy of the church fathers through acts of appreciation and appropriation of the heritage received to those who would come later; (3) provide a community place of instruction and nurture; (4) participate in and understand the importance of private meditation (prayer); and (5) remember that life's movement is a journey under God, a pilgrimage of faith. Branch told the Dexter Avenue audience that the best advice he could give to them would be "to look repeatedly at the methods and manner of the works of Christ." This sermon officially ended Branch's pastorate at Dexter Avenue. Despite his decision to leave, he maintained an amicable relationship with the church and he returned in October to participate in the ordination service of a group of deacons he had trained.[46]

After a year of guest preachers and searching for new pastoral leadership, members called Reverend Robert Dickerson Jr. Born in Pine Bluff, Arkansas, Dickerson was a graduate of the University of Arkansas and later received a master of divinity degree from the Southwestern Baptist Theological Seminary in Fort Worth, Texas. The son of a Baptist minister, Dickerson had not formerly pastored at a church, but had grown up in the Baptist faith and had been a national president of the Baptist Training Union (BTU) and had served as director of the Mobile, Alabama, Baptist Fellowship.

Like Martin Luther King Jr., Dickerson officially became the pastor of Dexter Avenue Baptist Church at an installation service preached by his father, Robert Dickerson Sr., on October 28, 1973. Similar to King, as well, Dickerson developed a set of recommendations that served as a kind of manifesto for his ministry, which endeavored to revitalize and coordinate church leadership and to improve the youth ministry. More important, during Dickerson's pastorate, Dexter Avenue proceeded in planning its centennial celebration.[47]

The first area of the church that received attention during the Dickerson pastorate was church organization and leadership. Dickerson encountered some of the same frustrations Branch had experienced—namely, having only a small nucleus of faithful workers doing much of the work of the church. His solution was to develop a leadership nominating council. Under the direction of Virginia Gary, the council was to find congregants with leadership potential and train them in the duties of leadership at Dexter Avenue. Gary organized a series of workshops not only to train potential leaders but also to improve the skills of those already vested with authority. As the church moved closer to its centennial celebration, the issue of dependable and capable leadership became more and more important.[48]

Dickerson also hoped to improve attendance at regular church services and, particularly, special church events. The problem, as he saw it, was one of planning ahead. In the 1970s, as in its earlier history, Dexter Avenue was a church of much activity, albeit the attendance at many events was sparse. A month of programming at the church involved —in addition to the two services each Sunday and a midweek prayer service—meetings of the monthly clubs, the Missionary Society, the BTU, the ushers, the trustees, the deacons, the choir, and family fellowship dinners. Then, there were seasonal meetings, like the spring lecture series, annual revivals, Youth Day, Women's Day, and Men's Day.

Dickerson appointed a committee to "co-ordinate, attract, and give leadership" to Dexter Avenue members by planning a calendar for the year. Through this the members would have the opportunity to do long-range planning, and to make firmer commitments to attend both regular church and special-event occasions.

Dickerson also hoped to make the Sunday morning church services more meaningful for young people, so he instituted a youth sermon. At the beginning of the sermon, he invited church youth to come to the front for a special ten-minute talk geared toward the issues, concerns, and struggles of young Christians. To provide young people with more opportunities to participate in church services, the board voted to allow the youth choir to sing on the second and fourth Sundays for the morning service. Perhaps more noteworthy, the youth choir often sang gospel music, and for the sacred offertory music on youth Sundays, church youth were permitted to play different musical instruments—other than the traditional organ and piano. Committed to regularly training church youth in the rituals of Baptist worship, Dickerson designated that each second Sunday shall be Youth Sunday, "meaning our Youth will be in charge of all services and functions of the Church, Sunday School, ushers, announcements, training union, Night services." These new ministries signaled a change at the church. In some ways the Dexter Avenue congregation and leadership had developed different, perhaps less rigid, attitudes than those it possessed during the Johns pastorate in the 1950s. Its problems and its struggles to remain an effective religious agent in the Montgomery community, nonetheless, persisted.[49]

The area of greatest activity during Dickerson's pastorate was the planning and execution of Dexter Avenue's centennial celebration. In the preparation for and celebrating of this occasion, members of the church began to experience the privileges and responsibilities of their decision to become a memorial to the late Dr. King. As early as 1971, a centennial committee chaired by deacon Robert F. Jones and consisting of Jerome Morris, Emmerette Austin, Desserene Holloway, Reva Allman, Addre Bryant, William Gary, Lurana Kelly, Katherine Maddox, R. D. Nesbitt, Bertha Williams, and G. Murray Branch had begun making plans. Committee members suggested that the official centennial celebration take place on December 11, 1977, and that Zelia Evans and J. T. Alexander research and write the church's history. Members also decided to seek pledges from current and former members to pay for all of the activities. Almost immediately, committee chair Jones was able to secure pledges totalling thirty thousand dollars.[50]

Furthermore, as part of its centennial celebration, church members voted to pursue having Dexter Avenue Baptist Church declared a national historic monument. In their application to the U.S. Department of the Interior's National Park Service, members requested that the church be designated a historical site for two reasons. First, the building itself was an architectural monument to the European eclecticism that characterized public buildings in Alabama in the nineteenth century. Supporting Dexter Avenue's contention, Warner Floyd, executive director of the Alabama Historical Commission, stated that "Dexter Avenue Baptist Church was an excellent architectural landmark as well as historical site." Second, and perhaps more significant, members explained, "It has often been said that Dr. King's success as a black leader in the South was the result of his ability to fuse mass movements and direct confrontation … the link which had sustained the black man since slavery—the black church. Dexter Avenue is one such link." Within two months, the Department of the Interior officially designated Dexter Avenue Baptist Church a national historic landmark. Although designation was granted immediately, perhaps to make the centennial celebration even more special, the official presentation was scheduled as part of the centennial afternoon's activities.[51]

While the regular order of church services and activities continued, the celebration of the church's centennial had now begun in earnest. For the five years leading up to the culminating celebration in 1977, church members invited prominent persons from the African American community to speak at its church anniversary each December. For example, then U.S. congressman Andrew Young spoke at the church anniversary in 1975. In his message "Confluence of God, Past, Present, Future" Young told those gathered that "as a continual people of God, having come to this point in history by faith and the grace of God that they should take possession of the land." Young suggested that Dexter Avenue members and other concerned Americans must do their part to ensure justice in the world. He asserted that a nation with America's resources should be able to provide a quality education for all. "In taking possession of the land," Young concluded, "we must redeem it for the purpose of fulfilling the American Dream of putting America's Rights before America's might, thus securing jobs, health, housing and education for all." Young's message, like much of the history of Dexter Avenue, sought to apply Christian principles to the idea of seeking justice and equality in America.[52]

Just a few months before the actual centennial celebration, when it seemed that all was in order, Dexter Avenue faced a crisis. Pastor Robert Dickerson accepted a call to Barogue Street Baptist Church in

Pine Bluff, Arkansas. He told members that taking the Barogue Street pastorate would allow him to teach philosophy at the University of Arkansas, which he found very appealing. In June 1977 he resigned, leaving Dexter Avenue without a pastor. Understandably shaken, deacon Robert Jones, chairman of the Centennial Project approached Murray Branch and requested that he serve as interim pastor from June through the anniversary celebration in December. Branch agreed to serve as interim pastor for the balance of the year, and once again all was in order for the big celebration.[53]

December 11, 1977 arrived amid great excitement and anticipation. The centennial committee designed an elaborate celebration. On their special day, Dexter Avenue members received messages wishing the church well from a number of prominent public officials including Joe Reed, chairman of the Alabama Democratic Black Caucus; Emory Folmar, Montgomery mayor; Governor George C. Wallace; and, finally, President Jimmy Carter. The large audience began the morning service by singing "The Church's One Foundation," followed by "God of Our Fathers." The centennial committee selected members from various organizations at Dexter Avenue to participate in the program: Desserene Holloway, a BTU officer, led the responsive reading; Deacon Severne Frazier led church members in prayer; Virginia Gary read the official centennial statement; and as he had been doing for more than thirty years, R. D. Nesbitt read the church announcements. Deacon F. W. Taylor introduced the speaker for the eleven o'clock service: eighty-three-year-old Benjamin Elijah Mays, president emeritus of Morehouse College. In many ways, Mays was an appropriate choice. Described by historian Lerone Bennett Jr. as "the last of the great school masters and the embodiment of a great part of black history," Mays had presided over Morehouse during Martin Luther King Jr.'s student days, and a large number of church members had graduated from Morehouse during Mays's tenure. Mays spoke on the theme selected by the centennial committee, "Retrospection, Introspection, Prospection." The idea was to look back, examine the present, and plan for the future. Members closed the morning service singing the hymn "Forward through the Ages."[54]

Convening in the auditorium at Carver High School for the afternoon service helped to create more of a patriotic than religious tone for the second part of the centennial celebration. The Dexter Avenue choir led the patriotic songs, opening with "My Country 'Tis of Thee." Then the church youth choir performed gospel selections. There was no sermon at this service; rather, members invited Benjamin Brown, deputy vice chair of the National Democratic Committee, to speak. The highlight of this ceremony was the presentation by the National Park Service, in which deputy director of national parks Ira J. Hutchison formally presented Deacon Robert F. Jones with a bronze plaque and a certificate designating Dexter Avenue Baptist Church a national historic landmark. Following musical selections by the church choir and remarks by interim pastor Reverend Branch, the ceremony closed. This celebration, having taken years of planning on the parts of dedicated members, was a grand occasion in the life of Dexter Avenue Baptist Church. It seemed appropriate that the church would have both a spiritual celebration and a patriotic ceremony to recognize this milestone in its existence. After all, it had served as a spiritual haven and political free space to fight for the cause of justice and equality. Moreover, it had promulgated a faith in the "American dream" and a belief in the morality of democratic institutions.[55]

A year later, members of Dexter Avenue undertook two large projects: a renovation and a name change. The church's status as an official historic site rendered it eligible for funding from both the city of Montgomery and the federal government. To further authenticate its significance as a historical site, the congregation decided that the church should be renovated as closely as possible to resemble its original 1885 appearance. Although the primary structural change involved restoring the front steps to their original style, the ninety-two-year-old edifice was in need of repairs that totaled more that $350,000. The church received $100,000 from the City of Montgomery and the Alabama Historical Commission, with the balance coming from federal funds and some individual donations.[56]

More important than the renovation work, the members of Dexter Avenue Baptist Church voted officially to change the name of the church to Dexter Avenue King Memorial Baptist Church. In October 1978, members of Dexter Avenue and the Montgomery community gathered for a special ceremony. Appropriately, members invited Coretta Scott King to speak on this occasion. Having continued to maintain close relations with some of the members of the church since leaving Montgomery, Coretta King felt at home. She began by telling the Dexter Avenue audience, "I have a tendency to want to reminisce because of the five and one half years Martin and I were here." She thanked Dexter Avenue members for standing by her and her husband during dangerous and trying times, and she recalled with gratitude the courageous acts of several members, some of whom were no longer at the church but had returned for the ceremony. "A man and a movement in history converged as a long walk to freedom was begun," she told the audience. "My husband," she continued, "was able to translate God's love into action by trying to change the social order." She concluded by issuing a challenge to the Dexter Avenue congregation, to "live up to (King's) example as the church embraces his name. Do not use his name, as some have done, without regard for his philosophy." At the end of the day, Dexter Avenue Baptist Church became Dexter Avenue King Memorial Baptist Church. The church had a new name and a new responsibilities.[57]

The decision to rename the church, though thoroughly discussed and prayerfully considered by the congregation, had not been a difficult or controversial one for most members. "I thought King deserved it," said Nesbitt. Thelma Austin Rice concurred, adding, "King gave his life for the betterment of the nation." In some ways the renaming seemed an expected next step in celebrating the life of Dexter Avenue, and it brought to fruition a pledge church members had made almost ten years earlier to make the church a national shrine to honor its slain former pastor. Zelia Evans recalled that supporting the renaming of the church was a decision she had to think and pray about for a while. "I know Dr. King was a great man," she said, "but we don't usually name churches for people." Evans explained that since King "had given so much for the cause of justice," ultimately she and other members had no problems supporting the decision to rename the church. Though at peace with their decision, still members realized that the community would have heightened expectations of the church, for despite all of its efforts over the last one hundred years as a religious institution and as an organization committed to the struggle for justice, the harvest was still plentiful.[58]

CONCLUSION:
FIGHTING THE GOOD FIGHT

Fight the good fight of faith, lay hold on eternal life, whereunto thou art also called, and hast professed a good profession before many witnesses.

—1 Timothy 6:12 AV

"I hope they will be able to say that Dexter made a contribution toward the salvation of souls and the improvement of the social order, and did something to diminish antisocial behavior, violence, and undesirable conduct ... bringing forth a more peaceful society in harmony with Christian principles," proclaimed Dr. Zelia Evans when asked what she hoped people celebrating Dexter Avenue King Memorial Baptist Church's bicentennial in 2077 would be able to say about the church.[1] Evans's words privilege the same concern for Christian salvation and active citizenship that founding church members valued. The story of Dexter Avenue evinces many images: communion and discipleship, faith and struggle, freedom and power, endurance and affirmation. The formerly enslaved African Americans who founded Dexter Avenue, like many other African Americans in the first-generation postbellum South, transcended the legacy of slavery to set out on their own walk of Christian faith. Since its founding as a religious institution, Dexter Avenue has sought to meet both the spiritual and temporal needs of the black community in Montgomery, Alabama. Between 1877 and 1977, five generations of congregations at Dexter Avenue have, through protest (dramatic and day-to-day), prayerful and painstaking institution building, and creative self-expression, "fought the good fight" for a prophetic Christianity and against the political, economic, and social oppression of African Americans. In the course of its history, we see these assorted forms of protest, self-expression, and empowerment manifested in multifarious ways: through the establishment of place, the development of self-help programs, class struggles, ministries established during various pastorates, the church's role in the civil rights movement, and finally in church members' decision to make the church a national historic landmark and to rename it in honor of its slain pastor, the Reverend Dr. Martin Luther King Jr.

In the years between Dexter Avenue's founding and the turn of the twentieth century, congregants sought self-determination and self-expression through a variety of programs. Despite the abolition of slavery and the passage of the Thirteenth, Fourteenth and Fifteenth Amendments to the U.S. Constitution, African Americans' notions of what black emancipation meant contrasted sharply with those of most white Americans. For most whites, emancipation was simply a moment that led to the absence of legalized slavery with few if any tacit implications of equality or justice for African Americans. As Reginald Hildebrand has explained, for blacks emancipation was the beginning of a process that ceded the liberty to move about and make basic choices.[2] Perhaps even more significant, emancipation quickened the opportunity to act as free moral agents, and it evoked the occasion to seek political, economic, and social justice and equality. In no place were the conflicting notions of black emancipation more evident than in the religious institutions shared by formerly enslaved blacks and their erstwhile white owners. In order to express freely their religious as well as their political convictions and act in accordance with their own aspirations, African Americans created independent religious institutions.

African Americans quickly came to believe that their spiritual, intellectual, and social development demanded that they rely on themselves. The first step in facilitating their own emancipation was to create "free spaces"—affirming religious and educational institutions, independent of white control, where they could find spiritual and psychological nourishment and plan political strategies to broaden the horizons of their newly acquired freedom. Dexter Avenue was one such institution.

In many ways, the church's founding was a dramatic act of resistance and of self-determination. Opening its doors on a structure formerly used as a slave trader's pen transformed a profane facility of enslavement and bondage into a hallowed shrine from which to exercise self-expression and to fight for African American freedom. On the very space where blacks had been held awaiting a life of enslavement and illiteracy, the founders of Dexter Avenue established a religious institution that promoted education as indispensable to good Christian character, responsible citizenship, and enduring liberation. Also, permanently locating the church two blocks from the state capitol, where just sixteen years earlier Jefferson Davis had taken the oath of office as president of the Confederacy became, over time, a dramatic symbol of resistance. Over the years numerous important gatherings to contest racism would be held in this building: an early formation meeting of the National Association for the Advancement of Colored People (NAACP); an organizational meeting for the Montgomery bus boycott; a refreshment and renewal stop, in 1965, for the Selma-to-Montgomery marchers before they concluded the historic event on the steps of the Alabama state capitol building; and in the 1970s, one of the Scottsboro Boys, pardoned by the state after almost forty years as a fugitive, held a press conference at Dexter Avenue. In the era of Jim Crow segregation practices and in defiance to white opposition that complained "it is not right for them [African Americans] to build nor for us [whites] to assist them to build in every place," church members erected, in 1885, a permanent edifice on the corner of Dexter Avenue and Decatur streets. And it became an important fixture and symbol of resistance against white racism.[3]

Much of the activity of Dexter Avenue during the late nineteenth and early twentieth centuries was less dramatic than the church's founding, but no less important in furthering the process of African American emancipation and self-expression. Church members established ministries that allowed for day-to-day resistance to oppression. In 1901, members of the legislature in Alabama wrote a new state constitution that effectively restricted most African Americans from participating in the political life of the state. Even so, establishing an infrastructure to keep the church running effectively, with governing boards like the board of deacons and board of trustees, afforded African Americans important experience in leadership. Furthermore, the plethora of organizations and auxiliaries provided occasions for fellowship, affirmation, and the exercise of autonomy.

Likewise, an important part of Dexter Avenue's ministry at the turn-of-the twentieth century included self-help programs. Due in part to the increasing, though still small, number of African Americans graduating from colleges and also because of diminished activity on the part of Northern white missionaries, black churches such as Dexter Avenue developed educational and philanthropic programs. Often these efforts took the form of sending financial support to Baptist-affiliated colleges like Selma University and Morehouse College. Moreover, the Dexter Avenue missionary society, formed shortly after the church's establishment, sponsored numerous charitable initiatives, from providing free holiday meals for indigent community members to supporting the fresh air camp during the 1915 influenza epidemic, as well as providing health clinics for midwife training. All these efforts were part of the church's initiative to improve the lives of African Americans in the Montgomery community.

Dexter Avenue engaged in both dramatic and everyday forms of protest in challenging the racial stereotypes that depicted blacks as ignorant, immoral, and incapable of handling the responsibilities of full citizenship rights. Beginning in 1905, R. C. Judkins and the church congregation inaugurated a seasonal lecture series. Presented before the Montgomery community were some of the most prominent members of the black community: politicians, religious figures, novelists, opera singers, and even comedians. These people were models of accomplishment and proof that success was possible for African Americans. This image of African Americans as moral, intelligent, talented, and capable was an important component of the church's effort to offer models to shape black character and to counter images portrayed by a hostile white community.

All of Dexter Avenue's programs and ministries, between its founding and the early 1920s, helped members of Montgomery's black community survive oppression. But the approach of these programs varied from accommodation to resistance. Perhaps the best example of this spectrum is reflected in the range of editorials in the *Colored Alabamian* newspaper, considered an arm of the church's ministry. On the one hand, there was a common notion that blacks had to work to prove themselves worthy of the rights guaranteed all citizens in the U.S. Constitution. A 1907 editorial in the *Colored Alabamian* encouraging church members to participate in the Alabama State Fair demonstrates this accommodationist mind-set. It told the congregation that bringing their best crafts and produce to the fair "will give us an opportunity to show the white people of Alabama what we have been doing." More dramatic evidence of the accommodationist thinking that motivated many members was an editorial that appeared in the *Colored Alabamian* on December 14, 1912, in anticipation of the fiftieth anniversary celebration of Emancipation Day. R. C. Judkins wrote, "The eyes of the world will be turned upon the race with a deep and anxious inquiry: has the Negro manifested in this period sufficient evidence of his capability to be a full-fledged citizen of America?" This editorial was followed by a review of black progress since 1865, and argued that blacks had excelled in all areas, especially medicine, business, sports, literature, and education. Judkins concluded that African Americans had earned the right to citizenship.

At the same time, Dexter Avenue also offered measures of resistance through both the newspaper and other means. The church, for example, regularly held voter registration campaigns while Judkins frequently used his newspaper to remind blacks of the qualifications for voting and to alert them to the deadline for paying poll taxes. Judkins often ran editorials declaring that the injustice of African Americans' disfranchisement was "not a crime against man but a sin against man's maker."[4] Additionally, the epidemic of lynching and race riots in 1918–20 inspired Montgomery blacks to organize a local chapter of the NAACP. Meeting at Dexter Avenue, the group worked to ensure passage of a compulsory education law in Alabama, and requested that the amount of money the state paid for the education of each black child be increased.

Despite all of its efforts of protest against racial discrimination, the history of Dexter Avenue Baptist Church suggests that its preeminent goal was not to fight racism but to create a supportive spiritual and loving communion among church members. At Dexter Avenue, members covenanted to "walk together in Christian love; to strive for the advancement of this church in knowledge and holiness ... to watch over, to pray for, to exhort and stir up each other unto every good word and work; ... with tender sympathy to bear one another's burdens and sorrows...."[5] Toward the goal of maintaining these promises to one another, church members developed a range of ministries that included creating a ritual life in which members could come together to pray and meditate at Wednesday evening prayer services, monthly fellowship dinners, and special birthday celebrations. As well, Sunday night communion services, along with seasonal revivals and lecture series gave members the opportunity to come together often and to renew their commitment to Christianity as well as to one another.[6] This church life of sharing and caring, in turn, helped individuals to garner the confidence and power to go out into their society and make contributions as capable, worthy citizens. This church life also gave members the strength to act collectively as a benevolent community, committed to service.

Both as a religious institution and as a free space in which to develop strategies to further black emancipation, Dexter Avenue's ideal was the betterment of all blacks living in the Montgomery community;

still, it did not always successfully provide the same level of affirmation for poor blacks as it did for those in the elite. The issue of class at Dexter Avenue was complex. On the one hand, a religious institution responsive to the needs of Montgomery's black elite led to increased African American empowerment as the church helped more blacks move into positions through which they could help other blacks. On the other hand, notwithstanding the shared experience of racial discrimination, class distinctions caused divisions within an already fragile community, with one class of African Americans feeling a degree of alienation toward the other. For example, Dexter Avenue established a rather formal and staid worship format, frowning upon the slightest display of emotion during Sunday services. It was not difficult at times for the comparatively privileged group of African Americans at Dexter Avenue, with its gaze focused on achieving and maintaining middle-class respectability, to lose sight of the feelings of their less fortunate counterparts.[7]

As E. Franklin Frazier explained many years ago, the achievement of middle-class status, even within a larger racist context, led to a measure of complacency among some African Americans and perhaps diminished the passion with which they were willing to fight for racial equality. Over the years, despite the many benefits Dexter Avenue provided to blacks, including home missionary activities and benevolence programs, many African Americans in Montgomery complained that they did not feel welcome at the church. Despite the church's sustained efforts to bring the less fortunate into its membership by establishing neighborhood prayer circles throughout Montgomery's black community, these measures met with only marginal success.[8] A careful study of the significance of class distinction as it worked itself out in the Dexter Avenue congregation suggests that creating and sustaining a black elite was, at once, a benefit and a hindrance to the African American struggle for equality; for while it empowered the black community, it also caused division and alienation.

Women were an integral part of church life at Dexter Avenue and were involved in all components of the ministries except the deaconate and the pastorate. Dexter Avenue women began a tradition of political and community activism in the 1880s when Susie Stone and Sallie Wright took it upon themselves to spearhead the effort to raise money to build a college—Selma University—to train African Americans for the Baptist ministry. In a similar maverick fashion Henrietta Gibbs, who headed the Ladies' Missionary Society at Dexter Avenue during the early years of the century, not only established a kindergarten class for church youth but also was the first African American woman to cast a ballot in Alabama during the election of 1920. The activist tradition among women at the church continued into the 1940s and 1950s and beyond. Sadie Brooks, Mary Fair Burks, and Jo Ann Robinson founded the Women's Political Council and led the Social and Political Action Committee, organizations that were crucial in kindling the 1955 Montgomery Bus Boycott.

In congregational life, with few notable exceptions, women of Dexter Avenue Baptist Church chose not to share authority with men, but created a separate sphere to address women's concerns and to develop female leaders. Until the 1950s, two organizations were largely the domain of women: the missionary society and the H. A. Loveless Working Club. The missionary organization focused on benevolence and home missions. The Working Club, founded in 1921 to honor one of Dexter Avenue's founders, raised money for special projects within the church. Both of these auxiliaries gave women some voice and power over which programs and repairs would be funded; still, women's authority was circumscribed.

In at least one way, however, Dexter Avenue was more progressive than other Baptist churches in the leadership opportunities it provided for women. From the 1930s forward, the church counted women among the membership on its board of trustees. The first women trustees were Henrietta Gibbs and Agnes Lewis, who were active and vocal members of this organization. The real seat of power at the church was the official board, which combined the deacons, the trustees, and the pastor's advisory council. Therefore, women had a voice in searching for pastors and other important decisions concerning church life. Still, Dexter Avenue was conservative in the power it vested in women, when compared to holiness and Pentecostal traditions during the same period. "Sanctified" churches, as they were called, generally offered an alternative model of power and leadership that placed women in all positions of authority, including serving as deacons, ministers, pastors, and, in some cases, even bishops.[9]

After the era of the civil rights movement, Dexter Avenue took a further step to place women in the kind of leadership roles previously held by men. In the 1960s women such as Elizabeth Arrington, Zelia Evans, Louvenia Herring, and Thelma Austin Rice headed powerful and influential groups like the Board of Religious Education and the stewardship committee. At the time of the centennial celebration in 1977, prompted by Pastor G. Murray Branch, women began to explore the possibility of ordination to the deaconate. The budding of this movement at Dexter Avenue was indicative of a sea change in the way many Baptist churches regarded the proper role of women. Church historian

Leroy Fitts explains that, "unremittingly, the winds of change or transition are pressing hard on the doors of all aspects of the institutional life among black Baptists. This is nowhere truer than of black Baptists' response to the women's liberation movement." But long before this change, at Dexter Avenue it is clear that women's efforts and influence were pivotal in sustaining the life of the church in every possible capacity. As Jualyne Dodson and Cheryl Townsend Gilkes have written, "If anything characterizes the role of black women in religion in America, it is the successful extension of their individual sense of regeneration, release, redemption and spiritual liberation to a collective ethos of struggle for and within the entire black community."[10]

Between 1877 and 1977, Dexter Avenue Baptist Church was led by twenty-three pastors. While a short pastorate was not atypical in black Baptist churches, Dexter Avenue's sister church—First Baptist, Ripley Street—had just five pastors in the same time period. Two things account for the comparative tenure brevity of Dexter Avenue pastors. First, the church called ambitious men, who after a few years either moved to larger churches or moved into leadership positions in state and national Baptist organizations and conventions; still others chose careers in academics. Second (and equally important), Dexter Avenue has always had among its congregation strong personalities and vocal deacons and trustees who have been closely involved in the decision-making process. These members have often voiced their opinions of policies and procedures of the ministers. Sometimes this relationship between the pastor and the board led to disagreements, and ultimately the pastor's resignation. Nevertheless, the Dexter Avenue Baptist Church has remained a highly sought-after pulpit.

Most Dexter Avenue pastors had a vision of the kind of ministry they hoped to establish at the church. Beginning with Judkins in 1905 and continuing to Robert Dickerson in 1977, pastors encouraged members to be active Christians. Their approaches, management styles and philosophies, however, varied. Most pastors can generally be characterized as having an organizational focus or a prophetic focus. Ministers who focused heavily on organizational church life include Frank Jacobs, Arnold Gregory, Ralph Riley, and Herbert Eaton. They devised programs for fund-raising, organized missions and auxiliaries to improve community outreach, and developed elaborate training programs to ensure that church members received the proper instruction to effectively carry out the responsibilities of membership and leadership in the church's programs. This leadership style was reflected in activities of various pastors: Frank Jacobs ordered copies of *Bailey's Manual of Instruction for Baptists* for each new church member. A. E. Gregory used his administrative skill to help rescue the church from the financial ravages of the Great Depression. Ralph Riley met with Sunday School teachers to help them prepare for their lessons. Herbert Eaton introduced a yearlong course for new deacons. The activities and programs emphasized by these pastors focused on sustaining and improving the internal lives of church members through an emphasis on training, organization, and structure.

A few twentieth-century pastors combined a social gospel with black liberation theology to establish what can be characterized as prophetic ministries. Ralph Luker has noted that the Social Gospel movement was not just a response to industrial-urban relations in the United States but also was a proclamation, advocating the rightness and effectiveness of organizing society around Christian principles, an atavism from the voluntary societies and home missions of antebellum America.[11] Liberation theology posits that economic and social conditions inevitably shape collective theological perceptions; in other words, a group's notions of God are determined and influenced by the economic and social conditions of its life.[12] Four ministers had particularly powerful passions in establishing prophetic ministries that embraced the principles of the Social Gospel and liberation theology: R. C. Judkins, Vernon Johns, Martin Luther King Jr., and G. Murray Branch.

Judkins, Johns, King, and Branch had many things in common. Each arrived at Dexter Avenue hoping to improve life at the church and the social order. All continued a prophetic tradition dating back at least to the abolitionist movement—always keeping before the people the importance of righteousness and conscience over social and economic expediency.[13] These ministers came out of the larger American Protestant tradition of social reform, the idea that just as religious organizations have a responsibility to encourage individuals to be moral, so too must they hold the corporate actions of a nation to the moral standards of equality and justice.[14] Intensely committed to the idea of justice, through the *Colored Alabamian* as well as his educational programs and ministries, Judkins hoped to transform the church congregation by creating a cadre of affirmed and informed workers to go into the world and change it. Governments, Judkins complained, sometimes forget the basic principle of justice, so "Negro religious organizations have thus felt it their responsibility to point out the golden rule to the politicians of society."[15]

Martin Luther King Jr. himself acknowledged his great debt to the prophetic mission of Vernon Johns at Dexter Avenue Baptist Church. Johns's ministry sought to keep before both the congregation and the community the immorality of racial segregation and discrimination.

His approach, though harsh at times, was essential in shaking the Dexter Avenue congregation out of its complacency toward the white power structure. While his manner was more powerful and imposing than gentle or charismatic, Johns got his message across. His ministry did not swell into a full-blown social protest for a number of reasons. The times were still not ripe for such action—especially in Alabama, where just the mention of racial integration could incite riotous white behavior; indeed, the forced integration on military bases in Montgomery had prompted the city council to forbid racial integration even in the minutia of life. Meanwhile, at this time, much of Montgomery's black community was factionalized into competing social and political organizations. Perhaps above and beyond all else, by his own admission, Johns did not have a flair for the logistics important to carry out a social protest; rather, he was "prophet and dreamer, leaving the more practical affairs to those who have more time and love for details." Even so, Johns did a remarkable job of preparing the hearts and minds of Dexter Avenue members for what was soon to come in their journey to fight the good fight through self-expression and dramatic protest as well as day-to-day resistance.

Coretta Scott King referred to Martin Luther King's coming to Dexter Avenue Baptist Church as the meeting of "a man and a moment in history," and so it was.[16] King came to Dexter Avenue to establish a prophetic ministry, but neither he nor the congregation could have anticipated what happened. As we discuss King's ministry we must also consider Dexter Avenue's role in the civil rights movement. Even though King only had a year at Dexter Avenue before his activities gained national recognition, his success and the Dexter Avenue members' reception of him contributed significantly to his confidence in subsequently leading the larger national protest for civil rights. King possessed not only a prophetic vision and organizational skills but also the charisma to inspire the congregation's trust and its willingness to share in mobilizing the resources of the church and community to support the protest against racial segregation. King used his personal acumen to persuade church members of something that Vernon Johns had preached to them earlier: that they had a moral obligation actively to resist evil.

Murray Branch's prophetic mission differed from Judkins's, Johns's, or King's. It did not involve sending people out to change the political climate but instead challenged the congregation at Dexter Avenue to embrace changes that had taken place in the world outside of the church. Particularly, he advocated a change in the church's attitude toward women deacons and pastors. In a centennial letter to members designed to provide them direction for the next hundred years he wrote, "Nothing can be allowed to block or hinder the Godward reach of the human spirit, not race, color, nor class, nor nationality, nor ideological preference, nor language, nor sex." Branch explained, "For years I had developed the view that there was no more reason for people to object to women holding any office in the life and work of the church than there was for people to believe that blacks should not hold any office in the life and work of the church." Branch believed that the Baptist church should respond affirmatively and supportively to women's desire for more authority and recognized leadership in black churches. "Greater provisions [must be] made for women in significant leadership positions in the church ...," Branch admonished, "service in the deaconate ... and if called to the ordained ministry, should not be discouraged by brethen [sic]." Branch saw the pastor as leader-facilitator, encouraging the members to work together to develop and execute their own visions for the church. Church members seriously considered Branch's suggestions as they made preparations to celebrate its centennial, but it would be 1987, ten years later, before the church ordained its first women deacons.[17]

Dexter Avenue Baptist Church as a religious institution and part of the Montgomery community evoked important historical issues at the time of its founding and continued to raise important concerns as it celebrated its one hundredth birthday. At the centennial, the congregation repeatedly emphasized its many accomplishments. After all, members had raised a phoenix from the ashes of slavery.

The church's numerous programs and ministries to encourage Christian salvation and the fight for political and social reform were always underscored by its near proximity to the state capitol and the former white house of the Confederacy. Almost close enough to hear the segregationist and discriminatory legislation as it was being drafted by lawmakers, since 1877 the church has stood as an undeniable fixture, glaring in stolid red brick reproof at the gleaming white power structures that surround it. Day after day, the church persisted in both extraordinary and ordinary ways to buttress the black community from the crippling effects of many of the policies and practices being fomented and sanctioned next door. It provided Montgomery's oppressed community with the opportunity for self-expression and self-determination. In the first hundred years of its existence, most members held tightly to the early founding values of faith in the American ideal that hard work inevitably leads to progress and improvement, and a belief that democratic institutions were moral and capable of bringing forth a just society.

In 1978, the church officially renamed itself Dexter Avenue King Memorial Baptist Church, and in so doing forever identified itself as a symbol in the fight for civil rights. This change raised two unanticipated dilemmas. First, the embrace of the church by the larger Montgomery community would, at once, highlight and obscure the conflicting historical legacies of the community.[18] Second, the church would now have to struggle to resist becoming a museumlike institution rather than an active, living congregation. The renaming of the church and the celebration of its presence by the entire Montgomery community raises issues about the larger community's efforts to deal with its contradictory pasts. The City of Montgomery takes pride in representing itself as both the cradle of the Confederacy and the home of the modern civil rights movement. On the one hand, this contradiction it seems is a reasonable self-identity since the latter (the civil rights movement) could be interpreted as a response to the former (the Confederacy), and in reality these two pasts are indeed an undeniable part of one community. The Montgomery Heritage Organization proposed the joint celebration of the birthdays of Martin Luther King Jr. and Robert E. Lee "in the spirit of peaceful coexistence." Perhaps appropriately, this celebration began at noon at Dexter Avenue King Memorial Baptist Church with the theme "Hope for Unity in a Divided World." Those gathered explained that "celebrating the two men's birthdays is an example of Dr. King's dream of peaceful coexistence." And yet, conspicuously missing from the celebration was any explicit statement of Robert E. Lee's dream, or the seeming incongruence of conflating the dreams of two such different historical actors and circumstances. One of the many challenges for Dexter Avenue members in the next hundred years of its service to the community is to help facilitate discussions on race and morality as the United States continues to confront these issues of race in the twenty-first century.

Even more germane to the history, mission, and future of the church is how and what it must do to continue as a viable institution in the African American community. Since its centennial Dexter Avenue has struggled to remain a living church, especially among the young citizens of Montgomery. Perhaps the paucity of attendance at Dexter Avenue in some measure can be attributed to a general decline in church membership. And yet the possibility remains that the memory of the church prompted a kind of complacency. Murray Branch noted at the time of his resignation from his second tenure as pastor of Dexter Avenue that "too many of its well-educated and socially conscious members are 'basking in what used to be' and ignoring the mounting challenges that a church, especially a black church must face."[19] The struggle to remain a viable and effective religious organization is Dexter Avenue's great challenge for its next centennial of life. Despite the many struggles that lie ahead, there is no denying the importance and significance of its presence in the Montgomery community. Since 1877, the members of Dexter Avenue King Memorial Baptist Church have "fought the good fight" for the cause of Christian evangelism and full citizenship rights for all Americans.

NOTES

Introduction

1. Carter G. Woodson, *The History of the Negro Church*, 3d ed. (1921; reprint, Washington D.C.: Associated Press, 1985) is the pioneering study of black churches in the United States; see Albert J. Raboteau, David Will, Randall Burkett, Will Gravely, and James Melvin Washington, "Retelling Carter Woodson's Story: Archival Sources for Afro-American Church History," *Journal of American History*, 77 (1990): 183–99. See also Ethel L. Williams and Clifton F. Brown, *The Howard University Bibliography of African and Afro-American Religious Studies, with Locations in American Libraries* (Wilmington, Del.: Scholarly Resources, 1977); and Lester Scherer and Susan Eltscher, *Afro-American Baptists: A Guide to the Records in the Library of the American Baptist Historical Society* (Rochester, N.Y., 1985).

2. J. DeOtis Roberts, *Roots of a Black Future: Family and Church* (Philadelphia: Westminster, 1980), 39; Henry H. Mitchell, *Black Preaching*, C. Eric Lincoln Series in Black Religion (Philadelphia: J. P. Lippincott, 1970); E. Franklin Frazier, *The Negro Church in America* (New York: Schocken, 1963); C. Eric Lincoln, *The Black Church since Frazier* (New York: Schocken, 1974).

3. Benjamin Mays and Joseph Nicholson, *The Negro's Church* (New York: Arno Press, 1969), 281.

4. Donna L. Irvin, *The Unsung Heart of Black America: A Middle-Class Church at Midcentury* (Columbia: University of Missouri Press, 1992); Samuel G. Freedman, *Upon this Rock: the Miracles of a Black Church* (New York: Harper Collins, 1993); C. Eric Lincoln and Lawrence Mamiya, *The Black Church in the African-American Experience* (Durham, N.C.: Duke University Press, 1990), 7; Eugene Genovese, *Roll Jordan Roll* (New York: Random House, 1974), 232–4.

5. For a history of the white church from which all black Baptist churches in Montgomery can be traced, see Lee Norcross Allen, *The First 150 Years: Montgomery's First Baptist Church, 1829–1979* (Birmingham, Ala.: Oxmoor, 1979), 15, 19, 45–47, 88–89.

6. James Melvin Washington, *Frustrated Fellowship: The Black Baptist Quest for Social Power* (Macon, Ga.: Mercer University Press, 1986), 52–84.

7. Reginald Hildebrand, *The Times Were Strange and Stirring: Methodist Preaching and the Crisis of Emancipation* (Durham, N.C.: Duke University Press, 1996), 33.

8. For a discussion of black churches as "free spaces," see Sara Evans and Harry Boyte, "Crossing the Jordan," in *Free Spaces: The Sources of Democratic Change* (New York: Harper and Row, 1985). For a discussion of education in Alabama, see Robert G. Sherer, *Subordination or Liberation: The Development and Conflicting Theories of Black Education in Nineteenth Century Alabama* (Tuscaloosa: University of Alabama Press, 1977), 66.

9. Classic studies addressing class and African Americans include E. Franklin Frazier, *The Black Bourgeoisie* (New York: Macmillan, 1957); W. E. B. Du Bois, "The Talented Tenth," in *The Negro Problem: A Series of Articles by Representative Negroes of Today* (New York: James Prott, 1903), 33–75; Willard Gatewood, *Aristocrats of Color* (Bloomington: Indiana University Press, 1993).

10. Aldon Morris, *The Origins of the Civil Rights Movement: Black Communities Organizing for Change* (New York: Free Press, 1984), 4.

11. See Adolph Reed, "Mythology of the Church in Contemporary Society," in *The Jesse Jackson Phenomenon: The Crisis in Purpose in Afro-American Politics* (New Haven, Conn.: Yale University Press, 1986); Gary Marx, "Religion: Opiate or Inspiration of Civil Rights Militancy among Negroes," *American Sociological Review*, no. 32 (August 1967): 64–72; James Melvin Washington, "Jesse Jackson and the Symbolic Politics of Black Christendom," in *Annals of the American Academy of Political and Social Science*, vol. 480 (Philadelphia: A. L. Hummel), 88–105.

12. For an examination of liberation theology see James H. Cone, *Black Theology and Black Power* (New York: Seabury, 1969), and Gayraud Wilmore, *Black Religion and Black Radicalism: An Interpretation of the Religious History of Afro-American People*, 2d rev. ed. (Maryknoll, N.Y.: Orbis, 1983), 99–240.

Chapter 1

1. "How It Was," *Montgomery Daily Advertiser*, August 22, 1865. William Warren Rogers, Robert David Ward, Leah Rawls Atkins, and Wayne Flynt, *Alabama: The History of a Deep South State* (Tuscaloosa: University of Alabama Press, 1994), 226; James Melvin Washington, *Frustrated Fellowship: The Black Baptist Quest for Social Power* (Macon, Ga.: Mercer University Press, 1986), 49–83. The independent African American church movement began in the late eighteenth century with Richard Allen and other free Northern African Americans establishing autonomous black churches. Allen's efforts led to the establishment of the African Methodist Episcopal Church. It is worth noting that some white Southern churches, like First Baptist of Tuskegee, Alabama, had separate buildings for their African American worshipers. The religious vision and initiative that established black churches during the Reconstruction years were part of an emancipation movement that relied on African American churches to administer traditional functions associated with churches but also to serve as forums to address community concerns and as places to develop African American leaders. These churches, along with other institutions, like schools, consciously worked to define emancipation in the broadest possible terms.

2. For a discussion of the "prophetic" principle in black Christianity, see Peter J. Paris, *The Social Teaching of Black Churches* (Philadelphia: Fortress, 1995) 10–13; Cornel West, *Prophesy Deliverance: An Afro-American Revolutionary Christianity* (Philadelphia: Westminster, 1982) 15–20; C. Eric Lincoln and Lawrence Mamiya, *The Black Church in the African-American Experience* (Durham, N.C.: Duke University Press, 1990), 12.

3. It was officially named the Second Colored Baptist Church; the exact date of the name change is not recorded, but it was probably during the late 1880s when the name of the street on which the church was located—Market—was changed to Dexter Avenue to honor one of Montgomery's founders, Andrew Dexter. In 1973, church members voted to change the name to honor their former pastor, Martin Luther King Jr.

4. C. O. Boothe, *The Cyclopedia of the Colored Baptists of Alabama* (Birmingham, Ala.: Alabama Publishing, 1895), 239; Peter Kolchin, *First Freedom: The Responses of Alabama's Blacks to Emancipation and Reconstruction* (Westport, Conn.: Greenwood, 1972), 107–28; V. P. Franklin, *Black Self-Determination: A Cultural History of the Faith of the Fathers* (Westport, Conn.: Greenwood, 1984), 87; Reginald Hildebrand, *The Times Were Strange and Stirring: Methodist Preaching and the Crisis of Emancipation* (Durham, N.C.: Duke University Press, 1996), xiii–xxii.

5. Washington, *Frustrated Fellowship*, x–xi; Gayraud Wilmore, *Black Religion and Black Radicalism: An Interpretation of the Religious History of Afro-American People*, 2d rev. ed. (Maryknoll, N.Y.: Orbis, 1983), 78.

6. Lee Norcross Allen, *The First 150 Years: Montgomery's First Baptist Church, 1829–1979* (Birmingham, Ala.: Oxmoor, 1979), 88; *Minutes of the Forty-Third Annual Session of the Alabama Baptist State Convention, 1865* (Atlanta: Franklin Steam, 1866), Alabama State Historical Archives, Montgomery, Alabama (hereafter ASHA).

7. *Minutes of the First Baptist Church, Montgomery* (hereafter *FBC Minutes*), August 11, 1832; Special Collections, Samford University Archives, Birmingham, Alabama.

8. Allen, *The First 150 Years*, 45–47.

9. *FBC Minutes*, February 1, 1840, Book B 40. Rogers et al., *Alabama*, 147–48.

10. *FBC Minutes*, April 10, 1840. The actual vote taken at this particular church conference meeting does not show a black majority, but this was due to the absence of blacks at this particular church conference. By the time of the 1867 black exodus, there were 690 African American members and 320 white members.

11. *FBC Minutes*, January 10, 1850–November 3, 1857. Boothe, *Cyclopedia*, 112; William J. Wright, "Towering O'er the Wrecks of Time," souvenir booklet for First Baptist Montgomery (Ripley Street), Dexter Avenue King Memorial Baptist Church Papers (hereafter DAKMBCP), Montgomery, Alabama; Allen, *The First 150 Years*, 46.

12. Horace Mann Bond, "Social and Economic Forces in Alabama Reconstruction," in *Reconstruction: America's Unfinished Revolution, 1865–1877*, ed. Eric Foner (New York: Harper and Row, 1988), 374; Allen, *The First 150 Years*, 86; For a discussion of African Americans' decision to leave the churches of their former slave masters, see Carter G. Woodson, *The History of the Negro Church*, 3d ed. (1921; reprint, Washington D.C.: Associated Press, 1985), 61–85; William Montgomery, *Under Their Own Vine and Fig Tree: The African American Church in the South, 1865–1900* (Baton Rouge: Louisiana State University Press, 1993); Beulah Lewis, "Our Church History," program for the centennial celebration of First Baptist, Montgomery (black), DAKMBCP; Katherine Dvorak, *An African-American Exodus: The Segregation of Southern Churches* (Brooklyn, NY: Carlson, 1991).

13. *Montgomery Daily Advertiser*, August 5, 1865; W. E. B. Du Bois, *Black Reconstruction* (New York, Harcourt, Brace, 1935), 487.

14. Rogers et al., *Alabama*, 226.

15. United States Census Office, *Eighth Census: Population* 9, ASHA. The census showed that in the city of Montgomery, there were 4,502 blacks and 4,341 whites. According to the census of 1870, the scales tipped slightly with whites comprising 51 percent of Montgomery's population. More significantly, perhaps, 15.4 percent of the city's black population had migrated from rural areas. For a discussion of black presence in political life in Montgomery see Howard Rabinowitz, "Three Reconstruction Leaders: Blanche K. Bruce, Robert Brown Elliot, and Holland Thompson," in *Black Leaders of the Nineteenth Century*, ed. Leon Litwack and August Meier (Urbana: University of Illinois Press, 1988), 210.

16. Kolchin, *First Freedom*, 158; *Mobile Advertiser and Register*, May 3, 1867; *Montgomery Daily Advertiser*, August 15, 1868; *Montgomery Daily Advertiser*, September 14, 1866.

17. John Hope Franklin, *From Slavery to Freedom: A History of Negro Americans*, 6th ed. (New York: Alfred A. Knopf, 1988), 206–8.

18. Herbert Shapiro, *White Violence and Black Response* (Amherst: University of Massachusetts Press, 1985), 5; Du Bois, *Black Reconstruction*, 489; Rogers et al., *Alabama*, 3; Horace Mann Bond, "Social and Economic Forces," 371.

19. *FBC Minutes*, July 28, 1867 and August 15, 1867. Walter L. Fleming, *Civil War and Reconstruction in Alabama* (New York: Columbia University Press, 1905) 644; Beulah Lewis, "Our Church History," 1967 centennial program for the First Baptist Church (Colored); Owen D. Pelt and Ralph Lee Smith, *The Story of the National Baptists* (New York: Vintage, 1960), 163. At an unspecified date, Columbus Street Baptist Church took the name First Baptist (Colored).

20. Boothe, *Cyclopedia*, 112.

21. *Minutes of the Eight Annual Session of the Colored Missionary Baptist Convention of Alabama*, November 17–24, 1875, American Baptist–Samuel Colgate Historical Library Collection, Colgate Rochester Divinity School, Rochester, New York.

22. Zelia Evans, interview with the author, July 21, 1993; Edna Doak King, interview with the author, July 20, 1993; Janice Denton, interview with the author, July 15, 1993; R. D. Nesbitt, interview with the author, May 4, 1994; Addre Bryant, interview with the author, July 13, 1993; Taylor Branch, *Parting the Waters: America in the King Years* (New York: Simon and Schuster, 1988), 2; Mrs. Gertrude Campbell Phillips interview with J. T. Alexander, March 28, 1961, partial transcript, DAKMBCP.

23. The Campbells were an African American couple, and their children were among the first to be baptized at Dexter Avenue when it became a separate church. Zelia Evans and J. T. Alexander, *The Dexter Avenue Baptist Church* (Montgomery, Ala.: Dexter Avenue Baptist Church, 1978), 11; Phillips interview, DAKMBCP; Robert G. Sherer, *Subordination or Liberation: The Development and Conflicting Theories of Black Education in Nineteenth Century Alabama* (Tuscaloosa: University of Alabama Press, 1977), 66, 4.

24. Evans and Alexander, *Dexter Avenue*, 10; Book II of Deeds, January 30, 1879, ASHA.

25. Leroy Fitts, *A History of Black Baptists* (Nashville, Tenn.: Broadman, 1985); Woodson, *The History of the Negro Church*, 224–29; church program for the ninety-sixth anniversary of Dexter Avenue Baptist Church, DAKMBCP; King interview; Denton interview. See also Willard Gatewood, *Aristocrats of Color* (Bloomington: Indiana University Press, 1993); Evelyn Brooks Higginbotham, *Righteous Discontent: The Woman's Movement in the Black Baptist Church* (Cambridge, Mass.: Harvard University Press, 1993), 1–19; Branch, *Parting the Waters*, 11; Hans A. Baer and Merrill Singer, *African-American Religion in the Twentieth Century: Varieties of Protest and Accommodation* (Knoxville: University of Tennessee Press, 1992), x–xiv.

26. Theophilus G. Steward, *Fifty Years of the Gospel Ministry* (Philadelphia: A. M. E. Book Concern, 1915), 33.

27. W. E. B. Du Bois, *The Souls of Black Folk* (1903; reprint, New York: Johnson Reprint, 1969), 191.

28. Baptist churches set their own standards for qualifications of ministers and, at least among some Baptists, convincing a congregation of the authenticity of one's call to preach and personal relationship with God was more important than having formal credentials. There were no bishops or centralized bodies setting requisites for preachers. Dexter Avenue, however, did seem to seek out and hire educated pastors.

29. Henry H. Mitchell, *Black Preaching*, C. Eric Lincoln Series in Black Religion (New York: J. P. Lippincott Co., 1970) contains a general discussion of the role of black preachers from Reconstruction to the present. John Childs, *The Political Black Minister: A Study in Afro-American Politics and Religion* (Boston: C. K. Hall, 1980) provides a detailed treatise on the political power of African American ministers. David Swift, *Black Prophets of Justice: Activist Clergy Before the Civil War* (Baton Rouge: Louisiana State University Press, 1989) discusses how this tradition of authority and power developed among African American ministers during slavery.

30. Hildebrand, *The Times Were Strange*, 32, 15–27, 119–20. Hildebrand uses the term "Gospel of Freedom" to refer to the ideas preached by ministers who believed that emancipation from slavery was the secular equivalent to a sinner's redemption from sin. These ministers preached that new-found emancipation was "earthly" salvation—the opportunity to enjoy the same rights and privileges as other American citizens.

31. Kolchin, *First Freedom*, 128.

32. Sherer, *Subordination or Liberation*, 23.

33. Judith Hillman Paterson, *Sweet Mystery: A Book of Remembering* (New York: Farrar, Straus and Giroux, 1996), 22.

34. Evans and Alexander, *Dexter Avenue*, 15.

35. J. Mills Thornton, *Touched by History: A Civil Rights Tour Guide to Montgomery, Alabama* (Montgomery, Ala.: Black Belt Communications), 27.

36. Sherer, *Subordination or Liberation*, 23–32.

37. Booker T. Washington, *Up From Slavery: An Autobiography by Booker T. Washington* (Cambridge, Mass.: Houghton Mifflin, 1900), 106–33, 217.

38. Ibid., 106–33; Sherer, *Subordination or Liberation*, 45–64.

39. Evans and Alexander, *Dexter Avenue*, 15.

40. *Resolution upon the Occasion of the Death of Deacon William Watkins*, read at his memorial service on March 15, 1914, DAKMBCP.

41. Boothe, *Cyclopedia*, 266.

42. Kolchin, *First Freedom*, 153.

43. Rabinowitz, "Three Reconstruction Leaders," 210.

44. *Montgomery Daily Advertiser*, January 2, 1866.

45. Rabinowitz, "Three Reconstruction Leaders," 210.

46. Ibid., 211–14.

47. Boothe, *Cyclopedia*, 13.

48. Boothe fails to account for his resignation, only noting that "owing to embarrassments" he left Dexter Avenue after a short time; see Boothe, *Cyclopedia*, 1895.

49. Evans and Alexander, *Dexter Avenue*, 18. Boothe's works include *Plain Theology for Plain People* (1891), *Biblical Systematic Theology* (1925), and *Last Day Challenge in Last Day Voice* (n.d.), 18.

50. Boothe, *Cyclopedia*, 13.

51. *Minutes of the First Session of the Colored Missionary Baptist Convention of Alabama*, cited in Boothe, *Cyclopedia*, 36.

52. For a discussion on the issue of Baptists having an educated clergy, see Washington, *Frustrated Fellowship*, 173–77.

53. Donald Mathews, *Religion in the Old South* (Chicago: University of Chicago Press, 1977), 23, points out that as the Baptist faith was being established in the South, "Education … was for Baptists, a sign of worldly but not heavenly approval."

54. *Minutes of the Sixth Session of the Colored Missionary Baptist Convention of Alabama*, cited in Boothe, *Cyclopedia*, 36.

55. See Higginbotham, *Righteous Discontent*, for an in-depth discussion of the formation of the Woman's Baptist Convention.

56. Mary V. Cook, "The Work for Baptist Women," in *The Negro Baptist Pulpit*, ed. Edward Brawley (1890; reprint, New York: Books for Libraries, 1971); Boothe, *Cyclopedia*, 251; *Proceedings of the Twenty-Fourth Annual Session of the Alabama Baptist State Convention*, Peace Baptist Church, Talladega, Alabama, November 18–22, 1891; American Baptist–Samuel Colgate Historical Library, Colgate Rochester Divinity School, Rochester, New York.

57. For a detailed discussion of this struggle, see Washington, *Frustrated Fellowship*, 137–57.

58. Boothe, *Cyclopedia*, 13; Evans and Alexander, *Dexter Avenue Baptist Church*, 29.

59. For a discussion of the development of national Baptist conventions, see Washington, *Frustrated Fellowship*, 133–9. Fitts, *A History of Black Baptists*, 114; E. Franklin Frazier, *The Negro Church in America* (New York: Schocken, 1963), 29-47.

60. Wilmore, *Black Religion and Black Radicalism*, 92–95.

61. Evans and Alexander, *Dexter Avenue*, 23.

62. Montgomery City Directory 1880–1881; *Montgomery Daily Advertiser and Mail*, December 4, 1884.

63. Editorial, *Montgomery Daily Advertiser*, May 6, 1885; "ASHA," *Alabama Journal*, July 3, 1974; Nesbitt interview with the author, May 4, 1994; Thelma Austin Rice, interview with the author, May 16, 1995.

64. *Alabama Journal*, July 3, 1974; Nesbitt interview; Rice interview; Evans interview; "NAACP Holds Interesting Meeting at Dexter Avenue Baptist Church," *Emancipator*, June 21, 1919.

65. *Montgomery Advertiser*, August 20, 1980.

66. This information, cited in Evans and Alexander, *Dexter Avenue*, 13, is taken from a statewide, now defunct, African American newspaper, the *Argus of Alabama*.

67. U.S. Department of the Interior, *National Register of Historic Places Inventory-Nomination Form*, 1974, ASHA.

68. "Life in the Capital, Gossip From the Street and Sidewalk," *Montgomery Daily Advertiser*, July 16, 1885.

69. R. T. Pollard, "Baptists and Colportage," sermon, in Brawley, ed., *The Negro Baptist Pulpit*, 211–20. Colportage, literally translated, means "peddler of religious books."

70. Evans and Alexander, *Dexter Avenue*, 237, 265, 209.

71. In the early years of its existence, Dexter Avenue had a few white members, but by the turn of the century, it had an exclusively African American congregation.

72. Franklin, *Black Self-Determination*, 48–54, 67, 87, 193–94.

73. Hildebrand, *The Times Were Strange*, 50–75.

74. Lincoln and Mamiya, *The Black Church*, 2–15; Gayraud Wilmore, "Introduction: Black Theology and the Black Church," in *Black Theology: A Documentary History, 1966–1979*, ed. Gayraud Wilmore and James Cone (Maryknoll, N.Y.: Orbis, 1979), 241–57.

Chapter 2

1. Gayraud Wilmore, *Black Religion and Black Radicalism: An Interpretation of the Religious History of Afro-American People*, 2d rev. ed. (Maryknoll, N.Y.: Orbis, 1983), 78; James Melvin Washington, *Frustrated Fellowship: The Black Baptist Quest for Social Power* (Macon, Ga.: Mercer University Press, 1986), 83–89; William L. Andrews, "The Politics of African-American Ministerial Autobiography from Reconstruction to the 1920s," in *African-American Christianity: Essays in History*, ed. Paul E. Johnson (Berkeley and Los Angeles: University of California Press, 1994), 111–12.

2. Booker T. Washington, "Booker T. Washington's Platform of Accommodation: The Atlanta Exposition Speech, 1895," in *Negro Protest Thought in the Twentieth Century*, ed. Francis Broderick and August Meier (Indianapolis: Bobbs-Merrill, 1965), 3–18. For a brief survey of the dissemination of Washington's speech in the southern press, see Rayford Logan, *The Betrayal of the Negro from Rutherford B. Hayes to Woodrow Wilson* (New York: Da Capo, 1997), 275–313.

3. Carter G. Woodson, *The History of the Negro Church*, 3d ed. (1921; reprint, Washington D.C.: Associated Press, 1985), 103, 224–303; Sydney Ahlstrom, *A Religious History of the American People* (New Haven, Conn.: Yale University Press, 1972), 698–714, 785–804; Robert T. Handy, *A Christian America: Protestant Hopes and Historical Realities* (New York: Oxford University Press, 1971), 70–72, 106–10, 174–83; E. Franklin Frazier, *The Negro Church in America* (New York: Schocken, 1963); 23–25, 35–90; C. Eric Lincoln, *The Black Church since Frazier* (New York: Schocken, 1974), 101–34;

Benjamin Mays and Joseph Nicholson, *The Negro's Church* (New York: Institute of Social and Religious Research, 1933), 273; Aldon Morris, *The Origins of the Civil Rights Movement: Black Communities Organizing for Change* (New York: Free Press, 1984), 4–16; Hart M. Nelson, Royth L. Yokley, and Anne K. Nelson, eds., *The Black Church in America* (New York: Basic, 1971), 299–315; C. Eric Lincoln and Lawrence Mamiya, *The Black Church in the African-American Experience* (Durham, N.C.: Duke University Press, 1990), 7; Eugene Genovese, *Roll Jordan Roll* (New York: Random House, 1974), 20–46; Washington, *Frustrated Fellowship*, 135–207; Paul Harvey, *Redeeming the South: Religious Cultures and Racial Identities among Southern Baptists, 1865–1925* (Chapel Hill: University of North Carolina Press, 1997), 45–74.

4. Logan, *The Betrayal of the Negro*, 275–313; William Warren Rogers, Robert David Ward, Leah Rawls Atkins, and Wayne Flynt, *Alabama: The History of a Deep South State* (Tuscaloosa: University of Alabama Press, 1994), 343.

5. Rogers et al., *Alabama*, 345; *Daily Advertiser*, May 15, 1901; Malcolm Cook Macmillan, *Constitutional Development in Alabama 1798–1901: A Study in Politics, the Negro and Sectionalism* (Spartanburg, S.C.: Reprint Company, 1978), 264.

6. Rogers et al., *Alabama*, 347; State Constitution of Alabama, 1901, copy, Alabama State Historical Archives, Montgomery, Alabama. By 1913, according to the *Colored Alabamian* (March 8, 1913), of the fifty-six thousand African Americans living in Montgomery County, less than one hundred were registered to vote. Of the almost one million living in the state of Alabama, about five thousand were registered to vote.

7. Macmillan, *Constitutional Development in Alabama*, 348.

8. Joseph M. Brittain, "Negro Suffrage and Politics in Alabama since 1870" (Ph.D. diss., University of Indiana, 1958), 132; Virginia Van Deer Ver Hamilton, *Alabama: A Bicentennial History* (New York: W. W. Norton, 1977), 93; Rogers et al., *Alabama*, 343; *Colored Alabamian*, October 8, 1907.

9. Zelia Evans and J. T. Alexander, *The Dexter Avenue Baptist Church* (Montgomery, Ala.: Dexter Avenue Baptist Church, 1978), 36–37. Clement Richardson, *The National Cyclopedia of the Colored Race* (Montgomery, Ala.: National, 1919), 22–23; Dwight Oliver Wendell Holmes, *The Evolution of the Negro College* (College Park, Md.: McGrath, 1943), 8: Maxine D. Jones and Joe M. Richardson, *Talladega College: The First Century* (Tuscaloosa: University of Alabama Press, 1990). Robert G. Sherer, *Subordination or Liberation: The Development and Conflicting Theories of Black Education in Nineteenth Century Alabama* (Tuscaloosa: University of Alabama Press, 1977), 135–37; "The Graduates of Talladega College and What They Are Doing," (Birmingham, Ala: Press of Our Mountain Home, 1900), 5–8.

10. W. E. B. Du Bois, *The College Bred Negro* (Atlanta: Atlanta University Press, 1900), 13. A college was rated on the basis of the number of Carnegie units it required for admissions (a Carnegie unit was given for any secondary course that lasted an academic year, with meetings weekly over five periods). Colleges varied in their requirements. Virginia Union required 14 units. The University of North Carolina required 14.7 units, while the University of Virginia required 11.5. First, Wayland Seminary and Richmond Theological Seminary united. They were joined by Hartshorne Women's College in the 1920s; in 1964, a fourth institution, Storer College, was added (*University Journal of Virginia Union University* 3, no. 8 [1903]); W. P. Thirkfeld, "Crisis in the Ministry," *University Journal of Virginia Union University* 4, no. 7 (1904): 97; Washington, *Frustrated Fellowship*, 173–77; Sutton E. Griggs, *Imperium in Imperio* (1889; reprint, Miami: Mnemosyne, 1969), 49, 51.

11. Thirkfeld, "Crisis in the Ministry," 97, 99; Virginia Union University, *Annual Catalogue of Virginia Union University, 1910–1911* (Richmond: Williams, 1911), Virginia Union University Archives, Richmond, Virginia.

12. "Question of Justice," *Colored Alabamian*, May 16, 1908.

13. "Last Sunday at Dexter Avenue Baptist Church," *Colored Alabamian*, September 3, 1910; *Colored Alabamian*, October 17, 1907.

14. All Bible quotations herein are from the Authorized (King James) Version.

15. "Question of Justice."

16. Two important works offer the role of jeremiads in historical analyses: see Sacvan Bercovitch, *The American Jeremiad* (Madison: University of Wisconsin Press, 1987) and David Howard-Pitney, *The Afro-American Jeremiad: Appeals for Justice in America* (Philadelphia: Temple University Press, 1990). "Last Sunday at Dexter Avenue," *Colored Alabamian*, December 14, 1912.

17. Lincoln and Mamiya, *The Black Church*, 20–47; Woodson, *The History of the Negro Church*, 259; Wilmore, *Black Religion and Black Radicalism*, 78; William Montgomery, *Under Their Own Vine and Fig Tree: The African American Church in the South, 1865–1900* (Baton Rouge: Louisiana State University Press), 267.

18. *Colored Alabamian*, June 21, 1913; R. C. Judkins, "The Call and Equipment of a Disciple," sermon, Dexter Avenue Baptist Church, June 15, 1913, Dexter Avenue King Memorial Baptist Church Papers (hereafter DAKMBCP), Montgomery, Alabama; "Last Sunday at Dexter Avenue," *Colored Alabamian*, June 21, 1913; Woodson, *The History of the Negro Church*, 198–223.

19. Edna Doak King, interview with the author, July 14, 1993; Dexter Avenue Baptist Church Sunday school program, 1892, DAKMBCP; *Colored Alabamian*, August 22, 1908; Archivist at John Hayes Archives, Brown University, telephone interview with the author, September 29, 1995; Richardson, *National Cyclopedia*, 33; "Professor J. W. Beverly, Elected President of State Normal School to Succeed the Late Professor W. B. Patterson," *Colored Alabamian*, July 3, 1915; "Dexter Avenue Baptist Notes," *Emancipator*, October 20, 1917.

20. Edna Doak King, interview with the author, July 20, 1993. Judkins was a distributor of the memorial anthology *The Life and Works of Paul Lawrence Dunbar*; see *Colored Alabamian*, October 26, 1907.

21. The University Journal, Virginia Union University, "Theological Department" 1911. Virginia Union University Archives, Richmond, Virginia.

22. Evans and Alexander, *Dexter Avenue*, 37, 225; King interview, July 14, 1993; obituary of R. T. Grant, July 11, 1927, DAKMBCP.

23. "Miss Elizabeth Brown Graduates from the Boston Conservatory of Music," *Colored Alabamian*, November 18, 1910; King interview, July 14, 1993.

24. Edna Doak married in 1917; see Evans and Alexander, *Dexter Avenue*, 227; Richardson, *National Cyclopedia*, 33; obituary for Edna Doak King, December 1, 1994, DAKMBCP.

25. J. Mills Thornton, "Touched by History: A Civil Rights Tour Guide to Montgomery, Alabama," pamphlet sponsored by the Dexter Avenue King Memorial Baptist Church, the Landmarks Foundation, and the Southern Regional Council (n.d., c. 1980s), DAKMBCP; King interview, July 20, 1993; Evans and Alexander, *Dexter Avenue*, 227; Richardson, *National Cyclopedia*, 33; King obituary.

26. King interview, July 20, 1993. "Handsome New Pipe Organ," *Colored Alabamian*, March 5, 1910.

27. "Great Musical Event of the Season," *Colored Alabamian*, September 12, 1914; "A Beautiful Operetta," *Colored Alabamian*, September 12, 1914; "Madame Margaret Egbert," *Colored Alabamian*, April 8, 1911; "Madame Martha Broadus-Anderson," *Colored Alabamian*, July 3, 1915.

28. "Resolutions of Respect of the late Deacon William Watkins," *Colored Alabamian*, March 28, 1914; Evans and Alexander, *Dexter Avenue*, 38.

29. C. O. Boothe, *The Cyclopedia of the Colored Baptists of Alabama* (Birmingham, Ala.: Alabama Publishing, 1895), 33; Montgomery, *Under Their Own Vine and Fig*

Tree, 260; "Seventh Anniversary Celebration," *Colored Alabamian*, June 18, 1912; *Colored Alabamian*, April 17, 1909; *Colored Alabamian*, December 14, 1907; *Colored Alabamian*, March 9, 1912; *Colored Alabamian*, June 5, 1912; *Colored Alabamian*, November 23, 1912; *Colored Alabamian*, February 22, 1913; *Colored Alabamian*, March 8, 1913; Frank Lincoln Mather, *Who's Who of the Colored Race: A General Biographical Dictionary of Men and Women of African Descent* (1915; reprint, Detroit: Gale, 1976), 217.

30. *Colored Alabamian*, December 14, 1907; *Colored Alabamian*, August 22, 1908.
31. *Colored Alabamian*, October 26, 1907.
32. "Colored Ministers and Leaders Make Protest Against Cruel and Inhuman Treatment of Their Race: They Condemn Crime and Plead for the Protection of the Law," *Colored Alabamian*, August 22, 1908.
33. *Colored Alabamian*, February 8, 1913.
34. Washington, *Frustrated Fellowship*, 196; Glenda Gilmore, *Gender and Jim Crow* 3.
35. "Emancipation Day in Birmingham," *Colored Alabamian*, January 15, 1910.
36. See *Dictionary of Negro Biography*, ed. Raford Logan and Michael R. Winston (New York: W. W. Norton, 1982), 271.
37. "The Great Mass Meeting at Dexter Avenue Baptist Church," *Colored Alabamian*, November 23, 1907; "Reverend Sutton E. Griggs of Nashville, Tennessee Gives Speech on Race Problem, "*Colored Alabamian*, November 16, 1907.
38. "The Great Mass Meeting"; "Literary and Social Circles Enlivened by Coming of Webster Davis," *Colored Alabamian*, August 15, 1908; "Kelly Miller Appears in the Great Lecture Course at Dexter Avenue Baptist Church," *Colored Alabamian*, February 27, 1909.
39. "Fifth Anniversary of the Pastorate of Rev. R. C. Judkins," *Colored Alabamian*, June 18, 1910.
40. "A Notable Gathering at Dexter Avenue Baptist Church," *Colored Alabamian*, February 22, 1913.
41. For a discussion of the work of Nannie Helen Burroughs see Evelyn Brooks Higginbotham, "Religion, Politics and Gender: The Leadership of Nannie Helen Burroughs," in *This Far by Faith*, ed. Judith Weisenfeld and Richard Newman (New York: Routledge, 1996), 140–54; "Miss N. H. Burroughs in Montgomery," *Colored Alabamian*, March 29, 1913.
42. "Two Great Southern White Men Discuss Race Problem," *Colored Alabamian*, October 26, 1912.
43. "Honorable J. C. Manning in Montgomery," *Colored Alabamian*, March 14, 1914.
44. Evelyn Brooks Higginbotham, *Righteous Discontent: The Woman's Movement in the Black Baptist Church* (Cambridge, Mass.: Harvard University Press, 1993), 1; Based on a listing of membership (see *Colored Alabamian*, October 19, 1907), approximately 68 percent of the congregation were women.
45. "Woman's Missionary Society at Dexter Avenue Met Last Tuesday," *Colored Alabamian*, April 23, 1910. King interview, July 14, 1993. Higginbotham, *Righteous Discontent*, 200.
46. "Articles of Incorporation," July 25, 1887, cited in Evans and Alexander, *Dexter Avenue*, 204–7.
47. "Christmas Dinner for the Poor," *Colored Alabamian*, December 25, 1909. "Xmas Dinner," *Colored Alabamian*, January 4, 1913.
48. "Health Week Program at Dexter Avenue Baptist Church," *Colored Alabamian*, March 27, 1915. See also Tara Hunter, *To Joy My Freedom: Southern Black Women's Lives and Labors after the Civil War* (Cambridge: Harvard University Press, 1997), especially the chapter "Tuberculosis as the 'Negro Servant Disease,'" 187–219; for a discussion of how endemic and epidemic illnesses become infused with cultural meanings, see

Susan Sontag, *Illness as Metaphor* (New York: Farrar, Straus and Giroux, 1977); for a discussion of disease and social thought during the late nineteenth and early twentieth centuries see Charles E. Rosenberg, *No Other Gods: On Science and American Social Thought* (Baltimore: Johns Hopkins University Press, 1997), 25–54.

49. Obituary for Henrietta M. Gibbs, December 1, 1960, DAKMBCP; Cynthia Neverdon-Morton, "The Black Woman's Struggle for Equality in the South, 1895–1925," in *The Afro-American Woman: Struggles and Images* (Port Washington, N.Y.: Kennikat, 1978), 43; "Miss Cornelia Bowen's Appearance at Dexter Avenue Baptist Church," *Colored Alabamian*, May 9, 1914.

50. *Colored Alabamian*, September 28, 1912; Gibbs obituary. For a discussion of African-American women and suffrage see Rosalyn Terborg-Penn, "Discontented Black Feminists: Preludes and Postscript to the Passage of the Nineteenth Amendment," in *We Specialize in the Wholly Impossible: A Reader in Black Women's History*, ed. Darlene Clark Heine, Wilma King, and Linda Reed (New York: New York University Press, 1995), 487–505.

51. "Negro Preacher Resigns Charge of Local Church—Pastor of Dexter Avenue Baptist Congregation Quits after 11 Years of Continuous Service," *Montgomery Advertiser*, 1916.

52. "A Review of the Pastor and Labor of Dr. R. C. Judkins for the Last Three Years," *Colored Alabamian*, June 20, 1908; *Colored Alabamian*, June 17, 1911.

53. Alexis de Tocqueville, *Democracy in America* (New York: Doubleday, 1969), 287; *Colored Alabamian*, December 14, 1907; *Colored Alabamian*, February 8, 1908.

54. *Colored Alabamian*, January 7, 1911; John Brown Childs, *The Political Black Minister: A Study in Afro-American Politics and Religion* (Boston: G. K. Hall, 1980), 1; Woodson, *The History of the Negro Church*, 248.

Chapter 3

1. *Minutes of the Twentieth-First Annual Session of the Alabama Baptist State Convention held at The African Baptist Church, Tuscaloosa, Alabama, July 18–21, 1888.* American Baptist–Samuel Colgate Historical Library, Colgate-Rochester Divinity School, Rochester, New York.

2. William Warren Rogers, Robert David Ward, Leah Rawls Atkins, and Wayne Flynt, *Alabama: The History of a Deep South State* (Tuscaloosa: University of Alabama Press, 1994), 354–55, 411, 371; Sheldon Hackney, *Populism to Progressivism in Alabama* (Princeton, N.J.: Princeton University Press, 1969), 32–47; Allen J. Going, *Bourbon Democracy in Alabama, 1874–1890* (Tuscaloosa: University of Alabama Press, 1951), 49–52; Malcolm Cook Macmillan, *Constitutional Development in Alabama 1798–1901: A Study in Politics, the Negro and Sectionalism* (Spartanburg, S.C.: Reprint Company, 1978); Joseph M. Brittain, "Negro Politics in Alabama since 1970" (Ph.D. diss., University of Indiana, 1958); R. D. Nesbitt, interview with the author, May 4, 1994.

3. Randall Burkett, "The Baptist Church in the Years of Crisis: J. C. Austin and Pilgrim Baptist Church, 1926–1950," in *African-American Christianity: Essays in History*, ed. Paul Johnson (Berkeley and Los Angeles: University of California Press, 1994), 134.

4. See C. Eric Lincoln and Lawrence Mamiya, *The Black Church in the African-American Experience* (Durham, N.C.: Duke University Press, 1990), 30, 97, 118–21 for a discussion of the significance of the northern black migrations on the black churches in the South.

5. Arthur H. Fauset, *Black Gods of the Metropolis* (Philadelphia: University of Pennsylvania Press, 1994).

6. Gayraud Wilmore, *Black Religion and Black Radicalism: An Interpretation of the Religious History of Afro-American People*, 2d rev. ed. (Maryknoll, N.Y.: Orbis, 1983), 152–60. See also Howard Bortz, "Rabbi Matthew: Black Judaism in Harlem," 399–403;

"The First Afro-American Catholic Congress, 1889," 267–71; Father Divine, "The Realness of God, to You-wards ...," 404–12; Wallace Muhammad, "Self-Government in the New World," in *Afro-American Religious History: A Documentary Witness*, ed. Milton Sernett (Durham, N.C.: Duke University Press, 1985), 413–20.

7. Wilmore, *Black Religion and Black Radicalism*, 166.

8. Burkett, "The Baptist Church in the Years of Crisis," 134–35.

9. Ibid., 135.

10. According to the U.S. Department of Commerce, Bureau of Census, *Census of Religious Bodies: 1936* (Washington D.C.: U.S. Government Printing Office, 1941), 1: 900–903, between 1926 and 1936 there was a 9 percent increase in membership in black churches (from 5.2 million to 5.7 million), while membership in black Baptist churches increased from 3.2 million to 3.8 million.

11. See Benjamin Mays and Joseph Nicholson, *The Negro's Church* (New York: Institute of Social and Religious Research, 1933), 10; Lincoln and Mamiya, *The Black Church*, 92–115; Edna Doak King, interview with the author, July 20, 1993. In 1916, Reverend W. W. Colley filled the Dexter Avenue pulpit for several months. Even though he is listed in the celebration history as a pastor, no record of the church's activities during his pastorate exists.

12. "Dexter Avenue Baptist Church Notes," *Emancipator*, November 10, 1917; U. S. Department of the Interior, *National Register of Historic Places Inventory-Nomination Form*, pastorium for Dexter Avenue Baptist Church, 1982, Dexter Avenue King Memorial Baptist Church Papers (hereafter DAKMBCP); "Young Men Organize for Effective Work," *Colored Alabamian*, October 17, 1914. In the 1920s the Men's Church Aid Band became the Brotherhood. The First Congregational Church was founded by the American Missionary Association after the Civil War to help educate newly freed slaves.

13. "Big Revival at Dexter Avenue Baptist Church," *Emancipator*, April 13, 1918; Nesbitt interview, May 4, 1994.

14. The *Emancipator* was published from 1917 to 1920; its credo was, "This publication is dedicated to the Colored people of America, and to all other peoples fettered by visible or invisible chains."

15. *Emancipator*, October 6, 1917; *Emancipator*, October 13, 1917; "Mammoth Chorus of Colored Citizens Organized," *Emancipator*, October 20, 1917; *Emancipator*, November 17, 1920.

16. *Emancipator*, December 8, 1917; *Emancipator*, November 17, 1917; *Emancipator*, October 6, 1917; *Emancipator*, December 8, 1917.

17. "National Association for the Advancement of Colored People Holds Interesting Meeting," *Emancipator*, August 31, 1918; "Memorial to Alabama Legislature Aroused Keen Interest," *Emancipator*, February 8, 1919; "NAACP Holds Interesting Meeting at Dexter Avenue Baptist Church," *Emancipator*, June 21, 1919.

18. The lecture series did not reappear until the pastorate of Martin Luther King Jr.

19. "Death Claims Prominent Preacher: R. C. Judkins, Former Resident of Montgomery Dies in New Jersey," *Emancipator*, August 16, 1919.

20. "Memorial Held in Honor of Late Reverend R. C. Judkins Tuesday Evening," *Emancipator*, November 11, 1919.

21. See Chapter 2 of this volume for examples of the many times Loveless spoke on behalf of the congregation. Also, see his biographical sketch in Clement Richardson, *The National Cyclopedia of the Colored Race* (Montgomery, Ala.: National, 1919), 47, for examples of his representing the church in civic and public life.

22. Estate of Henry A. Loveless, 1921, Alabama State Historical Archives, Montgomery, Alabama (hereafter ASHA).

23. Zelia Evans and J. T. Alexander, *The Dexter Avenue Baptist Church* (Montgomery, Ala.: Dexter Avenue Baptist Church, 1978), 242.

24. Ibid.; Last Will and Testament of Bertha Loveless, ASHA.

25. Evans and Alexander, *Dexter Avenue*, 42–43.

26. Resolutions from the Pastor for the Church, May 17, 1926, DAKMBCP; Minutes of the Official Board of the Dexter Avenue Baptist Church (hereafter MOB), October 29, 1926, DAKMBCP. The official board consisted of the joint meeting of three organizations: the board of deacons, the pastor's advisory board, and the board of trustees.

27. Every Member Canvass, Dexter Avenue Baptist Church, June 20–27, 1926, DAKMBCP.

28. The salaries and expenses were as follows: pastor, $1,800; organist, $300; chorister, $120; clerk, $60; secretary, $60; sexton, $180; supplies and utilities, $1930; benevolence, $700; and parsonage, $650 (DAKMBCP).

29. Every Member Canvass.

30. Annual Message of the Pastor to the Congregation, June 1927, DAKMBCP.

31. MOB, March 7, 1927, DAKMBCP; "The Formal Opening of the Ladies Restroom," program, February 20, 1927, DAKMBCP; Program for The Dedication of the New Steps, June 19, 1927; DAKMBCP.

32. Church Bulletin, August 26, 1926, DAKMBCP; Recommendations for Church Quarterly Conference, October 3, 1928, DAKMBCP. Jacobs calculated that they should be able to raise $1,500 to be distributed as follows: $600 for bank notes; $250 for Selma University; $100 to repair the church furnace; $40 to repair the church automobile; and $390 to be used for expenses during the winter months.

33. Record of Missionary Meeting of Dexter Avenue Baptist Church, 1926, DAKMBCP.

34. Quarterly Report of Auxiliaries of Dexter Avenue Baptist Church, DAKMBCP.

35. Homecoming Day Program, Dexter Avenue Baptist Church, October 10, 1926, DAKMBCP. It was not officially decided until October 7, 1930, by common consent of the board to combine a memorial service along with the annual homecoming service.

36. F. W. Jacobs to the American Baptist Publishing Society (letter), April 8, 1929, DAKMBCP; MOB, August 8, 1931, DAKMBCP.

37. MOB, January 5, 1931, DAKMBCP; Dexter Avenue Baptist Church Bulletin, August 22, 1926 and May 29, 1927, DAKMBCP.

38. Resolutions from the Pastor for the Church, May 17, 1926, DAKMBCP; MOB, October 4, 1926, DAKMBCP.

39. Rogers et al., *Alabama*, 465–66; MOB, October 18, 1926 and November 22, 1926, DAKMBCP; Reverend F. W. Jacobs to Loveless Undertaking Company (letter), April 15, 1929, DAKMBCP.

40. Obituary for R. T. Grant, July 11, 1928, DAKMBCP.

41. F. W. Jacobs, "Negro Church Life in Montgomery," DAKMBCP; MOB, March 21, 1931; DAKMBCP. Rogers et al., *Alabama*, 411–43; Evelyn Brooks Higginbotham, *Righteous Discontent: The Woman's Movement in the Black Baptist Church* (Cambridge, Mass.: Harvard University Press, 1993), 200.

42. MOB, December 8, 1930 and January 19, 1931, DAKMBCP; Frank W. Jacobs to Joseph Taylor (letter), July 17, 1933, DAKMBCP.

43. Minutes of Regular Church Conference of Dexter Avenue Baptist Church, April 13, 1932, DAKMBCP; MOB, March 1932, DAKMBCP; Jacobs to Taylor, July 17, 1933; Report of the Committee on Resolutions, Dexter Avenue Baptist Church, April 24, 1932, DAKMBCP.

44. For a discussion of the details of the negotiations between Jacobs and Dexter Avenue, see the following letters: F. W. Jacobs to J. H. Taylor, Clerk of Dexter Avenue, June 8, 1933; Joseph H. Taylor to F. W. Jacobs, June 20, 1933; F. W. Jacobs to Joseph Taylor, July 17, 1933; W. W. Blocker, Clerk of Dexter Avenue, to F. W. Jacobs, August 7, 1933;

F .W. Jacobs to W. W. Blocker, August 23, 1933: all DAKMBCP. MOB, June 6, 1932 and May 21, 1932, DAKMBCP.

45. MOB, June 6, 1932, DAKMBCP.

46. MOB, June 6, 1932, October 17, 1932, and August 22, 1932, DAKMBCP.

47. MOB, November 21, 1932 and December 11, 1932, DAKMBCP; Nesbitt interview, May 4, 1994; Oberlin College Alumni Catalogue, 1936, Oberlin College Archives, Oberlin, Ohio.

48. MOB, July 3, 1933, DAKMBCP.

49. Church Bulletin, January 30, 1937, June 6, 1947, November 14, 1937, and July 31, 1938, DAKMBCP; MOB, May 7, 1934, DAKMBCP.

50. Church Bulletin, October 22, 1935, February 14, 1937, April 18, 1937, April 24, 1937, May 30, 1937, December 12, 1937, April 10, 1938, DAKMBCP; MOB, July 17, 1933 and July 3, 1933, DAKMBCP.

51. Church Bulletin, March 13, 1937 and April 24, 1938, DAKMBCP; Men's Day Program, April 24, 1938, DAKMBCP; MOB, March 20, 1938, DAKMBCP.

52. Women's Day Program, May 22, 1938, DAKMBCP.

53. Obituary for J. A. Lawrence, January 3, 1937, DAKMBCP.

54. While Streety and Nesbitt played significant roles, leaders elected from the then younger generation included J. T. Alexander, C. C. Beverly, William McGhee, Lillian Shannon, R. Smiley, and W. J. Wood; DAKMBCP.

55. Special Meetings of the Board of Deacons, December 1936, DAKMBCP.

56. Evans and Alexander, *Dexter Avenue*, 253.

57. R. D. Nesbitt, interview with the author, May 5, 1994; King interview.

58. MOB, 1938 (precise date not specified), DAKMBCP.

59. MOB, June 2, 1939, DAKMBCP.

60. MOB, June 19, 1939 and July 23, 1939, DAKMBCP.

61. MOB, July 23, 1939, September 24, 1939, and October 9, 1939, DAKMBCP.

62. MOB, September 24, 1939 and October 9, 1939, DAKMBCP.

63. J. A. Wilson to R. D. Nesbitt (letter), September 8, 1939; W. Y. Bell to Mrs. H. M. Gibbs (letter), August 29, 1939; Ralph Riley to R. D. Nesbitt (letter), September 19, 1939; all DAKMBCP.

64. MOB, October 9, 1939, DAKMBCP; Evans and Alexander, *Dexter Avenue*, 58.

65. MOB, October 22, 1939, DAKMBCP. Ralph Riley to R. D. Nesbitt (letter), October 27, 1939, DAKMBCP; Ralph Riley to R. D. Nesbitt (letter), November 28, 1939, DAKMBCP; MOB, November 5, 1939, DAKMBCP.

66. MOB, December 4, 1939, DAKMBCP.

67. Minutes of Church Meeting, December 10, 1939, DAKMBCP.

68. Minutes of the Quarterly Church Conference, December 19, 1939, DAKMBCP.

69. Ibid.

70. MOB, July 1941, DAKMBCP; Rogers et al., *Alabama*, 510; Minutes of the Quarterly Church Conference, August 14, 1941, DAKMBCP; MOB, January 13, 1942, DAKMBCP.

71. Minutes of Dexter Avenue Board of Deacons, December 18, 1939, DAKMBCP.

72. Evans and Alexander, *Dexter Avenue*, 60.

73. Program for Youth Day, March 9, 1941, DAKMBCP.

74. Annual Report of the BTU, 1941, DAKMBCP.

75. Annual Report of the Sunday School, 1941, DAKMBCP.

76. Ibid.; Sunday School Program, 1941, DAKMBCP.

77. Church Bulletin, May 1, 1943, DAKMBCP.

78. Interracial Day Program, February 8, 1942, DAKMBCP. Sources do not reveal the precise nature of these occasions; it seems that Dexter youth made up the largest percent of the audience, but it is unlikely that their white contemporaries joined them in this pursuit.

79. Ibid.
80. Church Bulletin, April 5, 1942, DAKMBCP.
81. Rogers et al., *Alabama*, 511; Church Bulletin, May 5, 1942, DAKMBCP; MOB, January 13, 1942, DAKMBCP; Church Bulletin, January 18, 1942, August 1, 1943, and October 13, 1943, DAKMBCP; Wesley Phillips Newton, *Montgomery in the Good War: Portrait of a Southern City, 1939–1946* (Tuscaloosa: University of Alabama Press, 2000), xviii.
82. Sermon given by Reverend Ralph Riley at Dexter Avenue Baptist Church, December 19, 1943, DAKMBCP.
83. Church Bulletin, March 26, 1944, DAKMBCP; Nesbitt interview, May 5, 1994.
84. Minutes of Special Meeting of the Church Officers, April 30, 1944, DAKMBCP; Minutes of the Official Board of Dexter Avenue Baptist Church, May 7, 1944, DAKMBCP.
85. MOB, June 5, 1944, DAKMBCP.
86. MOB, August 7, 1944, DAKMBCP.
87. Evans and Alexander, *Dexter Avenue*, 62.
88. Nesbit interview, May 4, 1994.
89. "Memorial Service for Franklin D. Roosevelt" (program), April 15, 1945, DAKMBCP.
90. MOB, May 14, 1945 and June 11, 1945, DAKMBCP.
91. MOB, October 10, 1946, DAKMBCP; Church Bulletin, March 16, 1946, DAKMBCP; Evans and Alexander, *Dexter Avenue*, 62.
92. MOB, October 10, 1945 and April 7, 1947, DAKMBCP; Taylor Branch, *Parting the Waters: America in the King Years* (New York: Simon and Schuster, 1988), 5.
93. Church Bulletin, March 3, 1946, DAKMBCP; MOB, December 8, 1947, DAKMBCP.
94. Nesbitt interview, May 4, 1994; MOB, January 7, 1948, DAKMBCP.
95. Minutes of Special Church Meeting, February 1, 1948, DAKMBCP.
96. Interview with R. D. Nesbitt, May 4, 1994, DAKMBCP; King interview.
97. Bulletin for Church Anniversary, 1968, DAKMBCP.

Chapter 4

1. Godphrey Hodgson, *America in Our Time* (New York: Vintage, 1976), 20; William Warren Rogers, Robert David Ward, Leah Rawls Atkins, and Wayne Flynt, *Alabama: The History of a Deep South State* (Tuscaloosa: University of Alabama Press, 1994), 510–11; 515–16; 524–44; 578–79; William D. Barnard, The Old Order Changes: Graves, Sparks, Folsom and the Gubernatorial Election of 1942," in *From Civil War to Civil Rights*, ed. Sarah Woolfolk Wiggins (Tuscaloosa: University of Alabama Press, 1987), 413–31; Virginia Hamilton, *Alabama: A Bicentennial History* (New York: W. W. Norton, 1977), 96–102; Lawrence Scott, *Double V: The Civil Rights Struggle of the Tuskegee Airmen* (East Lansing: Michigan State University Press, 1994), 3–15; Charles E. Francis, *The Tuskegee Airmen: The Men Who Changed a Nation* (Boston: Brandon, 1993), 40–66. The Air Corps did not accept black airmen on an integrated basis, but created a separate unit.
2. Carl Grafton, "James E. Folsom and Civil Liberties in Alabama," *Alabama Review*, no. 32 (1979); see also William D. Barnard, *Dixiecrats and Democrats: Alabama Politics, 1942–1950* (Tuscaloosa: University of Alabama Press, 1974).
3. For more on *Smith v. Allwright*, see "Voting Rights," in *The Supreme Court and the Constitution: Readings in American Constitutional History*, 3d ed., ed. Stanley Kutler (1969; reprint, New York: W. W. Norton, 1984), 589–92. For a discussion of liberalism as a political ideology see Geoffrey Hodgson, *America in Our Time* (New York: Vintage, 1976); David Plotke, *Building a Democratic Political Order: Reshaping American Liberalism in the 1930s and 1940s* (New York: Cambridge University Press, 1996); James Young, *Reconsidering American Liberalism: The Troubled Odyssey of Liberal Ideas* (Boulder, Colo.: Westview, 1996); and Stephen Defoe, *Arthur M. Schlesinger, Jr. and the Ideological History of American Liberalism* (Tuscaloosa: University of Alabama

Press, 1994). For a discussion of liberalism in Alabama see, Rogers et al., *Alabama*, 524–66; Hamilton, *Alabama: A Bicentennial History*, 96–102; Thomas J. Gilliam, "The Second Folsom Administration: The Destruction of Alabama Liberalism, 1954–58" (Ph.D. diss., Auburn University, 1975.

4. For an excellent, comprehensive, and detailed discussion of Montgomery city politics during the 1940s and 1950s see J. Mills Thornton III, *Dividing Lines: Municipal Politics and the Struggle for Civil Rights in Montgomery, Birmingham and Selma* (Tuscaloosa: University of Alabama Press, 1902), 20–52.

5. Alfred Lewis Bratcher and Charles Stakely, *Eighty-Three Years: The Moving Story of Church Growth* (Montgomery: Paragon, 1950), 40–41.

6. Rogers et al., *Alabama*, 524–66; Hamilton, *Alabama: A Bicentennial History*, 97.

7. C. Eric Lincoln and Lawrence Mamiya, *The Black Church in the African-American Experience* (Durham, N.C.: Duke University Press, 1990), 164–96. Aldon Morris, *The Origins of the Civil Rights Movement: Black Communities Organizing for Change* (New York: Free Press, 1984); Donna Irvin, *The Unsung Heart of Black America* (Columbia: University of Missouri Press, 1992); H. Richard Niebuhr, *The Social Sources of Denominationalism* (New York: World, 1957); Edwin Gausted, *Dissent in American Religion* (Chicago: University of Chicago Press, 1973), 34–35, 100–111; Taylor Branch, *Parting the Waters: America in the King Years* (New York: Simon and Schuster, 1988), 1–64. See Adolph Reed, *The Jesse Jackson Phenomenon: The Crisis in Purpose in Afro-American Politics* (New Haven, Conn.: Yale University Press, 1986), especially the chapter "Mythology of the Church in Contemporary Society," for an alternative position on the role of the black church in the civil rights movement.

8. Church Constitution, 1891, Dexter Avenue King Memorial Baptist Church Papers (hereafter DAKMBCP).

9. Milton Sernett, ed., *Afro-American Religious History: A Documentary Witness* (Durham: Duke University Press, 1985), 229–489. For a discussion of black migrations after World War II see Nicolas Lehman, *The Promised Land* (New York: Vintage Books, 1991); Joe William Trotter, Jr., *The Great Migration in Historical Perspective: New Dimensions of Race, Class and Gender* (Bloomington: Indiana University Press, 1991) 90–92; Lincoln and Mamiya, *The Black Church in the African American Experience*, 164–196; Gayraud Wilmore, *Black Religion and Black Radicalism: An Interpretation of the Religious History of Afro-American People*, 2d rev. ed. (Maryknoll, N.Y.: Orbis, 1983), 134; E. Franklin Frazier, *The Negro Church in America* (New York: Shocken, 1974); C. Eric Lincoln *The Church since Frazier* (New York: Schocken, 1974); Rogers et al., *Alabama*, 445–52; and Morris, *The Origins of the Civil Rights Movement*. Martin Luther King Sr., *Daddy King: An Autobiography* (New York: William Morrow, 1980); Samuel Lucius Gandy ed., *Human Possibilities: A Vernon Johns Reader* (Washington, D.C.: Hoffman, 1977); Charles Boddie, ed., *God's Bad Boys* (Valley Forge, Pa: Judson Press, 1972).

10. E. Franklin Frazier, *The Black Bourgeoisie* (New York: Macmillan, 1957), R. D. Nesbitt, interview with the author, May 13, 1994; Thelma Austin Rice, interview with the author, May 16, 1994; Dr. Ralph Bryson, interview with the author, October 5, 1994.

11. R. D. Nesbitt, interview with the author, May 5, 1994. Edna Doak King, interview with the author, July 20, 1993. Branch, *Parting the Waters*, 7–27.

12. Minutes of the Official Board of the Dexter Avenue Baptist Church (hereafter MOB), September 7, 1948, DAKMBCP; alumni record of Vernon Johns, Oberlin College, Oberlin College Archives, Oberlin, Ohio; Nesbitt interview, May 13, 1994.

13. Nesbitt interview, May 5, 1994; Charles Hamilton, *The Black Preacher in America* (New York: William Morrow, 1972), 148–87; Joseph A. Johnson Jr., *The Soul of the Black Preacher* (Philadelphia: Pilgrim, 1971) 13–31; 143–67; MOB, September 7, 1948, DAKMBCP.

14. MOB, October 11, 1948 and September 12, 1948, DAKMBCP.

15. Vernon N. Johns to R. D. Nesbitt (telegram), October 1, 1948, DAKMBCP.

16. Boddie, *God's Bad Boy*, 62; see also Branch, *Parting the Waters*, 4-15; *Jet*, July 22, 1965, 47.

17. Altona Trent Johns, "As I Remember," in Gandy, ed., *Human Possibilities*, see also Vernon Johns, "The Jew Discovers the Ground the Negro Should," in Gandy, ed., *Human Possibilities*.

18. For an in-depth discussion of the Virginia Seminary see Lester F. Russell, *Black Baptist Secondary Schools in Virginia: 1887–1957* (Metuchen, N.J.: Scarecrow, 1981), 49–57; Johns, "As I Remember," viii.

19. Robert Fletcher, *A History of Oberlin College from its Founding through the Civil War* (Oberlin, Ohio: Oberlin College, 1948); John Barnard, *From Evangelicalism to Progressivism at Oberlin College, 1866-1917* (Columbus: Ohio State University Press, 1969). Johns recalls Bosworth's help in a letter to Bosworth dated July 27, 1922, Oberlin College Archives, Oberlin, Ohio. Robert Hutchison became president of the University of Chicago.

20. Vernon Johns to George W. Fiske (letter), February 24, 1919, Oberlin College Archives, Oberlin, Ohio; George Fiske to Walter H. Byrd (letter), April 10, 1926, Oberlin College Archives, Oberlin, Ohio; Boddie, *God's Bad Boys*, 62; Vernon Johns to George Fiske (letter), August 15, 1920, Oberlin College Archives, Oberlin, Ohio.

21. There is extensive literature on the social gospel in America; see, e.g., Sydney Alstrom, *A Religious History of the American People* (New Haven, Conn.: Yale University Press, 1972); Robert T. Handy, "The Protest Quest for a Christian America, 1830–1930," *Church History* 22, no. 1 (1953): 8–20; Sidney Mead, "Denominationalism: The Shape of Protestantism in America," *Church History* 23, no. 4 (1954): 291–320; A. Kathryn Rogers, *The Social Gospel and the Idea of Progress* (Chicago: University of Chicago Press, 1937); Robert White and C. Howard Hopkins, *The Social Gospel: Religion and Reform in Changing America* (Philadelphia: Temple University Press, 1976); Ralph Luker, *The Social Gospel in Black and White: American Racial Reform, 1885–1912* (Chapel Hill: University of North Carolina Press, 1991); and Curtis Robert Grant, "The Social Gospel and Race" (Ph.D. diss., Stanford University, 1968); For a thorough discussion of the development of the social gospel at Oberlin College, see Barnard, *From Evangelicalism to Progressivism*, 109–56.

22. Johns, "As I Remember," vii; Vernon Johns to George W. Fiske, March 6, 1919 and March, 1920 (letters), Oberlin College Archives, Oberlin, Ohio.

23. Flyer for the Southern Mercantile and Development Company, Vernon Johns Collection, Howard University Archives. Vernon Johns to George Fiske, March, 1920, March 22, 1920, and George Fiske to Vernon Johns, March 22, 1920 (letters), Oberlin College Archives, Oberlin, Ohio.

24. Vernon Johns to George W. Fiske, August 5, 1920, and Deacon Board of Court Street Baptist Church to Edward Increase Bosworth, August 12, 1921 (letters), Oberlin College Archives, Oberlin, Ohio. It should be noted here that there is some confusion over the recipient of the latter; it may have been George Fiske or Kemper Fullerton.

25. Vernon Johns to Edward Increase Bosworth (letter), August 17, 1920, Oberlin College Archive, Oberlin, Ohio.

26. Johns, "As I Remember," vii.

27. *Best Sermons, 1926*, ed. Joseph Fort Newton (New York: Harcourt, Brace, Jovanovich, 1926), 332. For a classic discussion of black middle-class life, see Frazier, *Black Bourgeoisie*; see also Earl Lewis, *In Their Own Interests: Race, Class and Power in Twentieth Century Norfolk* (Berkeley and Los Angeles: University of California Press, 1991); and Charles Banner-Haley, *The Fruits of Integration: Black Middle-Class Ideology and Culture, 1960-1990* (Judson: University Press of Mississippi, 1994).

28. See Johns's sermons: "A Jew Discovers the Ground the Negro Should," and "A Negro Agrarian Culture," in Gandy, ed. *Human Possibilities*, 129–36.

29. Alumni Records, Oberlin College Archives, Oberlin, Ohio. Branch, *Parting the Waters*, 10.

30. Nesbitt interview, May 5, 1994; Zelia Evans, interview with the author, July 21, 1993; Rice interview; Vernon Johns to George Fiske (letter), August 5, 1920, Oberlin College Archives, Oberlin Ohio.

31. Thelma Rice, "Retrospection, Introspection and Prospection," 7, DAKMBCP; Vernon Johns, "A Negro Agrarian Culture," 129–36; Vernon Johns, "Religion and the Open Mind," in Gandy, ed., *Human Possibilities*, 84–89.

32. Church Bulletin, December 5, 1948, DAKMBCP.

33. MOB, October 11, 1948, DAKMBCP.

34. Nesbitt interview, May 13, 1994; Evans interview, July 21, 1993; Rice interview; MOB, April 3, 1950 and December 11, 1950, DAKMBCP.

35. Nesbitt interview, May 13, 1994; Branch, *Parting the Waters*, 10. Zora Neal Hurston, "Spirituals," in *Negro Life*, ed. Nancy Canard (New York: Oxford University Press, 1969).

36. King interview.

37. Minutes of Church Conference Meeting, December 5, 1949, DAKMBCP; King interview; Nesbitt interview, May 13, 1994.

38. Johns, "Religion and the Open Mind," 85–89.

39. Vernon Johns, "What Ails the World?" in Gandy, ed., *Human Possibilities*, 78–83; Vernon Johns, "Transfigured Moments," in Gandy, ed., *Human Possibilities*, 49–59.

40. Johns, "Religion and the Open Mind," 85–89.

41. Nesbitt interview, May 13, 1994; Evans interview, July 20, 1993; Zelia Evans, interview with the author, March 24, 1994; King interview; Boddie, *God's Bad Boys*, 65.

42. Meeting of the board of deacons, December 11, 1950, DAKMBCP.

43. Vernon Johns, "A Plea for Confidence and Cooperation," in "A Jew Discovers the Ground the Negro Should: A Sermon Prospectus for A Corporation," August 1951, DAKMBCP.

44. Ibid.

45. Vernon Johns, "Rock Foundation," in Gandy, ed., *Human Possibilities*, 60–64; Johns, "Religion and the Open Mind," 85–89.

46. Nesbitt interview; Branch, *Parting the Waters*, 12, 22–23; Evans interview, March 24, 1994.

47. Jo Ann Robinson, *The Montgomery Bus Boycott and the Women Who Started It* (Knoxville: University of Tennessee Press, 1987), 23; Mary Fair Burks, "Women in the Montgomery Bus Boycott," in *Black Women in United States History*, vol. 16, ed. Darlene Clark Hine (New York: Carlson, 1990), 79.

48. Nesbitt interview, May 13, 1994; Branch, *Parting the Waters*, 15.

49. Lerone Bennett Jr., *What Manner of Man: A Biography of Martin Luther King, Jr.* (Chicago: Johnson, 1976), 50; Nesbitt interview, May 13, 1994.

50. MOB, December 17, 1950 and March 1951, DAKMBCP.

51. MOB, May 31, 1953, DAKMBCP; Minutes of Deacon Board, May 31, 1953, DAKMBCP; Resolutions Concerning the Resignation of Vernon Johns, June 1953, DAKMBCP; Church Clerk R. D. Nesbitt to Vernon Johns (letter), June 7, 1953, DAKMBCP.

52. Altona Trent Johns had moved back to Petersburg, Virginia, to accept a position in the music department at Virginia State University.

53. Branch, *Parting the Waters*, which includes the most comprehensive account of Johns's life, indicates that Johns leaves Montgomery in December 1952, but church records indicate that Johns preached his farewell sermon on May 3, 1953 (DAKMBCP).

54. Martin Luther King Jr., *Stride Toward Freedom: The Montgomery Story* (New York: Harper and Row, 1958), 36–39.

55. "Dr. V. Johns to Speak at Fries," *Winston-Salem Journal and Sentinel*, September 29, 1963; "Vernon Johns Speaks Here Next Week," *Norfolk* (Virginia) *Journal and Guide*, March 24, 1961; "Vauxhall Church Hosts Dr. Johns," *Union Leader*, October 1, 1959; "Emancipation Speaker," *Augusta Weekly Review*, January 29, 1962.

56. Vernon Johns, "The Romance of Death" in Gandy, ed., *Human Possibilities*, 124–25.

Chapter 5

1. "Racial Discrimination and the Search for Equality," in *The Supreme Court and the Constitution: Readings in American Constitutional History*, 3d ed., ed. Stanley Kutler (1969; reprint, New York: W. W. Norton, 1984), 548–53. Other important cases in education include *Missouri: ex rel Gaines v. Canada* (1938), *Ada Sipuel v. Oklahoma Regents* (1948), *McLaurin v. Oklahoma Regents* (1950), and *Sweat v. Painter* (1950); for a discussion of the impact of *Brown v. Board of Education* on public education, voting rights, public accommodations, and housing, see Derrick Bell, *Race, Racism, and American Law*, 3d ed. (Boston: Little, Brown, 1992); see also Michael R. Belknap, *Federal Law and Southern Order* (Athens: University of Georgia Press, 1987). For an excellent, thorough discussion of the life and contribution of Charles Hamilton Houston, see Genna Rae McNeil, *Groundwork: Charles Hamilton Houston and the Struggle for Civil Rights* (Philadelphia: University of Pennsylvania Press, 1983). *Birmingham World*, May 18, 1954; William Warren Rogers, Robert David Ward, Leah Rawls Atkins, and Wayne Flynt, *Alabama: The History of a Deep South State* (Tuscaloosa: University of Alabama Press, 1994), 524–47; Robert Smith, *They Closed Their Schools: Prince Edward County Virginia, 1951–1954* (Chapel Hill: University of North Carolina Press, 1965). For a discussion of the White Citizens Council, see John Bartlow Martin, *The Deep South Says "Never"* (New York: Ballantine, 1957), 1–43.

2. Minutes of the Official Board of the Dexter Avenue Baptist Church (hereafter MOB), March 6, 1950, January 8, 1951, and May 31, 1953, DAKMBCP. R. D. Nesbitt, interview with the author, May 5, 1994.

3. Crozer was a liberal Baptist Seminary, much in the tradition of Oberlin College in Ohio. The Seminary made a valiant effort to create a multiracial student body. In King's 1948 first-year class of thirty-two students, eleven were black, three were Chinese, one was Japanese, and several were American Indian. Walter McCall to Messrs. Randall and Nesbitt (letter), November 10, 1953, DAKMBCP; Nesbitt interview with author, May 13, 1994.

4. Martin Luther King Jr. was born Michael Luther King Jr., but his father changed his own names from Michael Luther to Martin Luther (an intentional reference to the sixteenth-century Protestant reformer), and then changed his son's name as well; there is a great deal of controversy surrounding the particular circumstances of the name change; see Taylor Branch, *Parting the Waters: America in the King Years* (New York: Simon and Schuster, 1988), 44–47; Nesbitt Interview; Walter McCall to Martin Luther King Jr. (letter), January 17, 1954, in *The Papers of Martin Luther King Jr.*, ed. Clayborne Carson (Berkeley and Los Angeles: University of California Press, 1994), 2:235–36 (hereafter cited as Carson, ed., *King Papers*); Nesbitt interview.

5. Martin Luther King Jr., *Stride Toward Freedom: The Montgomery Story* (New York: Harper and Row, 1958); David Levering Lewis, *King, A Biography* (Urbana: University of Illinois Press, 1978); Martin Luther King Sr., *Daddy King: An Autobiography* (New York: William Morrow, 1980). Currently, a professional history of Ebenezer Baptist Church does not exist, but a brief sketch is included in Carson, ed., *King Papers*, 1:6–26.

6. Martin Luther King Sr., *Daddy King*, 23–28, 15, 13; Willard Gatewood, *Aristocrats of Color* (Bloomington: Indiana University Press, 1993), 182–210.

7. Martin Luther King Sr., *Daddy King*, 62, 80.

8. Ibid., 82, 97; Branch, *Parting the Waters*, 40–44.

9. King began nursery school at age 3, then went to kindergarten and on to public elementary schools. In 1942 he enrolled in the Atlanta University Laboratory School, completing the grades 8 and 9 in a single year. He attended Booker T. Washington High School for the grades 10 and 11, but rather than return to complete grade 12 he enrolled early at Morehouse College. For accounts of King's education see Carson, ed., *King Papers*, 1:32-35; Greg Moses, *Revolution of Conscience: Martin Luther King, Jr., and the Philosophy of Nonviolence* (New York: Guilford, 1997); Benjamin Mays, *Born to Rebel: An Autobiography of Benjamin Mays* (New York: Charles Scribner's Sons, 1971), 172; see also Edward Jones, *A Candle in the Dark: A History of Morehouse College* (Valley Forge, Pa: Judson Press, 1967); Benjamin Brawley, *A History of Morehouse College* (Atlanta: Morehouse College, 1917); Addie Louise Joyner Butler, *The Distinctive Black College: Talladega, Tuskegee, and Morehouse* (Metuchen, N.J.: Scarecrow Press, 1977), 100–43.

10. See Martin Luther King Jr., "An Autobiography of Religious Development," in Carson, ed., *King Papers*, 1:361–63.

11. Martin Luther King Sr. to Charles E. Batten, Dean of Admission at Crozer Seminary (letter), March 5, 1948, in Carson, ed., *King Papers*, 1:150; Certification of minister's license for Martin Luther King Jr., February 4, 1948, in Carson, ed., *King Papers*, 1:153. Several biographical accounts of King suggest that his father pressured him to join him as copastor at Ebenezer; see Branch, *Parting the Waters*, 68; Stephen B. Oates, *Let the Trumpet Sound: The Life of Martin Luther King, Jr.* (New York: Harper and Row, 1982), 23–24; David Levering Lewis, *King, A Biography* (Urbana: University of Illinois Press, 1978), 25–26. Martin Luther King Sr., *Daddy King*, 144, notes, "I didn't oppose M.L.'s wish to continue his education with advanced graduate work … but my hope was that he'd soon join me as co-pastor at Ebenezer. He was a fine preacher."

12. Martin Luther King Jr., *Stride Toward Freedom*, 96.

13. Barbour and King were intellectual sparring partners. Barbour was blunt in his disapproval of King's decision to return to the South. When King wrote to tell Barbour of his great success at Dexter Avenue in the first months of his pastorate there, Barbour wrote back, "You need not tell me about Dexter; I know Montgomery [Barbour had pastored at Day Street Baptist Church in Montgomery during the 1920s] and its superficial intellectuality. A plant-head in the North has more WORLD WISDOM than a college Pres. in the SOUTH.… Something wrong with SOUTHERN INTELLECTUALITY. I Know what it is; it does not have the atmosphere that breeds profundity … all abstraction" J. Pius Barbour to Martin Luther King Jr. (letter), December 21, 1954, in Branch, *Parting the Waters*, 75–79; 94–99; King was fascinated by the idea of personalism (briefly, a philosophy that suggested that only personality—infinite and finite—is ultimately real) and intended to study under the foremost authority on this philosophical theory, Edgar Brightman, but Brightman died within a year of King's arrival on campus and so King transferred to the School of Theology, where he completed requirements for his Ph.D. Carson, ed., *King Papers*, 2:322–24; Coretta Scott King, *My Life with Martin Luther King, Jr.*, 50–90; Branch, *Parting the Waters*, 94–99; Martin Luther King Jr., *Stride Toward Freedom*, 15–25.

14. Nesbitt interview.

15. J. T. Brooks to Martin Luther King Sr. and Alberta Williams King (letter), November 16, 1953, in Carson, ed., *King Papers*, 2:211. Melvin H. Watson to Martin Luther King, Jr. (letter), November 19, 1953, in Carson, ed., King Papers, 2:212; Martin Luther King Jr. to J. T. Brooks (letter), November 24, 1953, DAKMBCP.

16. Nesbitt interview. For other discussions of the exchange between Nesbitt and King see Branch, *Parting the Waters*, 25–26; 104; David J. Garrow, *Bearing the Cross: Martin Luther King, Jr., and the Southern Christian Leadership Conference* (New York: William Morrow, 1986), 48–49.

17. G. A. Key, Chairman of Deacon Board, First Baptist Chattanooga, to Martin Luther King Jr. (letter), January 16, 1954, in Carson, ed., *King Papers*, 2:234; Nesbitt interview.

18. J. T. Brooks to Martin Luther King Jr. (letter), January 16, 1954, DAKMBCP.

19. Martin Luther King Jr., *Stride Toward Freedom*, 15–19; Branch, *Parting the Waters*, 104, 111; Ralph David Abernathy, *And the Walls Came Tumbling Down: An Autobiography* (New York: Harper and Row, 1989), 124.

20. Abernathy, *And the Walls Came Tumbling Down*, 116–30.

21. Branch, *Parting the Waters*, 108.

22. Martin Luther King Jr. *Stride Toward Freedom*, 17; Abernathy, *And the Walls Came Tumbling Down*, 126; Nesbitt interview; Zelia Evans, interview with the author, July 21, 1993, Mary Fair Burks, quoted in Coretta Scott King, *My Life with Martin*, 100.

23. Nesbitt interview; Walter McCall to Martin Luther King, Jr. (letter), January 17, 1954, in Carson, ed., *King Papers*, 2:235-6.

24. Coretta Scott King, *My Life with Martin*, 94–95; Martin Luther King, Jr. *Stride Toward Freedom*, 21.

25. R. D. Nesbitt, Chairman of the Pastoral Search Committee to the Board of Deacons (letter), March 1, 1954, DAKMBCP; R. D. Nesbitt to Martin Luther King Jr. (telegraph), March 7, 1954. DAKMBCP.

26. Joseph C. Parker Sr. to Martin Luther King Jr. (letter), March 10, 1954, in Carson, ed., *King Papers*, 2:257-8. On January 24, 1954, King preached his trial sermon, "The Three Dimensions of a Complete Life." The next week Walter McCall preached his second trial sermon at Dexter Avenue, "The Four Dimensions of a Complete Life." As Parker indicated, McCall's second sermon did not go over well at Dexter Avenue; DAKMBCP.

27. Martin Luther King Jr. to R. D. Nesbitt, March 10, 1954; R. D. Nesbitt to Martin Luther King Jr., March 15, 1954; and Martin Luther King Jr. to R. D. Nesbitt, March 24, 1954 (letters), DAKMBCP. Coretta Scott King, *My Life with Martin*, 88–89.

28. Martin Luther King Jr. to Members and Officers of Dexter Avenue Baptist Church (letter), April 14, 1954, DAKMBCP; Minutes of Special Church Conference, April 18, 1954, DAKMBCP; R. D. Nesbitt to Martin Luther King Jr. (letter), April 19, 1954, DAKMBCP.

29. Stephen B. Oates, *Let the Trumpet Sound*, 50; Branch, *Parting the Waters*, 112; Coretta Scott King, *My Life with Martin*, 102.

30. Coretta Scott King, *My Life with Martin*, 99–100.

31. Recommendations to the Dexter Avenue Baptist Church for the Fiscal Year 1954–1955, September 5, 1954, DAKMBCP.

32. Martin Luther King Jr., *Stride Toward Freedom*, 25–26; Minutes of the Church Conference Meeting, January 8, 1951, DAKMBCP; Recommendations to the Dexter Avenue Baptist Church for the Fiscal Year 1954–1955, September 5, 1954, DAKMBCP.

33. Recommendations to the Dexter Avenue Baptist Church for the Fiscal Year 1954–1955, September 5, 1954, DAKMBCP.

34. Zelia Evans, interview with the author, March 24, 1995; Nesbitt interview; Martin Luther King Jr., *Stride Toward Freedom*, 26; Coretta Scott King, *My Life with Martin*, 102; Martin Luther King Jr. to Walter McCall, October 20, 1954, in Carson, ed., *King Papers*, 2:302; Walter R. McCall to Martin Luther King Jr., October 21, 1954, in Carson, ed., *King Papers*, 2:304.

35. Melvin Watson to Martin Luther King Jr. (letter), October 21, 1954, in Carson, ed., *King Papers*, 2:302-3; Major J. Jones to Martin Luther King Jr. (letter), November 1954, in Carson, ed., *King Papers*, 2:306-8.

36. Minutes of the Montgomery-Antioch Association, November 4, 1954, in Carson, ed., *King Papers*, 2:33, 311–12; Nannie Helen Burroughs to Martin Luther King Jr. (letter), August 3, 1954, Carson, ed., *King Papers*, 2: 282–3; *Dexter Echo*, August 6, 1958, DAKMBCP; *Dexter Echo*, August 27, 1957, DAKMBCP.

37. Program of Installation Services for the Reverend Martin Luther King, Jr., October 31, 1954, DAKMBCP.

38. Martin Luther King Jr. to Walter R. McCall (letter), October 20, 1954, in Carson, ed., *King Papers*, 2:301–2; J. Pius Barbour to Martin Luther King Jr. (letter), December 21, 1954, in Carson, ed., *King Papers*, 2:322–24; Program of Installation Services, October 31, 1954, DAKMBCP.

39. Martin Luther King, Jr. to Ebenezer Baptist Church (letter), November 18, 1954; Martin Luther King Jr. to Ebenezer Baptist Church (letter), November 18, 1954; "King in Third Annual Pulpit Exchange," *Dexter Echo*, January 8, 1958, DAKMBCP.

40. Oates, *Let the Trumpet Sound*, 55–56; Clyde L. Reynolds to Martin Luther King Jr. (letter), October 9, 1954, DAKMBCP.

41. Coretta Scott King, *My Life with Martin*, 60; Branch, *Parting the Waters*, 118-119; Evans interview, March 24, 1994.

42. Zelia Evans and J. T. Alexander, *The Dexter Avenue Baptist Church* (Montgomery, Ala.: Dexter Avenue Baptist Church, 1978), 82; Program from the Women's Day ceremony, October 10, 1954, DAKMBCP; Martin Luther King Jr. to Walter R. McCall (letter), October 19, 1954, DAKMBCP.

43. Martin Luther King Jr. to Dr. Melvin Watson (letter), November 2, 1954, Carson, ed., *King Papers* 2:309; Program of 77th Anniversary of Dexter Avenue Baptist Church, December 11, 1954, DAKMBCP; Melvin H. Watson to Martin Luther King Jr. (letter), December 15, 1954, DAKMBCP.

44. "Baptist Youth Fellowship," pamphlet, January 27, 1955, DAKMBCP; Martin Luther King Jr. to Walter R. McCall (letter), October 19, 1954, in Carson, ed., *King Papers*, 2:301–2;

45. Program for the Annual Spring Lecture Series, April 27–29, 1955, DAKMBCP; Martin Luther King Jr. to Samuel Dewitt Proctor (letter), October, 1954, Carson, ed., *King Papers*, 2:297; Samuel Dewitt Proctor to Martin Luther King Jr. (letter), April 18, 1955, DAKMBCP.

46. Martin Luther King Jr. to Samuel Proctor (letter), April 11, 1955; Samuel Proctor to Martin Luther King Jr. (letter), April 18, 1955, DAKMBCP; Coretta Scott King, *My Life with Martin*, 106–7.

47. Press Release for Men's Day at Dexter Avenue Baptist Church, July 7, 1955, DAKMBCP. Martin Luther King Jr. to Dr. Benjamin Mays (letter), November 1954, DAKMBCP.

48. The Kings had four children: Yolanda, Martin Luther III, Dexter (named for the church), and Bernice Albertine (named for her grandmothers); Nesbitt interview; Annual Report for Dexter Avenue Baptist Church, 1954–55, DAKMBCP.

49. There is an extraordinarily large body of literature on the Montgomery Bus Boycott. My treatment of the boycott in this work will be necessarily limited and focused toward its direct intersection with the people of Dexter Avenue. For an in-depth discussion see David Garrow, ed., *The Walking City: The Montgomery Bus Boycott, 1955-1956* (Brooklyn, N.Y.: Carlson 1989); *Bearing the Cross: Martin Luther King Jr. and the Southern Christian Leadership Conference* (New York: William Morrow, 1986), 11–83; Jo Ann Robinson, *The Montgomery Bus Boycott and the Women Who Started It* (Knoxville: University of Tennessee Press, 1987), 53–167; Howell Raines, *My Soul is Rested: Movement Days in the Deep South* (New York: G. P. Putnam's Sons, 1977), 1–71; Martin Luther King Jr., *Stride Toward Freedom*; Coretta Scott King, *My Life with Martin*, 108-48; Branch, *Parting the Waters*, 143–206; Aldon Morris, *The Origins of the*

Civil Rights Movement: Black Communities Organizing for Change (New York: Free Press, 1984); Sarah Woolfolk Wiggins, *From Civil War to Civil Rights: Alabama, 1860–1960* (Tuscaloosa: University of Alabama Press, 1987) 463–520; Andrew Michael Manis, *Southern Civil Religions in Conflict* (Athens: University of Georgia Press, 1987) 60–67; Fred Gray, *Bus Ride to Justice: Changing the System; The Life and Work of Fred Gray, Lawyer for Rosa Parks* (Montgomery, Ala.: Black Belt, 1994); Robert Graetz, *Montgomery: A White Preacher's Memoir* (Minneapolis: Augsburg Fortress, 1991); and J. Mills Thornton III, *Dividing Lines*, 53–118; these works, though far from exhaustive, inform this work. "Negroes Urging Bus Boycott," *Alabama Journal*, December 3, 1955, Alabama State Historical Archives, Montgomery, Alabama (hereafter ASHA).

50. Over the years several chapters of the WPC formed throughout the city, but the first was founded by Mary Fair Burks at Dexter Avenue. Robinson, *The Montgomery Bus Boycott*, 23; Mrs. Johnnie Carr, interview with the author, May 13, 1994; Virginia Durr, interview with the author, February 17, 1994.

51. Carr interview; "Negroes Urging Bus Boycott."

52. Robinson, *The Montgomery Bus Boycott*, 15–17.

53. Pamphlet on Women's Political Council, n.d., DAKMBCP; David Garrow, "The Origins of the Montgomery Bus Boycott," *Southern Changes*, no. 7 (1985): 21–27; J. Mills Thornton, "Challenge and Response in the Montgomery Bus Boycott," *Alabama Review*, July 1980, 163–235; "Letter from Jo Ann Gibson Robinson to the Honorable Mayor W. A. Gayle, May 21, 1954," in Robinson, *The Montgomery Bus Boycott*, viii.

54. J. Mills Thornton III, "Touched by History: A Civil Rights Tour Guide to Montgomery, Alabama," pamphlet, (Montgomery: Dexter Avenue Baptist Church and the Southern Regional Council, c. 1980), 11; Pamphlet of the Social and Political Action Committee, 1957, DAKMBCP.

55. Martin Luther King Jr., *Stride Toward Freedom*, 47.

56. Church Bulletin, December 4, 1955, DAKMBCP; "Negroes Urging Bus Boycott," *Alabama Journal*, December 3, 1955; Carson, ed., *King Papers*, 3:35; Nesbitt interview.

57. Martin Luther King Jr., *Stride Toward Freedom*, 54; Bunny Honicker, "Bus Officials Agree to Meet With Negroes," *Alabama Journal*, December 6, 1955, ASHA.

58. Martin Luther King Jr., *Stride Toward Freedom*, 50–59; Joe Azbell, "Negro Groups Ready Boycott of City Lines," *Montgomery Advertiser*, December 5, 1955, ASHA; David Garrow, introduction to Garrow, ed., *The Walking City*, xiii–iv; The body of literature on the civil rights movement is staggering. For a good overview, see Stephen F. Lawson, "Freedom Then, Freedom Now: The Historiography of the Civil Rights Movement," *American Historical Review*, no. 96 (1991): 456–71; and James F. Findley, "Religion and Politics in the Sixties: The Churches and the Civil Rights Act of 1964," *Journal of American History*, no. 77 (1990): 66–92.

59. Martin Luther King Jr., *Stride Toward Freedom*, 63.

60. Evans interview, March 24, 1994; Coretta Scott King, *My Life with Martin*, 117; 106; Church Bulletin, October 6, 1957, DAKMBCP; Social and Political Action Committee Voter Registration Form, DAKMBCP; Social and Political Action Committee Description of Candidates and Positions, DAKMBCP.

61. Thelma Austin Rice to Martin Luther King Jr. (letter), copy provided to author by Thelma Austin Rice; Nesbitt interview; Coretta Scott King, *My Life with Martin*, 127; Martin Luther King Jr., *Stride Toward Freedom*, 132.

62. Joe Azbell, "Blasts Rocks Residence of Bus Boycott Leader," *Montgomery Advertiser*, January 31, 1956, ASHA; Coretta Scott King, *My Life with Martin*, 126–27.

63. "The Montgomery Protest as a Social Movement," in Garrow, ed., *The Walking City*, 83–98.

64. Martin Luther King Jr. to Ralph W. Riley (letter), December 21, 1955, DAKMBCP.

65. *King Papers*, 3:37.

66. See James M. Washington, ed., *The Essential Writings of Martin Luther King, Jr.* (San Francisco: Harper and Row, 1986), ix–xxiv; in the introduction to this work, Washington includes an excellent discussion of the traditions that contribute to the development of King as a minister and a prophetic voice. See also Keith Miller, *Voice of Deliverance: The Language of Martin Luther King, Jr. and Its Sources* (New York: Free Press, 1992).

67. Martin Luther King Jr., "The Death of Evil upon the Seashore," sermon, DAKMBCP.

68. Church Bulletin, August 4, 1957, DAKMBCP; Martin Luther King Jr., "Conquering Self-Centeredness," sermon, August 4, 1957, DAKMBCP; Martin Luther King Jr., "Paul's Letter to American Christians," sermon, November 4, 1956, DAKMBCP.

69. *Dexter Echo,* December 1956, DAKMBCP (note: in some cases, only a month and year are noted on the *Dexter Echo* masthead; *Dexter Echo,* December 17, 1958, DAKMBCP.

70. Program for Spring Lecture Series, April, 1956, DAKMBCP; J. Pius Barbour to Martin Luther King Jr. (letter), December 21, 1954, Carson, ed., *King Papers,* 2:322–3; J. Pius Barbour to Martin Luther King Jr. (telegraph), January 31, 1956, DAKMBCP; Press Release, Dexter Avenue Baptist Church Spring Lecture Series, 1956, DAKMBCP; Carson, ed., *King Papers,* 3:44.

71. Program for Dexter Avenue Baptist Church Spring Lecture Series, 1958, DAKMBCP; *Dexter Echo,* April 1958, DAKMBCP; Clarence Jordan, *The Substance of Faith and other Cotton Patch Sermons,* ed. Dallas Lee (New York: Association Press, 1972), 8. See also Tracey Elaine K. Meyer, *Interracialism and Christian Community in the Postwar South: The Story of Koinonia Farm* (Charlottesville: University of Virginia Press, 1997).

72. King's Explanation of Men's Day, 1955, DAKMBCP; Men's Day at Dexter Avenue Baptist Church, July 13, 1958, DAKMBCP; Men's Day at Dexter Avenue Baptist Church, July 12, 1959, DAKMBCP; "And Now Faith is the Substance: A Religious Drama in Eight Scenes," July 12, 1959, DAKMBCP.

73. *Dexter Echo,* October 7, 1959, DAKMBCP; Women's Day at Dexter Avenue, October 1957, DAKMBCP.

74. Women's Day at Dexter Avenue, October 1957, DAKMBCP; The Annual Women's Day Observance, Dexter Avenue Baptist Church, October 12, 1958, DAKMBCP. Daisey Bates to Martin Luther King Jr. (letter) July 3, 1958; *Dexter Echo,* October 1958, DAKMBCP; *Dexter Echo,* quoting Jo Ann Robinson on Women's Day, November 1958, DAKMBCP.

75. *Dexter Echo,* December 1956, DAKMBCP; *Dexter Echo,* January 22, 1958, DAKMBCP.

76. *Dexter Echo,* December 4, 1957, DAKMBCP. See also Graetz, *Montgomery: A White Preacher's Memoir.*

77. *Dexter Echo* February 11, 1959, DAKMBCP; Martin Luther King Jr. to Alberta King (letter), n.d.; Dexter Avenue Baptist Church Presents Coretta Scott King In Recital, September 30, 1956, DAKMBCP; *Dexter Echo,* April 1958, DAKMBCP; *Dexter Echo,* January 21, 1959, DAKMBCP.

78. Coretta Scott King, *My Life with Martin,* 154. *Dexter Echo,* April 1957, DAKMBCP; *Dexter Echo,* February 1957, DAKMBCP.

79. *Dexter Echo,* December 4, 1957, DAKMBCP; *Dexter Echo,* August 6, 1958, DAKMBCP.

80. *Dexter Echo,* August 6, 1958, DAKMBCP; *Dexter Echo,* 1956, DAKMBCP; Evans interview, March 24, 1994.

81. Annual Report of Dexter Avenue Baptist Church, 1957, DAKMBCP.

82. MOB, January 18, 1958, DAKMBCP; *Dexter Echo,* 1959, DAKMBCP; Evans interview, March 24, 1994.

83. Evans and Alexander, *Dexter Avenue,* 126. King's schedule that year was rather remarkable: sermons preached at Dexter Avenue, 28; sermons and lectures away from home, 54; community and civic meetings attended, 106; pastoral visits, 20; sick visits, 26; baptisms, 15; marriages, 6; funerals, 5; children's dedications, 3; personal inter-

views, 36; attendance at state, district, and national conventions, 9. Nesbitt interview; Thelma Austin Rice, interview with the author, May 16, 1994; Coretta Scott King, *My Life with Martin*, 181.

84. Minutes of the Church Conference at Dexter Avenue Baptist Church, November 29, 1959, DAKMBCP; *Dexter Echo*, December 9, 1959, DAKMBCP; Coretta Scott King, *My Life with Martin*, 181; Worship and Service Hymnal (Chicago: Hope, 1957), 168.
85. Evans interview, July 21, 1993; *Dexter Echo*, October 7, 1959, DAKMBCP; *Dexter Echo*, February 1960, DAKMBCP; Annual Message to Dexter Avenue Baptist Church, 1958, DAKMBCP; *Dexter Echo*, December 1958, DAKMBCP.
86. The church's annual income ranged from $23,000 to $25,200; Annual Report of Dexter Avenue Baptist Church, 1956–59, DAKMBCP; Recommendations for Dexter Avenue Baptist Church, 1954–1955, DAKMBCP.

Chapter 6

1. For an in-depth discussion of these topics and issues see Carl M. Brauer, *John F. Kennedy and the Second Reconstruction* (New York: Columbia University Press, 1977); Harvard Sitkoff, *The Struggle for Black Equality, 1954–1980* (New York: Hill and Wang, 1981); Robert Weisbrot, *Freedom Bound: A History of America's Civil Rights Movement* (New York: W. W. Norton, 1990); William O'Neill, *Coming Apart: An Informal History of America in the 1960s* (New York: New York Times, 1971); David Halberstam, *The Best and the Brightest* (New York: Random House, 1972); Todd Gitlin, *The Sixties: Years of Hope, Days of Rage* (New York: Bantam, 1987); J. T. Patterson, *America's Struggle against Poverty, 1900–1980* (Cambridge, Mass.: Harvard University Press, 1981); Betty Friedan, *The Feminine Mystique* (New York: W. W. Norton, 1963); G. G. Yates, *What Women Want: The Ideas of the Movement* (Cambridge, Mass.: Harvard University Press, 1975); Doris Kearns Goodwin, *Lyndon B. Johnson and the American Dream* (New York: St. Martin's, 1991); G. C. Herring, *America's Longest War: The U. S. and Vietnam, 1950–1975*, 3d ed. (New York: McGraw-Hill, 1996); Richard Nixon, *The Memoirs of Richard Nixon* (New York: Grosset and Dunlap, 1978). Clayborne Carson, *In Struggle: The SNCC and the Black Awakening of the 1960s* (Cambridge, Mass.: Harvard University Press, 1981); Harvard Sitkoff, *The Struggle for Black Equality* (New York: Hill and Wang, 1981); and Jacquelyne Clark, *These Rights They Seek: A Comparison of the Goals and Techniques of Local Civil Rights Organizations* (Washington, D.C.: Public Affairs, 1962).
2. See Virginia Van Deer Ver Hamilton, *Alabama: A Bicentennial History* (New York: W. W. Norton, 1977), 101; and William Warren Rogers, Robert David Ward, Leah Rawls Atkins, and Wayne Flynt, *Alabama: The History of a Deep South State* (Tuscaloosa: University of Alabama Press, 1994), 565–66.
3. C. Eric Lincoln and Lawrence Mamiya, *The Black Church in the African-American Experience* (Durham, N.C.: Duke University Press, 1990), 164–96.
4. See Aldon Morris, *The Origins of the Civil Rights Movement: Black Communities Organizing for Change* (New York: Free Press, 1984), 4, and especially his discussion of resource mobilization theory (180ff); Malcolm X, *The Autobiography of Malcolm X* (New York: Ballantine, 1992); Peter J. Paris, *Black Religious Leaders: Conflict in Unity* (Louisville, Ky.: John Knox, 1991), 183–220.
5. Martin Luther King Jr., *Stride Toward Freedom: The Montgomery Story* (New York: Harper and Row, 1958), 189–224.
6. Minutes of the Dexter Avenue Baptist Church Conference, January 3, 1960, Dexter Avenue King Memorial Baptist Church Papers (herafter DAKMBCP). See also "Recommendations for the Pastorate of Dexter Avenue Baptist Church," Minutes of the

Official Board of the Dexter Avenue Baptist Church (hereafter MOB), February 2, 1960, DAKMBCP.

7. *Dexter Echo*, May–June, 1965, DAKMBCP.

8. Robinson took a job at Dillard University in Louisiana for a year and then moved to Los Angeles, where she taught high school English until her retirement in 1976. Robert Williams also took a position at Dillard University, but later returned to Montgomery. Ralph Simpson went to the University of Illinois to pursue doctoral studies in organ music; upon graduation he worked at Dillard University for a brief period before returning to Montgomery. Obituary for H. Council Trenholm, *Birmingham News*, February 22, 1963; Jo Ann Robinson, *The Montgomery Bus Boycott and the Women Who Started It* (Knoxville: University of Tennessee Press, 1987), 168–70; *MOB*, 1963 (no day specified), DAKMBCP.

9. *Minutes of Pulpit Committee Meeting of Dexter Avenue Baptist Church*, February 6, 1960, DAKMBCP; MOB, February 27, 1960 and August 29, 1960, DAKMBCP.

10. MOB, August 15, 1960 and August 29, 1960, DAKMBCP. D. G. Hill to T. H. Randall (letter), July 24, 1960, DAKMBCP.

11. Allan Knight to J. T. Alexander, July 15, 1960, DAKMBCP; MOB, August 29, 1960, DAKMBCP.

12. Zelia Evans and J. T. Alexander, *The Dexter Avenue Baptist Church* (Montgomery, Ala.: Dexter Avenue Baptist Church, 1978), 146.

13. MOB, September 4, 1960, DAKMBCP; R. D. Nesbitt, interview with the author, May 5, 1994.

14. MOB, September 4, 1960, DAKMBCP. Early in his pastorate, Herbert Eaton married Delores Sankey, a member of Dexter Avenue.

15. MOB, September 19, 1960, DAKMBCP; Herbert Eaton to Elizabeth Arrington (letter), September 29, 1960, DAKMBCP; Program for the Installation of the Reverend Herbert Eaton to the Pastorate of Dexter Avenue Baptist Church, November 13, 1960, DAKMBCP; Herbert H. Eaton to Members of Dexter Avenue Baptist Church (letter), November 18, 1960, DAKMBCP.

16. Zelia Evans, "Board of Religious Education," pamphlet, DAKMBCP; Herbert H. Eaton to J. T. Alexander, Superintendent of Sunday School at Dexter Avenue Baptist Church (letter), October 12, 1960. Eaton to Board Members of Dexter Avenue Baptist Church, October 1960, DAKMBCP.

17. Evans, "Board of Religious Education."

18. Herbert H. Eaton to members of Dexter Avenue Baptist Church (letter), May 4, 1962, DAKMBCP; MOB, 1963, DAKMBCP.

19. Minutes of the Deacons' Meeting of Dexter Avenue Baptist Church, September 13, 1963, DAKMBCP.

20. Evans and Alexander, *Dexter Avenue*, 146–49; Nesbitt interview; Zelia Evans, interview with the author, July 21, 1993.

21. Herbert Hoover Eaton, "The Power of United Constructive Effort," sermon, January 14, 1962, DAKMBCP; Evans and Alexander, *Dexter Avenue*, 153.

22. Pastoral Recommendations for Dexter Avenue Baptist Church for 1964, January 6, 1964, DAKMBCP; 1964 Stewardship Pamphlet, DAKMBCP; Thelma Austin Rice to the Board of Deacons (memorandum), October 28, 1965, DAKMBCP.

23. MOB, January 20, 1964, DAKMBCP; Pastoral Recommendations for Dexter Avenue Baptist Church for 1964, January 6, 1964, DAKMBCP; Minutes of the Special Church Meeting, 1963, DAKMBCP. Minutes of the Special Church Meeting, February 3, 1964, DAKMBCP; Dexter Avenue Baptist Church Constitution, 1975, DAKMBCP.

24. Evans and Alexander, *Dexter Avenue*, 264; Letter of Resignation read at Special Church Conference, November 15, 1964, DAKMBCP.

25. Herbert Hoover Eaton, sermon, January 10, 1965, DAKMBCP.

26. MOB, December 7, 1964, DAKMBCP; Evans and Alexander, *Dexter Avenue*, 177; MOB, December 7, 1964, DAKMBCP; Zelia Evans to the Board of Deacons (memorandum), March 6, 1965, DAKMBCP. Deacon T. H. Randall died on February 23, 1965. It should be noted that this meeting included more than just the board of deacons, but also the trustees and other church leaders, as did most meetings of the official board. Only deacons could vote, however, for the next deacon chair.
27. Ministerial Appraisal Form, Dexter Avenue Baptist Church, March 6,1965, DAKMBCP; G. Murray Branch, interview with the author, March 24, 1994.
28. MOB, 1965, DAKMBCP.
29. Report of the Pulpit Committee, October 11, 1965, DAKMBCP; Nesbitt interview; Branch interview.
30. MOB, November 18, 1965, DAKMBCP.
31. Minutes of the Special Church Conference, November 11, 1965 and November 29, 1965, DAKMBCP. Dr. W. J. Wood, Chairman of Deacons and Mr. R. D. Nesbitt, Clerk to Dr. G. Murray Branch (letter), November 30, 1965, DAKMBCP; Reverend G. Murray Branch to W. J. Wood and R. D. Nesbitt (letter), December 2, 1965, DAKMBCP. Special Church Meeting, Dexter Avenue Baptist Church, January 9, 1966, DAKMBCP; Nesbitt interview; Zelia Evans, interview with the author, March 22, 1994.
32. MOB, February 7, 1966, DAKMBCP.
33. Branch interview; Minutes of the Annual Church Conference, January 8, 1967, DAKMBCP.
34. MOB, February 7, 1966, January 23, 1967, and December 5, 1965, DAKMBCP; Church Conference, January 16, 1969, DAKMBCP; Branch interview.
35. MOB, December 5, 1965, DAKMBCP; Dexter Avenue Baptist Church Constitution, 1975, DAKMBCP; Church Conference, February 5, 1968, DAKMBCP; Graduate and Retirees Recognition Banquet, May 1969, DAKMBCP; Branch interview.
36. MOB, April 1, 1968, DAKMBCP; Branch interview.
37. Evans and Alexander, *Dexter Avenue*, 162; Church Conference, March 11, 1968, DAKMBCP; Annual Letter from G. Murray Branch to Dexter Avenue Members and Associates, December 28, 1971, DAKMBCP.
38. Program for Youth Day Celebration at Dexter Avenue Baptist Church, July 13, 1969, DAKMBCP.
39. Church Conference, March 17, 1968, DAKMBCP.
40. Church Conference, March 17, 1968, DAKMBCP; MOB, April 1, 1968, DAKMBCP.
41. Nesbitt interview.
42. Resolution upon the Occasion of the Death of the Reverend Dr. Martin Luther King, Jr., by the Members of Dexter Avenue Baptist Church, April 5, 1968, DAKMBCP; MOB, April 29, 1968, DAKMBCP.
43. Branch interview; MOB, April 29, 1968, DAKMBCP.
44. MOB, April 29, 1968, DAKMBCP.
45. Church Conference, July 12, 1971, DAKMBCP; Thelma Austin Rice, interview with the author, May 16, 1996; Dr. Ralph Bryson, interview with the author, October 5, 1994; Zelia Evans, interview with the author, March 24, 1994.
46. Branch interview; G. Murray Branch, "Christ's Mission and Ours," sermon, September 3, 1972, DAKMBCP; Program for the Ordination of Deacons, October 15, 1972, DAKMBCP. Deacons ordained on this occasion included: Addre Bryant Sr., William Gary, Richard Jordan, William Minter, Wilbert J. Sheppard, Richmond Smiley, William Thompson, and Robert Williams.
47. "Dexter Church Names Pastor," *Montgomery Advertiser*, August 15, 1973. Theminutes of the church and board meetings and many of the other records between April 1972 and 1977 are missing. This makes it impossible to discuss many of the particulars of Robert Dickerson's call to the pastorate as well as his four-year tenure at Dexter

Avenue Baptist Church. Evans and Alexander, *Dexter Avenue*, 179; Program of Installation Services, October 28, 1973, DAKMBCP.

48. Rice interview; Thelma Austin Rice, "'Retrospection, Introspection, Prospection,' Centennial Souvenir for Dexter Avenue Baptist Church, 1977," DAKMBCP; Report of Recommendations of the Workshop for Lay Officials, February 18, 1974, DAKMBCP.

49. Church Bulletin, July 24, 1973, DAKMBCP; Nesbitt interview; Rice interview; Evans and Alexander, *Dexter Avenue*, 180.

50. Branch agreed to be an honorary member of the committee and continue to help and advise members as they saw need for his help. Church Conference, January 18, 1971 and July 12, 1971, DAKMBCP.

51. Nesbitt interview; Evans interview, July 21, 1993; National Register of Historic Place Inventory Nomination Form, May 30, 1974, DAKMBCP; "Dexter Baptist Church Named National Historic Landmark," *Alabama Journal*, July 3, 1974, Alabama State Historical Archives, Montgomery, Alabama (hereafter ASHA).

52. Program for the 98th Church Anniversary of Dexter Avenue Memorial Baptist Church, December 14, 1975, DAKMBCP; "Representative Young to Speak at Program," *Montgomery Advertiser*, December 15, 1975, ASHA.

53. "Dexter Avenue Baptist Church Pastor Leaving," *Alabama Journal*, June 10, 1977, ASHA; Nesbitt interview; Rice interview.

54. Alabama Democratic Conference to Dexter Avenue Baptist Church (letter), November 30, 1977, DAKMBCP; Emory Folmar to Dexter Avenue Baptist Church (letter), December 11, 1977, DAKMBCP; The White House to Dexter Avenue Baptist Church (letter), November 29, 1977, DAKMBCP; Centennial Program for Dexter Avenue Baptist Church, December 11, 1977, DAKMBCP; Rice, "Retrospection, Introspection, Prospection."

55. Centennial Program for Dexter Avenue Baptist Church, December 11, 1977; DAKMBCP; Evans interview, March 24, 1994;. "Dexter Church Landmark," *Alabama Journal*, December 5, 1977, ASHA; "Dexter Baptist Church Honored," *Montgomery Advertiser*, December 13, 1977, ASHA; Sara Evans and Harry Boyte, "The People Shall Rule," in *Free Spaces: The Sources of Democratic Change* (New York: Harper and Row, 1985), 17.

56. Rice interview; Evans interview, March 22, 1994; "Council OKs Funds for Black Churches," *Montgomery Advertiser*, November 23, 1977, ASHA.

57. "Coretta King Speaks at Dedication," *Montgomery Advertiser*, October 23, 1978, ASHA; "Dexter Church Renamed," *Alabama Journal*, October 23, 1978, ASHA.

58. Nesbitt interview; Rice interview; Evans interview, March 22, 1994.

Conclusion

1. Zelia Evans, interview with the author, March 22, 1994.

2. Reginald Hildebrand, *The Times Were Strange and Stirring: Methodist Preaching and the Crisis of Emancipation* (Durham, N.C.: Duke University Press, 1996), xiii–xx, 119–24.

3. *Montgomery Daily Advertiser*, May 6, 1885.

4. *Colored Alabamian*, October 15, 1907; *Colored Alabamian*, December 14, 1912; *Colored Alabamian*, December 14, 1907.

5. Church Covenant of Dexter Avenue Baptist Church, Dexter Avenue King Memorial Baptist Church Papers (hereafter DAKMBCP).

6. For a discussion of the significance the worship service in black churches see Wyatt Tee Walker, *The Soul of Black Worship: Praying, Preaching, Singing* (New York: Martin Luther King Fellows Press, 1984), 1–5.

7. William Montgomery, *Under Their Own Vine and Fig Tree: The African American Church in the South, 1865–1900* (Baton Rouge: Louisiana State University Press), 160–259.

8. Carter G. Woodson, *The History of the Negro Church*, 3d ed. (1921; reprint, Washington, D.C.: Associated Press, 1985), 270–71.

9. Cheryl Townsend Gilkes, "Together and in Harness: Women's Traditions in the Sanctified Church," *Signs: Journal of Women in Culture and Society*, no. 10 (1985): 680; Teresa Hoover, "Black Women and the Churches: Triple Jeopardy" in *Black Theology: A Documentary History*, ed. Gayraud Wilmore and James Cone (Maryknoll, N.Y.: Orbis, 1979. Zelia Evans and J. T. Alexander, *The Dexter Avenue Baptist Church* (Montgomery, Ala.: Dexter Avenue Baptist Church, 1978), 55.

10. Not all Baptist churches support the direction Dexter Avenue took in placing women in positions of authority. In fact, in 1987 when Dexter Avenue ordained its first women deacons, it was put out of its local association, the Montgomery-Antioch District Association. Zelia Evans, interview with the author, March 24, 1994; Leroy Fitts, *A History of Black Baptists* (Nashville, Tenn.: Broadman, 1985), 309; Jualyne E. Dodson and Cheryl Townsend Gilkes, "Something Within: Social Change and Collective Endurance in the Sacred World of Black Christian Women" in *Women and Religion in America*, ed. Rosemary Raford Ruether and Rosemary Skinner Keller (San Francisco: Harper and Row, 1986), 81.

11. Ralph Luker, *The Social Gospel in Black and White: American Racial Reform, 1885–1912* (Chapel Hill: University of North Carolina Press, 1991), 4–6, 312–24.

12. Gayraud Wilmore, *Black Religion and Black Radicalism: An Interpretation of the Religious History of Afro-American People*, 2d rev. ed. (Maryknoll, N.Y.: Orbis, 1983); James H. Cone, *Black Theology and Black Power* (New York: Seabury, 1969).

13. Washington, ed., *A Testament of Hope*.

14. Ibid.; Sydney Ahlstrom, *A Religious History of the American People* (New Haven, Conn.: Yale University Press, 1972), 670.

15. *Colored Alabamian*, July 14, 1907.

16. Kathy Hyde, "Dexter Church Renamed," *Alabama Journal*, October 23, 1978.

17. G. Murray Branch to the Members of Dexter Avenue Baptist Church (letter), November 1, 1977, DAKMBCP; G. Murray Branch, interview with the author, March 24, 1994.

18. For a discussion of another southern city also struggling to reconcile its racist past with its image as a harbinger of the civil rights movement, see Charles Rutheiser, *Imagineering Atlanta: The Politics of Place in the City of Dreams* (New York: Verso, 1996).

19. Ismael Ahmad, "Montgomery to Honor King, Lee," *Montgomery Advertiser*, January 16, 1989; Ismael Ahmad, "Dexter Avenue Minister Offers Bittersweet Goodbye," *Montgomery Advertiser*, April 7, 1989.

INDEX